Church Work in the City

CHURCH WORK
IN THE CITY

Frederick A. Shippey

ABINGDON PRESS
New York • Nashville

CHURCH WORK IN THE CITY

Copyright MCMLII by Pierce & Smith

Library of Congress Catalog Card Number: 52-8838

C

SET UP, PRINTED, AND BOUND BY THE
PARTHENON PRESS, AT NASHVILLE,
TENNESSEE, UNITED STATES OF AMERICA

To

CHANNING A. RICHARDSON, 1876-1950

Beloved pastor, able administrator, and understanding friend

PREFACE

DURING RECENT YEARS I HAVE TRAVELED MORE THAN A QUARTER of a million miles, going from city to city, from church to church, seeking a knowledge of religious work in urban places. A trip abroad, permitting on-the-spot examination of Protestant work in some of the leading cities on the Continent and in Great Britain, provided essential perspective and enrichment to the accumulating body of information. Out of this background the present volume was written, and into its pages are introduced some of the leading insights and ideas that I gathered. Because city church problems are relatively universal and derive from common urban conditions, it is possible to prepare a self-help manual for Protestant leaders.

This manual is intended for at least four groups of readers: (1) the *city pastor* who desires practical guidance in coping with problems; (2) the *denominational executive* who wishes to start new congregations, to relocate others, and to develop a city-wide or long-range strategy of work; (3) the *executive in a council of churches* who desires to cultivate more fully various patterns of Protestant church co-operation; and (4) the *seminary student* who needs a practical handbook on the urban church. Possibly other individuals concerned about the city church and its ministry may welcome this treatment of practical problems. The volume was prepared primarily for the many pastors, administrators, leaders, and students who are eager to make the Protestant church a more effective religious force in the American city.

This book has a practical aim. Each chapter is organized around one of the seven common city church problems. Each problem received careful analysis. Effective ideas related to such difficulties have been gathered from far and wide and then summarized for the busy pastor or administrator. Those selected for inclusion appear to offer the finest potential benefits in the urban situation. Thus an earnest endeavor has been made to answer the "how" of doing city church work. It is hoped that the religious leader confronted by a problem will find sufficient practical help in these pages to guide and encourage him in an intelligent course of action. From such experience come confidence and faith. An application of these ideas can yield notable advantages to local Protestantism.

Knowledge of the tangled conditions under which the local church must function is likewise essential to religious success in the city. For this reason an implicit orientation to urban sociology and to city planning is germane to the discussion. It is put there to enrich the treatment and to reassure the discerning reader that a church does not function in a vacuum but rather in a real environment which may be known and measured in objective terms. There is a vast urban revolution which is currently enfolding America, and we must not underestimate the significance of sociology in the work of the church. Sound sociological analysis should always undergird church strategy. Without it one wonders how blunders in religious work can be avoided. Who does not now realize that a vivid personality and mere aggressiveness hardly suffice to accomplish the high purposes of Protestantism in the city.

Principles of religious work described herein have emerged from the scientific study of several thousand city churches located in 150 cities. Although the data supporting such generalizations were purposely omitted from the text to facilitate practical use of the ideas, the reader should realize that painstaking research underlies the choice of principles which qualify as presuppositions for this book. All illustrations, instances, and charts appearing in these pages describe real situations which have been rendered anonymous by the removal of identifying clues. The inclusion of selected visual materials may increase the utility of the handbook.

I am indebted to many persons for suggestions, ideas, and kindly criticism. Frank discussions with pastors and laymen of many denominations on both sides of the Atlantic Ocean have furnished guidance in the selection of church problems to be treated. Because I have sought to listen to these authentic Protestant voices of the city and to record relevant insights, it is likely that the volume may prove interesting and helpful.

To call the roll of all friends, colleagues, and acquaintances who contributed directly or indirectly would be impossible. However, among the individuals who read and evaluated various chapters are the following: Leon M. Adkins, Alva R. Hutchinson, Recter W. Johnson, Bonneau P. Murphy, William D. Powell, Lawrence H.

8

Richards, and Ralph H. Richardson. Each of these persons made constructive suggestions for improving the arrangement of materials and for focusing the discussion. Further, the entire book was read and criticized by Earl R. Brown, who by virtue of extensive and successful experience in city pastorates and in urban church administration is highly qualified to evaluate the volume. Still further, valued assistance was given in the preparation of the manuscript by Barbara B. Bishop, Ruth O. Peterson, Ada M. Porter, and Elizabeth C. Lenz, who executed most of the drawings. Finally, without the continuous encouragement and forbearance of my wife and children the manuscript could scarcely have reached publication. Therefore it is a pleasant task to honor these persons who participated so significantly in the writing of this volume.

FREDERICK A. SHIPPEY

CONTENTS

LIST OF FIGURES

CHAPTER I

Changing Fortunes of the City Church

T HE RISE of the modern city has greatly complicated the task of organized religion. Though millions of people live closer together today, more people are further from God than ever before. Indeed, while civilization resided chiefly in open country and in relatively small communities, people not only were more accessible to the clergyman but also were more amenable to the demands of Christianity. Vast urban change has swept most of this away. As a result every phase of ministry, from pastoral visitation to burial of the dead, has been altered and rendered complex in a way which defies comparison. Man's need of God remains constant, however; yet to reach the individual in his prevailing condition and current environment poses a many-faceted problem. Thus the swift development of modern cities has disrupted traditional patterns and has opened a new phase of Protestant ministry. The church is in a new world.

RECENT URBANIZATION OF AMERICA

An urban revolution has settled upon America. The rather feeble population trends cityward noted at the beginning of the twentieth century have swollen into a mass migration, eclipsing any such previous development in the history of the nation. In 1900 only one third of America was urban. Today more than one half of the population resides in the city. The magnitude of the amazing changes which have been wrought by this recent revolution staggers one's imagination and stimulates a boundless hope for the future growth of Protestantism in cities. Yet the proportions of such an opportunity have but lately dawned upon the consciousness of religious leaders.

A serious scrutiny of the facts below may widen this important circle of awareness.

There are more urban residents. A recent study of population trends for cities of 5,000 and above reveals that U.S. urban inhabitants have increased 200 per cent or 55,000,000 persons during the period 1900-1950. To put the matter another way, where there was one urban resident in 1900, there are three today. How graphically is this fact revealed in Figure No. 1. Although during the past half century the general population doubled, the city population as defined above tripled in size over the same period.

More remarkable is the evidence of urban growth in every state. Data analyzed here disclose that net gains since the turn of the century ranged from 48,000 persons (Vermont) to 6,429,000 residents (New York). Contiguous states, curiously enough, reported the least and the largest growth. Further exploration of the trend situation reveals that fifteen states—California, Florida, Illinois, Indiana, Massachusetts, Michigan, Missouri, New Jersey, New York,

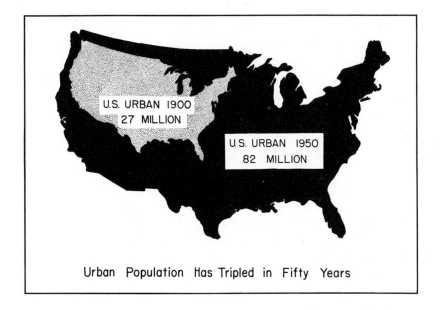

Urban Population Has Tripled in Fifty Years

FIGURE No. 1

CITY GROWTH IN THE U.S., 1900-1950

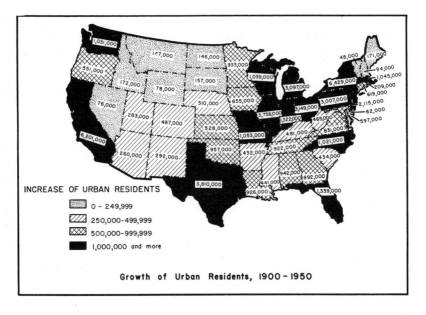

INCREASE OF URBAN RESIDENTS

- 0 – 249,999
- 250,000-499,999
- 500,000-999,999
- 1,000,000 and more

Growth of Urban Residents, 1900 – 1950

FIGURE No. 2

INCREASE OF CITY POPULATION BY STATES, 1900-1950

North Carolina, Ohio, Pennsylvania, Texas, Washington, and Wisconsin—reported increases of more than 1,000,000 urban inhabitants each during the past fifty years. Contrary to popular expectation ten of the states are located east of the Mississippi River.

Further, urban growth in twenty-seven states, cumulatively speaking, exceeded 500,000 persons each. In addition to the commonwealths mentioned above may be added the following: Alabama, Connecticut, Georgia, Iowa, Kansas, Louisiana, Maryland, Minnesota, Oklahoma, Oregon, Tennessee, and Virginia. Six of these states gained more than 900,000 city residents each. Surprisingly fifteen of the twenty-seven states in which most remarkable urban growth

17

occurred lie east of the Mississippi River. Clearly city growth is general rather than merely regional and as such supports the contention that America is currently gripped by a vast urbanization process. Increase of urban residents is widely distributed across the United States, with prominent accretions occurring in or near many older cities.

Supplementary evidence of the vitality of city growth is seen in the fact that this population group increased by more than 250,000 in thirty-seven states. A study of Figure No. 2 can reveal the amazing trends. Here is dramatized the story as unfolded in the preceding paragraphs. Even states traditionally rural reported the doubling and tripling of city growth. And this is a source of astonishment. Only five states—Delaware, Nevada, New Hampshire, Vermont, and Wyoming—showed urban growth of less than 100,000 persons, and yet here all increases constituted significant change since 1900. Wyoming quadrupled its urban population, while Nevada, with no cities above 5,000 fifty years ago, now boasts of five communities aggregating a total of 76,000 residents. More people now live under urban conditions than at any time since the founding of the nation. The situation leads many experienced observers to conclude that America is becoming urbanized.

There are more cities. Fifty years ago there were approximately 800 communities of 5,000 population and above in the United States. By 1910 the figure had risen to 1,200. More than 600 cities had been added by the end of the second decade. Over the half-century period a gain of several hundred additional communities each decade accounts for the present astounding total of 2,431 cities. This is an all-time high, and it eclipses by three times the number of incorporated places in existence in 1900. It is an increase of 1,600 communities, thus confounding the most reluctant skeptic who has remained dubious respecting the trend toward urbanization in America. There are more cities now than ever before.

Furthermore a study of materials presented in the accompanying table discloses support for another contention. There are more cities of every size. Little places grow larger, and larger communities become sprawling metropolises. Herein is shown a comparison of data for the years 1900 and 1950. Conventional classifications of communities by population size tell the factual story that remarkable

SIZE OF CITIES	NUMBER OF PLACES		PER CENT OF TOTAL POPULATION	
	1900	1950	1900	1950
5,000 - 9,999	415	1,174	3.7	5.4
10,000 - 24,999	260	780	5.3	8.0
25,000 - 49,999	83	246	3.7	5.8
50,000 - 99,999	40	125	3.6	5.9
100,000 - 249,999	23	65	4.3	6.3
250,000 - 499,999	9	23	3.8	5.4
500,000 - 999,999	3	13	2.2	6.1
1,000,000 or more	3	5	8.4	11.6
TOTALS	836	2,431	35.0	54.5

change has taken place since the turn of the century and that it has produced more municipalities in every category. Instead of fewer places the number has increased all down the line. This fact is clearly revealed by the table above. Never has America boasted of so many cities, nor has it possessed so many in each size classification. Likewise the percentage of the population has increased in every category. Such facts underlie the emerging conviction that a profound urbanization process has fastened itself upon America. Apparently for better or worse city life is here to stay.

Cities continue to grow. There are 2,431 places above 5,000 population in the United States. From a study of recent population trends (1940-50) it was found that nine tenths of the American cities are growing. Only one community out of ten reported loss.

Conspicuous growth describes the general situation within fourteen states—Arizona, Arkansas, Delaware, Florida, Georgia, Idaho, Louisiana, Maine, Nevada, North Dakota, Texas, Utah, Washington, and Wyoming—which commonwealths report every city growing. Next, eighteen states indicate that nine out of ten cities are growing —Alabama, California, Connecticut, Indiana, Iowa, Minnesota, Mississippi, Montana, Nebraska, New Mexico, North Carolina, Ohio, Oregon, South Carolina, South Dakota, Tennessee, Virginia, and Wisconsin. Further still, thirteen states reveal that eight out of ten cities are increasing in population, namely, Colorado, Illinois, Kansas, Kentucky, Maryland, Massachusetts, Michigan, Missouri,

New Jersey, New York, Oklahoma, Rhode Island, and Vermont. Finally, only New Hampshire, Pennsylvania, and West Virginia report fewer than 80 per cent of the urban communities growing during the past decade. The amazing growth of cities during the past ten years fixes attention upon the vast urbanization process.

Child population sets a record. Twice since 1940 a new all-time record for births has been established in the United States. More babies were born in 1943 (2,934,860 births) than in any previous year in the history of the nation. Three years later this record was eclipsed. For the first time in U.S. history the number of births reached and exceeded the 3,000,000 mark. From 1940 to 1947 there occurred a 31 per cent gain in the number of children under five years per thousand women fifteen to forty-nine years of age. The increase for urban areas was 47 per cent, of approximately four times that registered for rural farm areas.

Births are recorded according to the place of residence of the parents. No matter where the actual delivery takes place, the child' birth is reported in the community where the parents maintain legal residence. More babies are born in the city of Chicago than in the entire state of Iowa. More than one half of the births for the state of New York are to parents who reside within the corporate limits of the city of New York. More births are reported in the city of Los Angeles than in the entire state of Wisconsin, more in Philadelphia than in Kansas, more in Detroit than in Nebraska, more in Boston than in Nevada and Wyoming combined, and so on. More babies are born in the fifteen largest U.S. cities than the total number reported for the eleven states of Montana, Wyoming, North Dakota, South Dakota, Nebraska, Kansas, Oklahoma, Texas, Minnesota, Iowa, and Wisconsin. Today more children are born in the city and grow up under urban conditions than at any time in the history of the United States. A vast number of children and young parents reside in American cities, and many are available for a Protestant ministry.

The remarkable increase in births since the beginning of the current decade has resulted in an unprecedented number of elementary-school children. And the number is increasing. In a community I recently studied not only had the number of children climbed to an all-time high, but also an increase of one thousand pupils per year has been reported for the last five years, although the city has not been stimulated by new industry nor other unusual factors. This case is neither isolated nor exceptional. For wherever one goes in urban America, elementary schools are found to be overcrowded. Undoubtedly urban Protestantism has never before been afforded so propitious and so extensive an opportunity to minister to children. Millions of children and youth reside in the cities of America.

Urban growth is everywhere. Though the urban growth pattern is differential, increases are relatively universal. There are three times as many city residents now as in 1900. Large-scale and continuing inmigration of people to urban places is reported in every one of the forty-eight states. Population growth appears as a dominant pattern regardless of a city's regional location. Significant increases are reported for communities as remote from one another as Maine and California, South Carolina and Utah, Ohio and Nevada, Georgia and Oregon. This striking fact dispels the notion that urban growth is restricted to but one or two regions of the United States. Rather the auspicious trends prevail within the perimeter of every state. Surprisingly fifteen out of twenty-seven states reporting increases of more than a half million city residents each are located east of the Mississippi River.

The ubiquity of urban growth is further revealed by the widespread appearance of new cities. They have sprung up not only in Texas and California but also in New York, Rhode Island, New Jersey, Delaware, Wyoming, and Virginia. In fact new communities have arisen in every state in the union since the turn of the century. Not only are there more new cities than ever, but also they are scattered to all points of the compass. Even states traditionally thought of as rural report the birth of new places and the phenomenal expansion of existing communities.

Cities everywhere continue to increase in size despite common expectation to the contrary. Across the nation larger municipalities join in a common chorus respecting fast-growing suburbs and changing neighborhoods, whether Virginia or Washington, Michigan or Mississippi. In fact 90 per cent of all places of 5,000 population and above in the United States report growth during the past decade (1940-50). Amazingly enough every single city is growing in fourteen states, nine out of ten are gaining in eighteen states, and eight out of ten are increasing in thirteen states. This accounts for forty-five states. Obviously the prevailing pattern of increase is widely dispersed. Only three states—New Hampshire, Pennsylvania, and West Virginia—report fewer than four fifths of their cities growing since 1940. This astonishing phenomenon underlies the emerging realization that everywhere in America one may witness the urbanization process at work. The situation is forcing Protestantism to take a new look at itself.

There are other factors also. There is scarcely any debate respecting the far-reaching significance of the cityward trend of U. S. population, the extensive rise of new cities, the spectacular growth of older communities, the record-breaking prevalence of urban children, and the ubiquity of city growth. That the current situation is astonishingly large is revealed by Figure No. 3. Once the facts are noted, no thoughtful person will deny them. Rather attention turns toward supplementary lines of evidence.

That there are additional concomitant factors involved in the urbanization process is readily admitted. These are not so easily discerned, though keen observers would include in a list the vastly improved means of transportation and communication, the revolution in the home-building industry, war-stimulated economy, large-scale employment of women, increased mobility of Americans, improved methods of agriculture and industry, and kindred considerations. An adequate discussion of these factors would take me afield from the main theme of the book, and therefore the reader may be expected to extend the list for his own purposes and to trace out the relevant implications. Obviously the present account lifts the situation to attention without endeavoring to treat it exhaustively. For the majority of readers this will be regarded as an essential service.

DISTRESSING IMPACT UPON PROTESTANTISM

The rapid growth of cities has induced a state of crisis and confusion among Protestants. No matter what else may be said, all is not well with the city church. Frankly, Protestantism has been caught napping, and apparent disorder has entered the ranks of the denominations. The simple confidence of former days among leaders has given way to vacillating concern. So intense and so extensive is the urban impact it has shaken the institution to the very bottom of its life. Hardly a local congregation or a community has escaped the disturbing influence of this crisis, and the result is a stunned, foundering, and confused church. Manifold weaknesses have been laid bare, and to these prompt and thoroughgoing attention should be given. Caught in the throes of so great an urban metamorphosis, Protestantism is trying desperately to muddle through. Thoughtful leaders find in the situation at least five considerations of grave concern.

1. *Alarming Protestant Trends.* Urban church trends since the turn of the century reveal that Protestantism is in danger of losing the city. As a whole, church membership appears generally static or modestly increasing. In older cities, especially in New England and along the Atlantic seaboard, Protestantism is having a hard time to avoid membership loss. In the Midwest and the central states some growth is generally reported. On the West Coast and in the Southwest conspicuous growth is the typical pattern. Scattered commu-

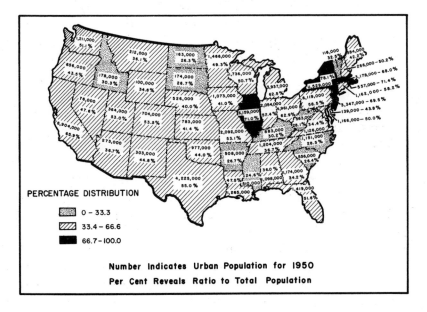

FIGURE No. 3

URBAN POPULATION BY STATES, 1950

23

nities across the United States vary from the general situation. Although growth is still the direction of trend, a significant deceleration of membership increase has been observed. This slowing down reveals that Protestantism is off the pace of gain reported in the general population trends. Since the turn of the century the faith has steadily fallen behind its opportunity. Cities stimulated to spectacular population growth during the recent war years and afterward recorded Protestant membership increases at the prewar leisurely rate. This lag remains as one of the distressing aspects of the trend situation.

The size of urban churches according to gross membership furnishes an important clue to the trends within Protestantism. Persistent feebleness is common to urban Protestantism. That a city church can be too small to be effective most research specialists agree, and they urge that in the practical situation rarely does the local church of less than five hundred active members make a significant religious impact upon its neighborhood environment. Small churches are marginal churches; that is, the quality, range, and duration of ministry are always problematical. In some cities 50 to 75 per cent of the institutions are below the level of effective strength necessary for city church work. Recent studies of this factor among several denominations indicate that the disproportionate ratio of small units has remained relatively constant during the past fifty years. The matter of persistent smallness has plagued Protestantism for decades. Recent accelerated growth of urban places has only accentuated the significance of this unsolved problem.

A Protestant catastrophe in embryo is revealed by the Sunday-school enrollment losses. In an inventory of the situation in eleven cities one major denomination reported an average loss of a thousand pupils per year during the past eighteen years. Many denominations have closed Sunday schools. Others have disclosed enrollment losses since 1930 running as high as 71 per cent. An examination of the trend status of Protestantism in a number of Midwestern communities reveals that enrollment losses from 10 to 20 per cent have been sustained in each city. In many urban places only one or two minor denominations report growth at all. The downward enrollment trend in urban Protestantism appears to be definitely established. It is no temporary fluctuation due to some transient factor. The forward

24

momentum of the Sunday school has apparently been dissipated. This enrollment decline presents a serious complication respecting the future of Protestantism. Spot studies reveal that some denominations have been recruiting from 50 to 100 per cent of their new Christians from this source, in as much as many thousands of children and youth find their way into the life of the church via the religious education program. Thus the large-scale shrinkage of the Sunday-school enrollment means a disastrous reduction of the most fruitful source of church growth. Such a development constitutes a potential Protestant catastrophe. Certainly the general trends reveal that all is not well with the city church.

2. *Lack of Over-all Planning.* Protestantism in the city grew up much like Topsy. Denomination after denomination, sect after sect, established preaching places and Sunday schools. Churches were built almost everywhere regardless of location, and religious rivalry appeared to be a prominent guiding objective. Further, some denominations across the years have subsidized competing units too weak to stand alone. This practice not only promoted competition and encouraged the survival of small units but also pauperized many of the congregations. Lack of orderly development and over-all planning is characteristic of the Protestant urban situation, a phenomenon which is common within the denominations also. The spectacular growth of American cities has but spotlighted this weakness, making it increasingly intolerable. Among other factors lack of an adequate knowledge of parish work has handicapped the faith, and this deficiency underlies repeated mistakes in church placement. Protestantism has been dollar wise and church foolish.

Within a relatively small neighborhood of a city known to me there are thirty-four Protestant churches. Not one of them is above 125 persons in member strength. A number of the leading denominations have several units each in the territory. Severe debilitating competition is the normal pattern of interchurch relationship, for wars of attrition are being fought continuously. Material resources and good will are being used up in prodigal fashion. Eventually many of the local churches will die. Several may withdraw belatedly to find a more promising ministry in an adjacent neighborhood. Some will persist by outlasting the Protestant opposition. None will find ecumenicity across the street.

25

Unfortunately this illustration does not describe an isolated phenomenon. Word from religious research specialists indicates that hardly a city above 50,000 population is free from religious competition. Interdenominational rivalry is still so common that it is generally condoned. Besides, overlapping parish work and duplication of ministries within denominations is also a frequent complaint of administrators and pastors. In a city recently studied one half of the major denominations reported churches competing within the religious body. Further, the study of a leading denomination's work in a hundred cities revealed intradenominational competition in three fourths of the communities. The distressing condition is more extensive than is generally acknowledged, and the current urban revolution reveals a fierce state of Protestant chaos.

3. *Inadequate Community Knowledge.* Absorbed in problems of church administration and general spiritual ministry, religious leaders have overlooked the importance of gathering up-to-date and reliable sociological information about the growing city. Chiefly because of this engrossment the far-flung urbanization of America has taken place almost unnoticed by the rank and file of Protestant executives, pastors, and laymen. Thus among other difficulties inadequate knowledge of community life continues as an embarrassment to urban religious leaders.

Only belatedly has serious concern arisen respecting the shameful predicament. The tremendous impact of the urban revolution has disclosed in the pastor and administrator incredible limitations of knowledge respecting population trends; patterns of city growth; neighborhood structure; areas of settlement by racial, ethnic, religious, and economic groups; places of extensive personal and social disorganization; territories of population mobility; differentiation among religious institutions; extent of parish outreach; and the pragmatic significance of such factors for city church work. Yet the leader is not altogether at fault. Unfortunately, published material treating these topics with a thoroughgoing orientation to organized religion is extremely scarce, and no amount of experience in the urban pastorate appears to avail in compensating for this deficiency in community knowledge. Further, many theological seminaries appear to have underestimated the importance of the urban revolution, for they have taken scant notice of the Protestant crisis which it has produced. In short, little knowledge of the modern city proves a dangerous asset.

That this deficiency is grave and costly may be noted in almost any American city. Lack of adequate sociological knowledge of parish work appears to produce many blunders. Such ignorance underlies repeated mistakes in church placement, in spacing between churches, in program adjustment, in provision of transitional ministries, and in basic conception of the urban religious task. How often, on the basis of a very superficial knowledge of community needs, vast sums of money have been invested in projects of dubious merit. Thousands of pastors have seen their devoted efforts reap frustration or produce pitifully meager results. Failure to discover a causal relationship between inadequate sociological knowledge and repeated churching mistakes accounts in part for the distressing impact of the urban revolution. Surely no beneficial revision of Protestant strategy and urban church tactics can come out of a deficiency in community knowledge. Rather a continuation of prodigal fumbling is the only warranted outcome. In view of the present crisis this is not a heartening eventuality.

4. *Dearth of Protestant Teamwork.* The splintered character of American Protestantism is so well known and so generally acknowledged that it needs only to be mentioned here. Proliferation within the faith is greatly aggravated in the city. Here the muliplication of sects and denominations throws off all reasonable restraint, and the development hardly furnishes a happy setting for Protestant cooperation. In fact the present urban revolution has turned the heretofore relatively placid church situation into a hectic scramble for new extension projects, relocation sites, better buildings, and wholesale withdrawal from slum areas. Neither the present mood nor the prevailing administrative policies of many bodies furnish fruitful soil for Protestant teamwork. This is another aspect of the crisis which enfolds American Christianity.

Parochialism usually starts at the local church level. Failure to make common cause with Protestantism plus undue emphasis upon the activities of one's own parish virtually eliminates the possibility of teamwork. Ecumenicity fails if it does not start across the street. In a city of three hundred thousand inhabitants a pastor was recently interrogated respecting the work of his denomination in the local

27

community. Despite a ministry of five years' duration neither he nor his officials could name more than several of the sister churches of that communion located within the community. Further, they were unable to describe membership size and other prominent characteristics. Such lack of information is difficult to justify, since the denomination under discussion is well organized and features intra-denominational co-operation. Clearly, poor teamwork originates where self-conteredness and ecclesiastical ignorance thrive. Though there are seventeen churches of the communion in the city referred to above, the pastor and officials estimated the number to be six or seven. The crowning gem of "knowledge" possessed by the leaders in question was, "Our church eclipses any other congregation in contributions to missionary causes." While high benevolent support constitutes an admirable achievement, it takes more than this to produce denominational teamwork. One would like to believe that instances of fragmentary knowledge and inadequate viewpoint as evidenced above are isolated or exceptional. Unfortunately the case is quite typical, thereby contributing importantly to the present Protestant crisis.

No longer can a single church, however strong or of whatever denomination, handle the entire city opportunity alone. Of necessity urban religious work is a shared task—shared with other Protestant churches and with other congregations within the denomination. Unilateral tactics are bound to prolong failure patterns and to in-duce additional demoralization of Protestant forces. The sheer facts in the case against a unilateral strategy are overwhelming. Factors of distance, primary barriers, topography, population density, types of housing, economic heterogeneity, racial differences, and ethnic background complicate the urban task beyond the reach of any single congregation to manage alone. Thus an individual city church at best has but a limited ministry. Recognition of this fundamental fact by Protestant leaders is likely to open the way for an enlightened pattern of co-operative urban church work.

Further, consider the plight of the denomination which boldly feigns to undertake the full ministry required by a city. The falseness of this pretension is soon discovered. At the outset the communion's historic specialization precludes ministry to manifold population groups. For where is the denomination which provides an adequate ministry to both rich and poor, to all racial groups, to all ethnic populations, to urban and suburban residents, and to persons of diverse cultural background? Answer to this disturbing question proves an embarrassment since the heterogeneity of the modern city escapes the scope of ministry offered by any communion I know of. Protestantism needs all denominations if all urban residents are to be served. Thus even under ideal circumstances a denomination can scarcely match the city with an adequate ministry. If this is true, why do not congregations within the communion learn to work together? Failure to co-operate at this level underlies the present dearth of teamwork.

Still further, denominations, though not officially antagonistic, are reluctant to work together very closely. Each goes its own separate way. Apparently a competitive spirit remains and is manifest in undeclared wars between communions. Co-operative indifference in the city arises from the diversification among Protestant bodies. The urban revolution discloses a need to co-ordinate denominational efforts and to harness these energies in a responsible teamwork pattern. This is the great unsolved problem. Teamwork on an interdenominational level is virtually nonexistent in hundreds of urban communities. In additional places co-operation is a word rather than a reality. To view the distressing situation in a realistic manner should in no way be construed as an attempt to belittle the importance of the ecumenical movement. Rather it should direct attention to the increased scope of the dilemma thrust upon Protestantism by the recent urban revolution. It is no longer optional to develop adequate patterns of co-operative activity. Inability to find ways of working together keeps Protestantism floundering needlessly in the midst of a propitious urban opportunity.

5. *A Sense of Failure.* The cumulative impact of the alarming Protestant trends, the lack of over-all planning, the inadequate community knowledge, and the dearth of Protestant teamwork shatter the easy confidence of religious leaders. Protestantism has reached a turn in the road. The urban revolution drives home the point that the denominations cannot drift along as before until the present crisis blows over. This situation is not going to blow over. The city is here to stay, and if Protestantism is to succeed with its magnificent

new opportunity, it must confront and solve the new problems. Along with the dawning of this profound realization may come a sense of failure. This is a natural initial reaction.

The new problems stemming from the urban revolution reveal how outmoded and unserviceable are many of the prevailing methods of city church work. As time passes, ways of doing things require thorough revision in order to mediate the Christian ministry under changed conditions. A new day calls for new techniques. Consider some of the changes which have come. Vast areas of the city are now built to apartments and tremendous public-housing projects. Commuter suburbs have multiplied in number and acquired a fresh importance which can no longer be disputed. Freeways, toll parkways, and boulevards crisscross the great metropolitan centers in an enormous spider web of fast transportation lanes. The ubiquity of the radio, television receiver, and automobile favors the progressive secularization of urban culture and seeks to reduce the influence of the church to a new low. In what ways shall religion now speak to man's condition? City residents take the church for granted but force the institution to make its own way into the lives of the people or else fall by the wayside. The rising urban tide has brought to light the outmoded character and general irrelevance of many urban church methods. Strangely enough, the passing of cherished techniques which once proved so effective engenders a nostalgia which contributes to a sense of failure. Change is resisted by the church, however beneficial the alterations promise to be.

Protestantism is shocked by the sweeping urban changes which have come. The emigration of millions of people, the spectacular growth of cities, the metamorphosis of small communities, and the wholesale alteration of urban neighborhoods—these developments have tumbled in upon the minds of leaders with such rapidity and suddenness that great distress has been generated. Naturally a sense of being overwhelmed has arisen. So much has to be accepted and adjusted to and so much has to be accomplished all at one time that the task appears impossible of solution. The muddling through with antiquated techniques in itself is hardly conducive to optimism. Repeated failure breeds discouragement. However, in spite of this distressing impact of the urban revolution there may be engendered

a saving sense of humility. If so, Protestantism can go from her knees out to meet the world's needs.

EMERGENCE OF COMMON CHURCH PROBLEMS

This rapid growth of cities has engulfed Protestantism in a new set of problems and put its hand to an enormously difficult task. The alert religious leader responds to the crisis by groping toward solutions. He is not content with a knowledge of what is wrong; he seeks a way out of the situation. Thus appropriately the present volume treats the work of the regular city church and endeavors to delineate paths leading to religious effectiveness. Further, an implicit orientation to sound principles of urban sociology may multiply the usefulness of the book to the pastor, lay officer, denominational administrator, interdenominational executive, and theological student. This hidden frame of reference furnishes an adequate scientific background for the discussions and underlies the numerous concrete suggestions for city church programs.

Wide acquaintance with urban Protestantism discloses that though the problems of the city church are manifold, the more common ones can be grouped roughly into seven basic classifications. From the practical viewpoint this set of categories will satisfy the needs of most readers. Herein are treated (1) extent of local church effectiveness, (2) discovery of unchurched city residents, (3) religious work in the downtown area, (4) a ministry to apartment dwellers, (5) role of the neighborhood church, (6) establishment of new congregations, and (7) co-operative Protestant activity.

Admittedly these do not exhaust the list of city church difficulties which might be drawn up, but rather serve to turn serious attention toward the work of organized religion in American cities. However, a satisfactory solution of these seven problems can go a long way toward restoring Protestantism to a place of leadership and influence in urban America. Chapter-length treatments of the topics given above comprise the subsequent pages of the present volume. Relevant information, basic analysis, and program ideas are featured. By means of this discussion religious leaders are furnished guidance in the study and exploration of local church problems.

From the outset Protestantism has found the city difficult to serve. However, where fundamental problems have been attacked with intelligence, resourcefulness, and adequate faith, solutions have been forthcoming. Every community possesses residents who believe that the faith can rise in this crisis and deliver its spiritual ministry to the churchless millions. Thus the present urban metamorphosis in America can become the occasion for a distinguished Protestant recovery if embattled leaders will but match the hour with appropriate knowledge and vital piety.

No matter how tangled and disheartening the present church situation appears, solutions can be found by gathering facts, by utilizing simple analyses, by studying the findings, and by applying tested courses of action. This practical approach can aid Protestant leaders in moving out across the face of the city with increasing effectiveness. To accomplish so praiseworthy an objective may seem a herculean task. Therefore one must turn to it with sincere awareness that his own wisdom and strength may prove insufficient for the day. Surely steadfast reliance upon God can bring the city church into a great new ministry.

CHAPTER II

Ways to Study a Local Church

HOW often the local congregation postpones taking an inventory of strengths and weaknesses until fully overtaken by a serious crisis. Meanwhile years of relatively uneventful ministry pass, years which might have been used for remedial action. Then, as though from nowhere, trouble appears; and suddenly things begin to go wrong within the local church. Consider several clues to emerging difficulty. A normal budget is harder to raise. Members in significant number move out of the neighborhood or out of town. Constituents do not appear to take responsibility in the church as during former days. Attendance at services declines. Irrespective of the pattern which the individual crisis takes, the pastor and church officers eventually begin to realize that a self-inventory is urgently needed. Church health and religious effectiveness become a burning issue, and maintenance of a significant ministry at the present site is now a matter of sharp concern.

Self-examination need not be deferred until a crisis appears. Religious experts affirm that church difficulties can be anticipated relatively early since processes of institutional disintegration can be traced and clearly identified. The haste with which a congregation appears to be swept suddenly into disaster and difficulty is only in the eyes of those who have not kept a discriminating watch over the church's life. For this reason a scientific inventory of the local church is relevant and useful. Such an approach permits a discovery of and a realistic attack upon fundamental problems. If seeds of deterioration are already within the religious institution, prompt cognizance of their damaging presence may be taken, and remedial measures can be launched in time. Thus weaknesses may be properly assessed.

Evidences of local church health may be discovered by a survey of membership and Sunday-school trends, of age-sex composition, of financial support patterns, of plant utilization, of parish dispersion, and of kindred phenomena. To pass over such data lightly, especially when findings are negative, opens the way to institutional disaster. In business detailed inventories are made regularly. Recent developments in the religious field indicate the relevance of pragmatic research methods and the need for frequent local church inventories. Thousands of dollars may be saved thereby and many common church mistakes avoided. Facts are of immense help to the puzzled religious leader. Where adequate objective data are available, fewer errors in judgment are made.

PURPOSE OF A LOCAL CHURCH INVENTORY

Many local churches can benefit immediately from a scientific inventory. The discovery and factual definition of weakness may stimulate action leading to a sounder pattern of churchmanship henceforth. Remedial measures may be launched in time, since a discovered weakness need not be tolerated indefinitely. Any current unsatisfactory condition can be changed by an intelligent course of action. A church can control its destiny.

Gaps in the total ministry of a local church often exist. The institution generally surmises mistakenly that its religious and fellowship service is rendered uniformly to persons of all ages and to both sex groups who reside in the community. Actually the ministry provided is often spotty and uneven and therefore should be tested by an inventory. Whether the findings prove to be negative or positive, the local church may be stimulated to broaden and to extend the ministries it proposes to provide. A church may inadvertently have a lopsided ministry.

Occasionally a church struggles almost vainly to become what is outside the range of its potentiality to achieve. In a neighborhood composed of residents engaged dominantly in the manual occupations, it unwisely strives to specialize in reaching upper-income and/or college-educated persons. Such an objective is not always stated but rather is implicit in the attitude of officers and leaders.

34

When an inventory is made of the local church and its neighborhood environment, a new sense of realism is commonly secured. Ultimately its ministry should be adapted to the neighborhood opportunity and tailored to fit the needs of residents within a mile service radius, regardless of the educational or economic achievements of the residents. A church may fail to serve its neighborhood.

Many local churches utilize but a fraction of the financial potential, the leadership power, and the participation ability of the congregation. If an undesirable condition with respect to finances, leadership, or participation is suspected to exist, the situation can be explored by means of a local church inventory. Special instruments for the analysis of various factors have been devised, tested, and standardized for use by pastors and church leaders. Data assembled reveal the segment of the membership which satisfactorily participates while pointing out specific age groups which need a more intensive parish cultivation. A church may function at minimum capacity.

Does the local church lack sufficient organizational structure to care for the needs of its membership? When a congregation grows rapidly in size, as many urban churches are now doing, it often endeavors to continue with the old outmoded structure unchanged. People generally look for and expect two things from the church: (1) membership in a purposeful congenial group and (2) an opportunity to exercise leadership. Rapid growth calls for prompt expansion of participation opportunities in Sunday-school classes, group work, choral music, leadership, and offices. Thus an inventory may uncover a condition which needs to be corrected. A church may not hold its members.

More than one half of the Protestant churches in the city are too small. A survey may reveal that the particular congregation is below the level of effective size required in the urban community. Persistent feebleness may be disclosed in a study of membership and Sunday-school trends, and this discovery may generate a desire on the part of the congregation to intensify evangelistic activity. An urban church may be inept in size.

Therefore manifold reasons and conditions may provide occasion for an inventory of the local church. No experienced minister or layman would deny that local churches contain primary weaknesses which impose serious limitations upon the effectiveness of the local institution. Information derived from field studies reveals that approximately one half of the urban Protestant churches are confronted with urgent problems, and for this reason it is hardly necessary to detail the critical nature of such problems as ineffective financing, inferior and inept leadership, losses in membership, declining Sunday-school enrollment, poverty of program, competition, unstrategic location, altered population opportunities, and kindred difficulties. Their fruits hobble the institution with ineffectiveness. What is called for at this juncture is a definition of the condition which obtains in a particular local church or community. This is the required initial step on the path which leads into intelligent action.

SELECTION OF A STUDY COMMITTEE

Satisfactory results are procured when a study committee composed of laymen is formed to set up and carry out the contemplated inventory. Six to twelve able persons are selected, but the group should be representative of the local church. Committee size is determined by the magnitude of the congregation. Eight or ten persons suffice for a church of a thousand members. Several women, several men, young adults, youth representatives, a church secretary, are normally selected to serve. Often the church treasurer or financial secretary and several persons from the membership committee are included. Though he is rarely chairman, it is customary for the pastor to be included also. Some churches name permanent forward-planning or study committees. In such instances long-term objectives may be formulated and eventually realized. Vigilance and planning are essential ingredients for effective urban church work.

Following organization the committee proceeds to define its task. Many questions are asked concerning the congregation, and factual answers are sought. How adequate is the present church plant? What are the nature and function of each church organization? What age groups are represented in the membership? Do women dominate numerically? What is the financial support pattern of members? Who contributes, and in what amounts? Is the Sunday school primarily a children's organization? What other conditions or traits merit investigation? Definition of task is normally achieved by a discovery of current fundamental problems. It is desirable to conduct a series of orientation meetings prior to launching an investigative program. Constituents need to become apprised concerning the project and encouraged to develop a lively interest in it since the attention of the entire church should be solicited. Eventually, however, the committee itself must assume responsibility for formulating the program of research and study.

Further, the committee may desire to delegate responsibility for gathering specific types of data to various individuals or subcommittees. In this manner many types of data may be gathered simultaneously. However, an overview of the entire project should be retained while detailed investigations of several areas of the church life are being carried on. Six types of analysis are described below, and subsequent pages contain suggestions for assembling the required data. A pastor or layman can set up the project within the local church and secure the benefits of an inventory without consultation with an expert.

PREPARATION FOR A STUDY

The general committee should discover the critical local church problems as soon as possible. An aid to this process consists in the gathering of a written statement of problems from each organization in the local church. No group, however small or large, may be omitted from the exploratory survey of problems. Within each organization several persons should share in the preparation of the statement. A description of the purposes, personnel, and current objectives espoused by the club or society should be written out. If plant space or facilities are inadequate to the needs of the organization, or other difficulties cause current embarrassment, appropriate reference to the matter should be included.

A Statement of Problem. Further, statements of problems should be prepared respecting morning worship services, the Sunday school, weekday religious education, choral music, as well as from the manifold organizations for children, youth, young adults, men and women. A careful definition of the elements to be included in such a statement is essential to uniformity, so important in the process of synthesis and analysis. In a designated board meeting comprised of officers and leaders, a written outline of suggestions can be presented to the heads of all organizations.

The first step in the committee's preparation for a local church study consists in a summary of the statements of problems. However uneven in quality they are, all should be carefully worked over and summarized to suit the purposes of the committee. The statements are drafted into a preliminary prospectus. This outline furnishes a preliminary clue respecting the program of research needed.

Normally four analyses—church trend, parish map, membership, and financial—are included in the research program. These four devices utilize objective information bearing on the fundamental structure of the local church. However, many situations require the six analyses described in this chapter. Primary weaknesses which might otherwise be overlooked in a less profound investigative approach are discovered. Analytical devices are selected on the basis of needs disclosed in the preliminary prospectus.

Community Background Materials. A second step in the committee's preparation consists in the procurement of certain materials and information about the community. A good street map of the city and up-to-date reports respecting population and housing can prove useful and enlightening. Doubtless an interview with the city engineer or city-planning executive may result in the discovery of additional available data. Further, the public library is a depository of a cumulative file of booklets, clippings, and articles describing aspects of the community's life. If a college or university is situated near by, perhaps the sociology department can direct attention to valuable supplementary materials. In many instances it is desirable to assemble data upon the territory adjacent to the local church. Since urban church members are commonly drawn from the adjoining neighborhood population, one may expect the congregation to reflect approximately the cultural composition of the community. A study of the people will provide insights respecting the persons who are affiliated with the church. Like neighborhood, like church.

SOURCES OF CHURCH MATERIALS

The reader may now be wondering about the location of source materials. Some data are in the local church and thereby immediately accessible, while other information will require the expenditure of time and patience before it is found. Hence the relevance of the following discussion which treats six sources: denominational yearbooks, membership roll, financial records, Sunday-school enrollment list, organization records, and knowledge possessed by individuals. Such facts underlie local church analysis.

Denominational Yearbooks. Trend data on local churches are found in the statistical yearbooks of the denomination. Most major and many minor denominations publish annual statistical reports and file copies in regional and national offices. Religious administrators and historians, as well as theological seminaries, normally assemble research data of this type. Occasionally a near-by pastor makes a hobby of collecting a file of yearbooks. A letter written to the national headquarters of one's denomination will help locate the needed materials.

From the statistical yearbooks can be taken trend figures by individual local church on membership, accessions to membership, Sunday-school enrollment, Sunday-school attendance, local church finances, benevolences, women's work, youth work, property values, ministerial support, and several additional items. Generally speaking, a period ranging from ten to twenty-five years is required to pick up a trend. Yearbooks which antedate the current year are utilized, and this provides a terminal point for the commencement of the trend. Over the period selected, data are taken off in five-year intervals. For an intensive study of trends information is tabulated for each year.

Church Membership Roll. Here is another important source of vital materials. The membership roll is kept almost universally in a large loose-leaf book with a page for each member-family. Variants from the typical pattern of record keeping include the card file system, a typed list of the members arranged in alphabetical order, and a chronological roll according to the date of affiliation. Whatever the method used, the name, address, and membership status of individuals is clearly indicated.

Several uses may be made of these records. Street addresses reveal the geographical distribution of church members and provide a basis for the preparation of parish maps. Duration of membership can be studied also. Further, individuals may be grouped according to age, sex, occupation, and leadership position. Church attendance traits and participation in organizational activities can be investigated by a competent committee utilizing procedures to be discussed in detail later on in the present chapter.

Church Financial Records. Almost universally records are kept of persons who contribute systematically to the financial support of the local church. Whether the information is kept in a conventional church finance book or in a card system, the study committee is afforded an important body of primary data. Since financial information is commonly recorded according to person or family and in specific amounts contributed over a year's period, it is relatively easy to discover how many church members give systematically, how old they are, and in what amounts they contribute. A serious analysis of the financial structure of the local church requires access to these relevant data. Occasionally a parish map is prepared showing where contributors reside and the amounts given summarized by geographical area.

Sunday-School Enrollment List. Sunday-school enrollment records exist variously as class lists, department lists, or master address files. These records are more variable in form than church membership lists and usually are revised annually.

If a complete master enrollment list does not exist, the information can be procured with the expenditure of but a little effort. Each teacher may be asked to prepare a complete list of her pupils the next Sunday, utilizing the assistance of members present to procure names of absentees. The department head and the pastor may check over the lists submitted, adding pupils who may have been inadvertently omitted. Data respecting the age and sex of each person can be placed before the name. In this manner a complete up-to-date Sunday-school enrollment list can be prepared within a week.

Several types of information are inherent in the enrollment list: addresses of the pupils may be utilized in the preparation of a map showing geographical distribution; the name may be traced to the individual in order to discover age and sex; and the number of adults involved in the religious education project may be determined. The over-all age-sex configuration of the Sunday school reveals the scope of that project. Information respecting financial support by individuals is of value where reliable records are kept. Gross fiscal figures are useful in trend studies. Enrollees who are affiliated with the church probably are listed on the membership financial books if a contribution is made.

Church Organization Records. In many local churches organized groups keep records of membership, attendance, dues collected, activities, and so on. Often such records are useful in preparing a church-wide participation analysis. The names of members can be traced through the various organizations of the local church in order to discover what activities are participated in and what leadership positions are held. Regularity of attendance at functions can be investigated. While funds raised by each group provide additional insight into the financial structure of the local church, the activities reveal the range and frequency of functions in the life of the local church for a given year.

Knowledge Possessed by Individuals. Vital information exists in the minds of the leaders of the local church. This consists in the accumulation of information pertaining to fellow members of the local institution which years of experience in the congregation has deposited. Such knowledge slips unnoticed into the minds of church leaders as they function in office.

Often these data have not been put down anywhere. There are no written records. A reliable access to the knowledge possessed by individuals is via group concurrence; six to ten experienced local church leaders are brought together for consultation. Objective information respecting age, sex, occupation, size of family, home ownership, use of telephone, automobile ownership, educational achievement, and so on, is requested pertaining to all members of the church congregation. The assembled leaders pool their information and determine objective answers based upon observation and personal experience across the years with the individuals under consideration. Names are examined one at a time and a written decision put down. Blind guessing should be scrupulously avoided, and therefore individuals about whom no trustworthy information is at hand should be skipped. However, if many names are skipped, the committee should be enlarged.

The approach itself is not novel, for this process is utilized regularly by canvassers representing the U. S. Bureau of the Census.

These trained interviewers do not make personal contact with every individual reported upon. Information respecting age, sex, place of birth, occupation, and so forth is provided by a member of the household who happens to be at home when the census taker calls. It is assumed that a mature occupant does possess sufficiently accurate information respecting other persons in the home to provide reliable answers. This assumption is usually justifiably grounded.

In a similar manner vital objective information can be procured from local church leaders. Extensive experience gained through working with religious committees has convinced me that these data constitute an important source of materials in the study of a local church. The information can be assembled under proper conditions and utilized within reasonable limits.

TYPES OF LOCAL CHURCH ANALYSIS

The data available from the various sources indicated in the preceding section become the basis for the analyses described below. Although a dozen or more different types of analysis have been developed and utilized in the study of the local church, the present discussion treats the six most commonly used: church trends, parish maps, membership age and sex, financial support, leaders and officers, and plant utilization.

1. *Church Trends.* The simplest and most useful device for analyzing the local church consists in a study of trends. Membership figures at five-year intervals are taken from the denominational yearbooks over a trend period of from fifteen to fifty years, depending upon the purposes of the project. Similar data respecting the enrollment of the Sunday school can be gathered. An examination of the trends in church finance, benevolences, accessions to membership, women's work, and youth work may prove enlightening. Where a close study of fluctuations within trends is required, data are assembled year by year. Growth or decline can be described in terms of numerical and percentage gains or losses.

An additional type of analysis which is based upon trend information is called the evangelistic index. This trend measure has been used extensively by religious researchers. It consists of a comparison of the average number of accessions (all types) to membership during the opening five years and during the closing five years of the

42

trend period selected. Further, in order to make the figures comparable among churches varying in size, it is necessary to translate the number of accessions into the average number of members received annually per one hundred church members. The comparison may be made by an individual church or by a group of churches in the community. If the evangelistic index is greater at the beginning of the trend period than at the end, it probably reveals that

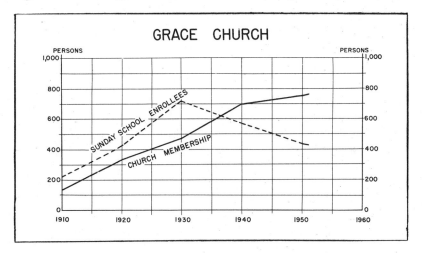

FIGURE No. 4

TREND CHART OF A CITY CHURCH

the church or denomination has become less aggressive evangelistically during recent years. Remedial measures can of course be taken to alter any condition found.

Local church trend materials of various types can be charted in a manner similar to that shown in Figure No. 4. This treatment visualizes the findings and aids measurably in galvanizing the congregation into action. Seeing is believing.

2. *Parish Map*. Some urban problems require an accurate knowledge of where church members live. The address of each person is looked up and located on a street map of the city. A tally mark or dot is placed in the proper city block for each member. This process is continued until all members have been located by place of residence. Sunday-school enrollees should be distributed in like manner. Tallies or dots are counted and replaced by a number within each

43

block. When completed the parish map may look similar to Figure No. 5. Church members are usually recorded with black ink and Sunday-school persons with red pencil. Contrasting colors reveal clearly the dispersion of persons connected with the local church in these two important relationships.

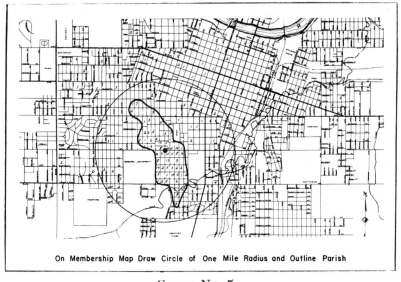

On Membership Map Draw Circle of One Mile Radius and Outline Parish

FIGURE No. 5
LOCAL CHURCH PARISH MAP

The outline of the area where the principal concentration of the local church members and Sunday-school enrollees reside is referred to as a parish configuration. Members and enrollees of most urban churches tend to cluster dominantly into a neighborhood pattern. However, a downtown church tends to have a scattered membership.

A Protestant church with a downtown location is likely to draw its congregation from the entire city. This generalization applies also to prestige churches, churches in transition, churches of bilingual background, churches recently involved in a merger or relocation, and churches of specialized ministry (theological, social service, and among handicapped persons). In such cases members are broadly scattered and wide dispersion is characteristic. On the other hand the neighborhood type (consult Figure No. 5 for sample analysis) generally shows the majority of its members huddled within a mile radius (service distance) of the church plant. Its outreach is delimited by barriers. The bounds of a residential neighborhood usually consist of primary barriers, that is, railroad tracks and yards, industrial installations, large parks or cemeteries, and prominent topographical features. Such barriers likewise constitute the boundaries of a parish.

To prepare a parish configuration of the local church a committee utilizes the membership list and a street map of the entire city. Maps can be procured in a bookstore or drugstore. All members living in each particular city block are indicated by a number. The procedure is described above. One should not record by families but by individuals. If the committee uses black ink for writing in members, a contrasting color should be used for recording Sunday-school enrollees. In instances of churches modest in size both types of data can be recorded on a single map. For churches of a thousand members or more, Sunday-school data are usually placed on a separate map.

After the parish map has been prepared, religious leaders can profitably study the configuration pattern with reference to its size, shape, and the influence of primary barriers upon it. The analysis will reveal an interesting battery of insights.

3. *Age and Sex of Members.*[1] The age-sex composition of the local church is amenable to scientific analysis. Preliminary preparation consists of a distribution of members according to chronological age and sex. The value of this analysis reposes in the revelation of current strengths and weaknesses within the membership structure. Church data should be compared with population data for the neighborhood or city to bring out contrasts.

Data for the membership analysis can be assembled by a committee of eight or ten persons. Individuals are selected on the basis of extensive contacts within the church and knowledge of the congregation. Committee personnel among them should know nearly the entire membership of the local church. Usually the following key persons are chosen: pastor, church secretary, church treasurer,

---

[1] The Sunday-school enrollment can also be analyzed respecting age and sex, following the processes herein described.

45

several women, several young adults, and a few persons at large from the congregation. Wide acquaintanceship among local church members is an important prerequisite for inclusion.

The constituted committee should be convened to estimate the chronological age of all church members. A typical membership list furnishes adequate space for abbreviated pencil notes. Therefore in front of each member's name are written a number corresponding to the person's age and a letter (*M* or *F*) corresponding to the person's sex. For example, in the committee's judgment George Adams is fifty-three years of age. Notes on the membership list would appear as follows: 53 *M* Adams, George R., 249 Main Street.

Thus the committee in accordance with its best working knowledge determines the approximate chronological age of each church member under consideration. Names are passed over and omitted only in instances where reliable knowledge is lacking. If the committee is compelled to omit more than 15 per cent of the church membership, other persons should be drawn in to augment the committee. Then the omitted individuals are reconsidered. When the membership roll has been completely covered, omitting only the few persons' names about whom the committee holds inadequate information, there remains the routine task of recording members by means of tally marks in the appropriate places on a work sheet. Tallies preserve the anonymity of members.

The procedure detailed above should be followed literally if the data for the present type of analysis is to be reliable. A distribution of the local church membership by age and sex is ultimately procured. The age categories used on the sample work sheet shown in Figure No. 6 are relatively simple but sociologically significant. Intervals below twenty-five years are in five-year units; from twenty-five to sixty-five years in ten-year units; and above sixty-five years in an estimated fifteen-year unit. Within each age group the distinction is retained between male and female. This is apparent from an inspection of the sample work sheet.

Membership data can be translated into percentages. Indeed they must be in order to reach the chart form of Figure No. 6. To accomplish this calculation the total number of members tallied on the work sheet is used as a divisor. The figure is divided into the number of persons found in each age group under each sex column. The

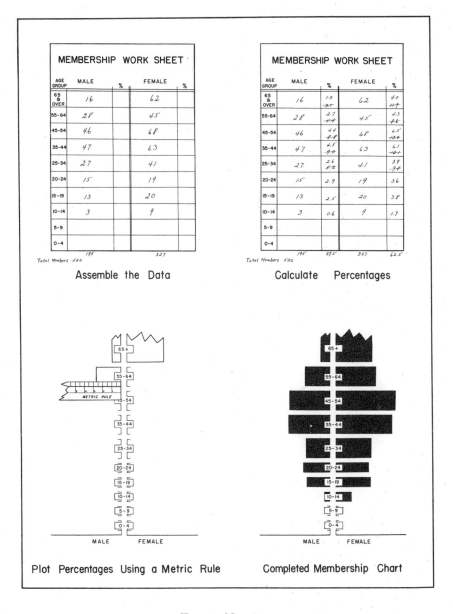

FIGURE No. 6

MEMBERSHIP ANALYSIS WORK SHEET AND CHART

quotient is written as a percentage, pointed off to the nearest tenth. Percentages should total one hundred if there are no errors in the work. This is a simple device for checking accuracy.

Findings should include the percentage of males and females, of members over fifty years of age, of members under twenty years of age, and so forth. Further, percentage calculations make possible the construction of a membership pyramid. This type of chart is useful in presenting a graphic report to the congregation and to the church officiary. A careful study may disclose readily points of strength and weakness in the membership as revealed diagrammatically on the pyramid. Findings should be fully discussed by the committee.

4. *Financial Support by Members.* A financial analysis is not intended to study the entire budget of the local church but instead investigates the extent to which systematic financial support characterizes the pattern of giving by members. Such information is accessible and can be procured with little difficulty.

The committee should have access to (a) the membership roll of full members and (b) the financial books of the local church, covering the latest completed fiscal year. A completed fiscal year is chosen in order that the total amount intended to be contributed to the local church during a specific twelve-month period by the individual can be recorded and the books pertaining thereto closed and audited. Some members give weekly, while others contribute amounts on a monthly, quarterly, semiannual, or annual basis. Only contributions which show evidence of continuity, year by year, or week by week, may be regarded as systematic. This realistic definition includes weekly support, tithing, and the miscellaneous types referred to above. In such cases the intent of the contributor may be inferred to by systematic support. He accepts fiscal responsibility toward the local church.

In the preceding section (*Age and Sex of Members*) a procedure was suggested by which to procure and record the estimated age and the sex of church members. That process constitutes the first step toward making a financial analysis. If the procedure has been followed, the membership roll should bear now the age and sex information for each member. Turning to the next step, the committee secures from the treasurer's books the amount in dollars contributed by each member during the completed fical year. This amount is written in pencil immediately in front of the name of the member under consideration.

For example, George Adams now has three entries before his name in the membership roll book: a 53 indicating estimated age, an *M* indicating sex, and a 26 indicating that he contributed twenty-six dollars during the latest completed fiscal year. In abbreviated form the entries preceding his name would appear as follows: 53 *M* 26 Adams, George R., 249 Main Street. In as much as George Adams and his wife contributed fifty-two dollars jointly during the closed fiscal year, and since both are members, the amount of the contribution is divided equally between them. Hence the entry of twenty-six dollars. Mrs. Adams receives credit for the remaining half of the total amount.

This bifurcation of contributions is followed only in cases where husband and wife are both members of the local church. Otherwise whoever is the member receives credit for the total amount. Children who are members must have made a contribution individually in order to receive credit for systematic financial support. So-called family contributions should be credited only to husband and wife if both are members. It must be remembered that the primary purpose of the financial analysis is to discover how many persons actually support the church in a systematic way, in what age and sex groups they occur, and in order to ascertain the amount or size of such contributions.

The entire membership roll is covered in the manner outlined above. Data are written in pencil before each name. Obviously members who do not contribute to the local church will not be listed in the church treasurer's book. When the membership roll has been worked over in the manner described, there remains the routine task of recording the performance of members by means of tallies in the proper places on a work sheet. Amounts of money are written in the appropriate sex column and age box on the work sheet. In general the tallying procedure parallels that outlined for the preceding section.

Data on contributors may be translated into percentages and charted on a membership pyramid. This chart (Figure No. 7) visualizes in graphic form the principal findings of the local church financial

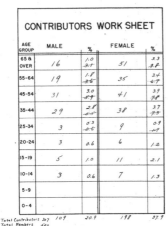

CONTRIBUTORS WORK SHEET

AGE GROUP	MALE	%	FEMALE	%
65 & OVER	16	1.0 / 3.1	51	3.3 / 9.8
55-64	19	1.8 / 3.6	35	3.4 / 6.7
45-54	31	3.0 / 5.9	41	3.9 / 7.8
35-44	29	2.8 / 5.6	38	3.7 / 7.3
25-34	3	0.3 / 0.6	9	0.9 / 1.7
20-24	3	0.6	6	1.2
15-19	5	1.0	11	2.1
10-14	3	0.6	7	1.3
5-9				
0-4				

Total Contributors 307   109   20.9   198   37.9
Total Members 522

Assemble Data & Calculate Percentages

FINANCIAL WORK SHEET
AMOUNTS GIVEN IN DOLLARS

AGE GROUP	MALE	÷100	FEMALE	÷100
65 & OVER	363 / 1090	3.6	813 / 2440	8.1
55-64	260 / 520	2.6	570 / 1140	5.7
45-54	755 / 1510	7.6	885 / 1770	8.9
35-44	417 / 835	4.2	468 / 936	4.7
25-34	52 / 104	0.5	182 / 364	1.8
20-24	52	0.5	104	1.0
15-19	104	1.0	156	1.6
10-14	26	0.3	52	0.5
5-9				
0-4				

Total 11,201   4,239   6,962

Convert Dollar Amounts into Ratios

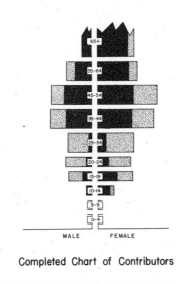

Completed Chart of Contributors

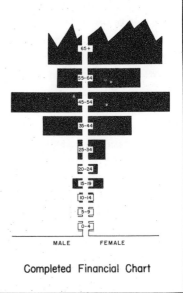

Completed Financial Chart

FIGURE No. 7
VISUAL ANALYSIS OF LOCAL CHURCH FINANCES

analysis. The percentage of members who contribute, the percentage of contributors under thirty-five years of age, the percentage of contributors in each age group and in each sex category, comprise information useful to church officials. Other items will suggest themselves to the committee. High lights should be selected for presentation and discussion.

The amount or size of contributions calls attention to another important aspect of the analysis. A step-by-step procedure for the charting of these data is suggested by Figure No. 7. The graphic result is instructive. One may observe in which age groups the total contributions are largest or smallest. Further, materials can be charted to show the distribution of contributions by size. Small contributions per capita usually indicate members of modest income or child contributors or token supporters. A token giver is a member who contributes as little as possible to the support of the local church and thereby hopes to dismiss his responsibility on minimum terms. Such individuals need to be re-educated.

Findings procured by an analysis of financial support by members provide insights into the fiscal structure of the local church. Therefore the finance committee should utilize such information for guidance in the next every-member financial canvass. An analytical approach based on facts is an effective way to educate the congregation to a higher level of fiscal support, for it elicits a hearty response among laymen.

5. *Leaders and Officers.* Frequently a scientific inventory of the local church leadership situation is called for. Pastors and administrators sense the need but lack the technique. A few practical suggestions in this sphere will prove helpful. Data respecting officers and leaders can be gathered on age, sex, occupation, place of residence, amount of church fiscal support, number of officers and leadership positions currently held, years of tenure in each position, and duration of membership in the local church. Other items may be added to suit the purposes of the committee.

The task of assembling information on officers and leaders is simplified through the use of a questionnaire. Such an instrument is customarily mimeographed and distributed among leaders in a public meeting or mailed to the homes. The questionnaire should be designed simply and circulated among all workers. To guarantee adequate coverage a designated committee should fill in the information on officers and leaders who fail to return the work sheet. Further, there may be instances where the committee is required also to complete the information on work sheets that have been returned. These contingencies should be provided for. The individual should conscientiously report all offices and leadership positions held currently or in the past and write in the number of years' tenure for each position. Information of course should be limited to statements of fact.

When the data from all local church leaders are in hand, the committee can summarize the materials in various ways. The age and sex distribution may be tallied and charted, following the pattern described under (3) *Age and Sex of Members*. A map showing the geographical dispersion of leaders may be prepared according to the specifications detailed under (2) *Parish Map*. A chart showing the extent of financial support among leaders may be prepared, following the suggestions given under (4) *Financial Support by Members*. These three types of materials should be carefully studied for possible clues pertaining to strengths and weaknesses in the local church. If possible, comparisons should be made with the rank-and-file members. In this manner many significant contrasts are likely to be discovered.

Further, the analytical process may be broadened to include an examination of the number of leadership positions held per capita and the period of tenure in each. Charting such information can be done in a pattern similar to the sample shown in Figure No. 8. Here is an ordinary bar graph which nearly anyone can draw to scale with but limited facilities. In no way, however, does the elementariness of the draftsmanship diminish the importance of the data. Relationships between items of information are set up in sharp silhouette via this technique.

Some experts urge that factors such as prominence in the community, vocational activity in the white-collar occupations, advancing age, and kindred characteristics dominantly influence candidacy for leadership position in the local church. Whether or not this contention is true, the leadership situation merits a periodic inventory. Surely the committee will wish to take into account all aspects of the problem and follow the facts toward a fuller understanding of the

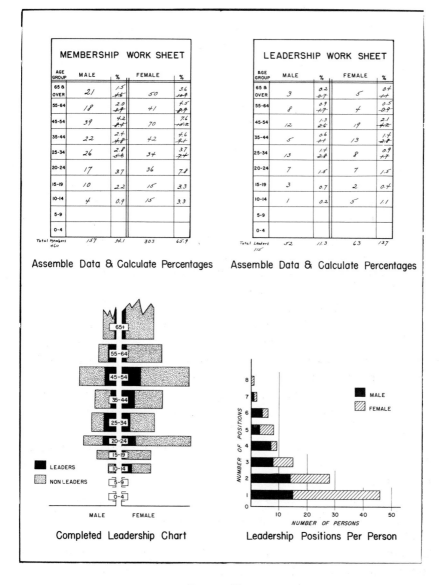

MEMBERSHIP WORK SHEET

AGE GROUP	MALE	%	FEMALE	%
65 & OVER	21	1.5 ~~1.6~~	50	3.6 ~~10.9~~
55-64	18	2.0 ~~3.9~~	41	4.5 ~~8.9~~
45-54	39	4.2 ~~8.4~~	70	7.6 ~~15.2~~
35-44	22	2.4 ~~4.8~~	42	4.6 ~~9.1~~
25-34	26	2.8 ~~5.6~~	34	3.7 ~~7.4~~
20-24	17	3.7	36	7.8
15-19	10	2.2	15	3.3
10-14	4	0.9	15	3.3
5-9				
0-4				
Total Members 460	157	34.1	303	65.9

Assemble Data & Calculate Percentages

LEADERSHIP WORK SHEET

AGE GROUP	MALE	%	FEMALE	%
65 & OVER	3	0.2 ~~0.7~~	5	0.4 ~~1.1~~
55-64	8	0.9 ~~1.7~~	4	0.5 ~~0.9~~
45-54	12	1.3 ~~2.6~~	19	2.1 ~~4.2~~
35-44	5	0.6 ~~1.1~~	13	1.4 ~~2.9~~
25-34	13	1.4 ~~2.8~~	8	0.9 ~~1.9~~
20-24	7	1.5	7	1.5
15-19	3	0.7	2	0.4
10-14	1	0.2	5	1.1
5-9				
0-4				
Total Leaders 115	52	11.3	63	13.7

Assemble Data & Calculate Percentages

Completed Leadership Chart

Leadership Positions Per Person

FIGURE No. 8

LEADERSHIP ANALYSIS CHART

officiary of the local church. A thorough inventory may disclose ways of strengthening the leadership situation.

6. *Plant Utilization.* The extent to which the local church building and facilities are actually used is a relevant analysis in many urban situations. This consideration should underlie plans for program change and for new construction. Pressure upon the existing church plant is measured in terms of average use-hours per month per room. How astonishing it is to discover that few urban churches utilize completely the building and facilities at their disposal. Therefore an inventory becomes a relevant prelude to sound future planning.

To gather materials for a plant-utilization analysis one must either secure a blueprint showing the floor plan of the church buildings or else draw to scale a chart showing the room layout for each floor. The sketch need not be an elaborate drawing; the simpler the better. An examination of Figure No. 9, which shows a sample analysis of the type under discussion, may prove instructive at this point. In large churches it may be necessary to assign a code number or letter to each room.

Next prepare sheets of paper (typewriter size, 8½"x11", preferred), providing one sheet for each room. Place the room's appellation and code number at the top of the sheet. Then write down three items of information respecting the use of each room: (1) name of each church organization or group using the room, (2) number of persons in attendance for each function, and (3) duration of each use in hours per year. For example, a woman's society with an average attendance of forty-three persons may use a particular room ten times per annum for two hours on each occasion. Therefore the entry on the appropriate room tally sheet would appear as follows: *Ladies' Aid, 43 persons, 20 hours.* This procedure should be followed for every room in the church plant excepting halls, storage space, heating, utility room, and rest rooms.

Care should be exercised to include the activity of every organization, group, and Sunday-school class. Several leaders should check over the work sheets for omissions. Further, special functions such as weddings, funerals, baptisms, special meetings, study groups, and so forth should be included. The purpose of the analysis is to show in both statistical and graphic forms the extent to which each room of the church plant is used. Data are first gathered on a yearly basis and then divided by twelve to procure an average use per month quotient. This places the materials before the committee in a form readily understood, and from this point the findings are easily communicated to the congregation.

Use-hours per month per room are shown on a chart (Figure No. 9). In an enlarged outline form the room layout for each floor of the church plant is drawn. Then when the rooms have been identified by name or code symbol, the differential in use-hours is revealed in a scale similar to the legend shown in Figure No. 9. Rooms used less than one hour per month are left white. Rooms shown slight use (1-3 hours) are designated with widely spaced dots. Rooms used at least once a week on the average (4-9 hours) are hatched with slanting lines. Finally rooms most commonly used (10 hours and more) are shaded in with a dark color.

The resultant chart provides the committee and congregation an easily discerned analysis of plant utilization. Should additional elements be added to the ongoing church program, it will be possible now to discover which room space is immediately available. Further, progressive churches may discover how to relieve pressure on the plant by shifting some groups or organizations over to other rooms, thereby staggering the use of its good equipment and space. This procedure may relieve the congestion at the bottlenecks of plant use.

In instances of projected new construction, that is, either remodeling of older buildings or the erection of a new religious education building or sanctuary, the plant-utilization analysis may demonstrate the need for prompt and decisive action. In some instances it may call for significant modification of existing plans. These visualized facts can guide religious leaders in making important decisions.

The six basic types of local church analysis described in the preceding pages commend themselves for inventory use either singly or in battery. For either approach, the methodological procedure outlined should be closely followed in order to avoid needless and damaging bias in gathering data. Further, pastors may desire to examine the local church periodically (at five-year intervals) and thereby measure the modifications which have been wrought in

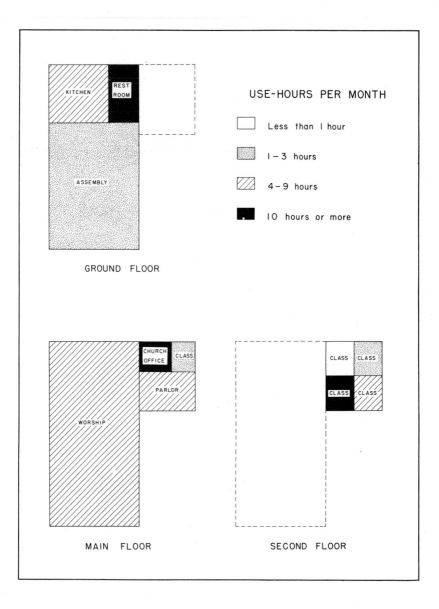

KITCHEN

REST ROOM

ASSEMBLY

GROUND FLOOR

USE-HOURS PER MONTH

Less than 1 hour

1 – 3 hours

4 – 9 hours

10 hours or more

CHURCH OFFICE

CLASS

PARLOR

WORSHIP

MAIN FLOOR

CLASS

CLASS

CLASS

CLASS

SECOND FLOOR

FIGURE No. 9
A PLANT UTILIZATION STUDY

trends, in parish geography, in membership recruitment respecting age and sex, in systematic financial support, in leadership tenure and effectiveness, and in plant utilization. A discovery of these changes may lead to remedial action vital to the ongoing life of the congregation.

Here then are six important ways to study the effectiveness of the local church. Additional insights respecting the relationship between the church and its community are scattered through the remaining chapters of the book and deal with the particular urban situation under discussion. What commends the present chapter to the reader is that a minister and a lay committee can set up and conduct an adequate inventory of a church without additional professional assistance.

SUMMARIZATION AND APPLICATION OF FINDINGS

The study committee must select the analyses which are apposite to the problems which have been so sharply defined and then gather the essential data, following the procedures detailed above. When these steps have been concluded, a general report should be prepared. This document normally consists of at least two essential ingredients: a battery of charts and maps, and a written summary of the materials.

Visual Materials. Graphic aids to the report consist of maps, charts, pictures, and miscellaneous exhibits of data. Generally speaking, charts and maps are prepared on a scale suitable for display purposes. Configurations and lettering need to be large enough to be read easily from the rear of a room. The objective in graphics is to summarize swiftly and accurately significant aspects of the data. Only the more important information is put in visual aid form. Since techniques of charting have been described as the previous discussion unfolded, the committee needs no additional instruction. To arrange the visual materials in a logical sequence is its next important task.

The significance of each chart or map should be written out in terms of three or four vital points. These preliminary notes may be organized later by the leader into an outline of comments and explanations. Prior to a public meeting, a small committee should prepare a statement respecting the visual materials. Thus reasonable unanimity may be procured relating to points of emphasis and order of discussion. Best results are secured when careful preparation is made.

A Written Report. The written report should consist of (1) a statement of problems, (2) a description of the analyses utilized, (3) a discussion of the representativeness of the materials, (4) a summary of the data, and (5) a set of recommendations based upon the findings. Ample opportunity should be provided to discuss both the charts and the statistical data before a preliminary draft of the report is mimeographed or printed in final form for general circulation. Eventually several copies of the revised document should be filed with the committee on local church records.

The opening section of a written report describes the basic and critical problems which called forth the research project. The original statement of problems should now be re-examined in the light of the fresh facts which have been gathered and analyzed. Where desirable the statement should be modified and recast to conform with the present knowledge of the committee.

Turning to the next section, we note the necessity of a brief description of each analytical device (church trends, parish map, and so on) utilized and the relationship it bears to the problems under consideration. A concise explanation of the purpose of dealing with these bodies of data can satisfy the requirements here.

To guide the auditor and reader in arriving at a correct evaluation of the report, a third section delineates the limitations and representativeness of the materials used. The methodology outlined in the present chapter has been carefully tested and therefore constitutes an adequate set of scientific controls in gathering data. Religious leaders should know the limits of the data and compose their findings accordingly. Generalization is only as reliable as the background information against which it is cast.

The body of the report should contain statistical tables with relevant exposition plus a written account of the materials which have been mapped and charted. Here the author or authors walk around the problems by presenting in turn data on the community (population trends and composition, housing conditions, land use and zoning, barriers, and so on) and materials on the church situation (membership trends, financial information, and so on). Such information contributes notably to an objective understanding of conditions and thereby affords the reader an opportunity to become acquainted with the facts, processes, and principles involved in the situation.

This section is followed by a list of findings stated in brief compass and usually in outline form. The points made should have rather direct bearing upon the problem under consideration. Tangential and marginal matters possess more academic than pragmatic significance and hence should be omitted from the present report.

Finally recommendations based upon and deriving from the findings are drawn up. Usually in the form of alternate lines of action each constitutes a bona fide possibility. These merit complete and thorough discussion on the part of leaders and laymen.

Problem-solving Action. Procedures described in the present chapter stress the use of facts in solving problems. Church difficulties are carefully defined and utilized as a directive for the assembling of relevant objective information. No person's pet bias, prejudice, or sentiment is permitted to influence significantly the processes by which facts are collected, manipulated, and arranged in final form. Facts are followed to whatever intelligent solution of the problem is required, and this approach underlies a trustworthy philosophy of local church study. Faith in facts is demanded by present urban church conditions.

It is difficult to justify the effort expended in a local church study unless action of an intelligent and derivative sort follows the inventory. The purpose of religious research is to provide an adequate factual background for intelligent action, since the stimulation of the project itself often prepares the individual to act. Purposive action is intelligence in motion.

The local church committee should take the principal findings of the project and apply them to the solution of specific difficulties. Problems related to plant remodeling or new construction, those related to newly needed program elements, and those related to supplemental ministries of varying types may call for prompt action. Since attention is focused upon the problem, no delay should intervene between the completion of the study and the launching of remedial measures in local church work. Improvement of any unsatisfactory situation can be secured by intelligent action.

Follow-up by Delegated Committees. Sustained effort is required in treating some urban problems. Therefore small functional committees need to be entrusted with the task of applying the study findings to the problem—whether it is the erection of a new church, the extensive recruitment of new members, the financial re-education of noncontributing church members, the expansion of the Sunday-school program, the revision of church records, the reorganization of church leadership opportunities, and other duly required changes in church life.

A report of committee progress may be expected after six months in order to guarantee prompt action. Further, an annual checkup may be desirable since action is the desired result of all religious research.

There is not a single problem which harasses the urban local church which cannot be solved by intelligent action. A scientific inventory is a welcome antidote for religious uncertainty and ineffectiveness. Protestantism in the city is often weaker than it needs to be.

CRITERIA FOR AN EFFECTIVE CITY CHURCH

The selection of local church analyses treated and illustrated in the preceding pages furnishes a serviceable orientation for the account of city church norms which follows. Admittedly no set of criteria for determining urban church effectiveness has won universal approval. Heir to the usual limitations ascribed to norms in the pragmatic field is the decalogue presented below. Therefore it may be regarded as tentative though relevant. Clearly its merit arises from the possibilities of comparison with the regular findings on a particular congregation which has utilized the analyses detailed in this chapter. For this reason chiefly the criteria contribute importantly to the discussion. Perhaps some city church may aspire to achieve:

1. *Reasonable membership size*—at least five hundred active members; in order to provide an adequate potential for a complete church life.

2. *Proper Sunday-school enrollment size*—at least matching active church membership; to produce and train sufficient Protestants for tomorrow's church.

3. *Vital trends*—growth of membership and Sunday-school en-

rollment exceeding that for the population, percentagewise; to keep pace with the expanding city Protestant opportunity.

4. *An adequate budget*—at least a living salary for pastor and staff members plus a matching amount for benevolences; in order to procure a competent staff and to share in the work of Christianity around the world.

5. *An indigenous ministry*—a thoroughgoing penetration of the neighborhood around the church; in order to minister to people residing within a one-mile service radius.

6. *An up-to-date program*—quality and range matching the religious and fellowship needs of the constituency; to mobilize and channel all the talents, interests, and energies of constituents into Christian activtiy.

7. *Full participation of constituents*—at least every person a spiritual dynamo, a worshiper, a leader, and financial supporter; to stimulate true religion at the grass roots.

8. *Required special ministries*—at least relevant service to handicapped persons and to persons in special circumstances; to furnish a practical spiritual frame of reference for tragedy and hardship.

9. *Enlightened continuous public relations*—bringing the cause of organized religion before the general public through press, radio, television, the theater, and so on; to let Christ be known among the multitudes.

10. *Vital relationship with Protestantism*—at least local and national affiliation through denominational teamwork along with participation in and support of the ecumenical movement; to aid in procuring a better world.

CHAPTER III

How to Conduct a Religious Census

THE religious census is a simple, direct method for discovering the religious composition of the population of a city, a town, or a neighborhood. Numerous clergymen and laymen have experience in this field and consequently are unlikely to encounter serious difficulty in the organization and administration of such a project. However, some practical suggestions may be appreciated not only by the novice but also by other interested Protestant leaders.

The purpose of this chapter is to collect into an ordered system the tested procedures in common use. Since my emphasis is pragmatic, sufficient detail is included to guide the reader in launching a project. Experience shows that ministers and laymen can set up and conduct a religious census with a minimum of professional guidance.

The religious census is but one of the number of research devices designed to procure religious information. However, the intrinsic values and practical relevance for evangelistic outreach commend this type of project especially to church leaders. Although the undertaking may be conducted on an interfaith, an interdenominational, or a local church basis, best results for problems involving comity are procured when it is launched on the interdenominational basis.

TYPES OF RELIGIOUS CENSUS

By definition the religious census is a door-to-door visitation of households in a city or neighborhood whereby volunteer workers gather information through a brief personal interview. Normally facts respecting religious attendance, membership, or preference of the inhabitants are secured. The project aims at a direct contact with the population. Data gathered are summarized and interpreted so that the religious characteristics according to faith and denomination may be discovered. The up-to-dateness of such information is a significant value.

A religious census can be conducted in several ways. Commonly every household in the survey area is contacted. No residential territory is left out; no family is omitted. Several call-backs may be necessary at households where residents were absent on the first visit. This comprehensive type of religious census reaches practically all of the people and provides a detailed knowledge of the community. Many cities and towns in the United States have been surveyed in this fashion. Where acute churching problems exist, the community should have this exhaustive type of religious census.

The second type of religious canvass is known as a sample block census. In such an undertaking only selected families (one out of ten or one out of five) or selected city blocks are covered. As a time-saving and work-reducing short cut to needed religious knowledge of the community, this type of census is trustworthy and significantly useful when under the direction of a competent researcher. Certain assumptions lie behind the sample block or sample family approach. The committee should possess a thorough working knowledge of the community under investigation and therefore demonstrate competence in selecting the blocks or families to be canvassed. Some of the committee's personnel should be trained in research and able to set up the project following scientific sampling procedure. If there is any uncertainty respecting a committee's competence, the sociology department of a near-by college or university should be contacted for technical assistance. Recent religious censuses in various U. S. communities reveal the limitations of this approach where adequate sociological knowledge of the community is lacking. The U. S. Bureau of the Census uses the sample block census for many of its special studies. In the religious field, however, one important limitation of this method consists in failure to locate more than a fraction of the unchurched families. To set up a reliable sample block census is always an intricate procedure, one which is not commonly recommended for amateurs.

PROBLEM SOLVING BY A RELIGIOUS CENSUS

A house-to-house religious census may be applied to the solution of manifold important problems. Pastors and administrators need a detailed knowledge of the religious composition of a community or neighborhood in order to resolve a variety of churching difficulties which arise in part from a lack of such vital information. Ultimately it is unwise to make decisions respecting church extension, church relocation, church merger, church program change, and kindred problems without reference to the community's religious composition. Protestantism has often been remiss at this point. A religious census is often an appropriate course of action preliminary to the disposition of a churching problem.

Results from religious censuses in the city reveal that from one fourth to one half of the population are unchurched. Thousands of urban residents for one reason or another have drifted away from organized religion. And the number is increasing. A practical objective justifying the work involved in a religious census is to locate and to identify the unchurched. A follow-up program of evangelistic visiting should then be launched to recover the unchurched to religion.

Residential mobility is a prominent characteristic of urban dwellers. Persons in some parts of a city have more frequent changes of address than do residents elsewhere. In certain types of neighborhood people move often. Recently a pastor reported to me the loss of sixty member families from the local church neighborhood in a single year. This diminution of indigenous Protestant potential emphasizes the ever-present fact of mobility in the city. In spite of well-kept records churches lose tracks of many families. A periodic inventory of the community at five-year intervals, utilizing a religious census, would prove valuable to the work of Protestantism.

The migration of thousands of people from one community to another has become the occasion for new concern on the part of the government. In no less a degree does the nomadic multitude become a concern of organized Christianity, since the influx of population to many urban places has resulted in a remarkable enlargement of religious opportunity. Numerous new churches must be built to bring the ministries of religion to the city's newcomers. A religious census is useful here in determining the center of the new church opportunity and in appraising its numerical extent.

Often when local churches are currently below the level of effective size for an urban ministry, many unchurched persons reside within the area adjacent to the church plant. In a situation recently brought to my attention a sufficient number of unchurched evangelical Protestants was found to permit a twofold increase in member strength of the local church involved. Persons who have been inactive for years, persons who are lost between churches, persons who are newcomers to the city, may be discovered by means of a religious census. The pastor concerned about the opportunity in his own parish may ascertain the religious prospects in the neighborhood with relative ease, accuracy, and promptness. Here again a religious census applied to a particular neighborhood may prove as useful as one for the city as a whole.

Records show that an inadequate knowledge of the community has been a fruitful source of churching mistakes. No church should be closed or relocated before a thorough religious census of the neighborhood has been made; no suburb should be entered by a denomination or a faith prior to an adequate analysis of the current religious opportunity. This gathering of religious information is an important step preliminary to the effective solution of many churching problems.

The religious census has additional Protestant significance. Materials gathered in the undertaking can be placed in summary tables by geographical areas and analyzed. If an area needs a new church, the findings of the census may indicate which denomination, working under comity agreement, should take responsibility for the extension work. Thus councils of churches especially require mastery of this technique as regular procedure in dealing with churching problems. Findings can be placed on file and denominational leaders invited in to utilize the reference materials.

SELECTION OF THE CENSUS AREA

The area selected for a religious census is determined by the kind of problem under consideration. If a new church is contemplated, the census territory is likely to consist of a developing residential suburb on the edge of the city or perhaps new housing along radial highways leading out into the countryside. If a large-scale public or private housing project has been recently erected in the urban community, a religious canvass may be needed to determine whether the residents are adequately churched. If a merger of local churches is contemplated, a religious census of the area may reveal the surmised diminishing Protestant opportunity. If a church relocation is under consideration, knowledge of the religious composition of the neighborhood to be abandoned, as well as of the neighborhood adjacent to the contemplated relocation site, is essential to an intelligent discussion of the matter. For the solution of these and kindred problems the religious census has proved to be significantly relevant.

After defining the problem to be solved a local committee determines the geographical area to be covered. This analytical process prepares the committee to observe the structure of the city and its principal neighborhoods. The location of prominent topographical features such as rivers, bluffs, ravines, creeks, lakes, hills, parks, and cemeteries is noteworthy. Existence of industrial establishments, railroad tracks and sidings, public institutions, substandard residential territory, and kindred uses of land is important. Such features assist the committee in setting the natural boundaries of the neighborhood to be canvassed.

In instances where the entire city should be covered, use of the current municipal boundaries is accepted procedure. However, even under such circumstances it is necessary to subdivide the community into its natural neighborhoods. Since topographical and industrial barriers generally bound the neighborhoods on one or more sides, boundary streets and highways for the census areas should be fixed with these considerations in mind. Suburban territory is subdivided according to concentrations of population. Formation of extremely large census areas is to be avoided.

A Census of the Entire Community. Frequently the local council of churches or a single denomination desires an inventory of the religious composition of the city or town. Therefore the entire community within its corporate boundaries is selected for a religious census. In such an undertaking effort is made to procure the cooperation of the majority of the major and minor denominations in order to guarantee the facile completion of the canvass. Many workers will be needed. Since all denominations stand to benefit, the census is wisely put on an interdenominational basis and under interdenominational auspices, with expenses distributed as broadly as possible. A council of churches is ideally set up to sponsor and to supervise such an undertaking. Most communities require a city-wide project.

A Census in an Older Section of the Community. The officials of a local church in an area where housing has begun to deteriorate may wonder whether a relocation to more promising territory should be contemplated. Before a withdrawal is seriously considered, the local church leaders should discover the religious composition of the territory within a mile radius of the present church site. Further, perhaps the council of churches has a request from several denominations demanding an inventory of an older section of the city. Some denominational administrators wonder if the neighborhood remains sufficiently Protestant in composition to justify continuance of existing church work. In such instances reliance upon a religious census will assist in securing a solution to the problem.

A Census in an Overchurched Neighborhood. There may appear to be too many churches in a particular neighborhood. In the minds of some church officials a severely competitive situation seems to exist among several denominations, and the question of the future of the several local churches is properly raised. Perhaps national mission funds from several denominations are being put into a competitive situation with the result that financial support from outside the community keeps the feeble institutions alive. If so, is it desirable to continue the mission support? A recent study of an urban subsidy program for a large denomination revealed the hopelessness of maintaining churches which have no extensive opportunity for Protestant ministry. This finding parallels results of other studies in the field. The use of a religious census in an overchurched neighborhood is appropriate, since data procured will indicate the extent of Protestant opportunity and provide a list of unchurched persons residing in the territory. From such information church officials may ascertain the extent of Protestant parish overlapping and competition.

A Census in the Suburbs. Many cities and towns have reported conspicuous population increases during recent years. The evidence of such growth, generally speaking, appears on the periphery of the

67

city. Frequently, organized religion fails to keep pace with the expanding community; it commonly falls behind its opportunity in the suburbs. Therefore underchurched areas may exist on the city's edges. An examination of such territory by means of a religious census is pragmatically desirable. The project can be undertaken under the auspices of the council of churches or by one or several denominations, and findings derived from the canvass will provide factual knowledge pertaining to the nature and extent of denominational opportunity. Areas which show a substantial concentration of unchurched Protestants may be entered successfully by a denomination. Many major and minor denominations work under comity agreements, and all such denominational allocations should be cleared through the local council of churches. Manifold urban areas need the detailed analysis provided by a religious census.

ORGANIZATION OF THE RELIGIOUS CENSUS

What practical organization is essential to a religious census? A general committee, a director (volunteer), and several subcommittees are three essentials of the organization. The general committee should be comprised of an inclusive group of co-operating religious bodies. If a council of churches is to set up the organization, effort ought to be made to draw into the committee representatives of religious sects not normally co-operative. Many groups and independent churches are willing to share in this type of project, and usually the "old line" denominations participate readily. If a single denomination undertakes to set up the organization, as many local churches as possible need to assume responsibility for the project. At the local church level prominent leaders and organizations need to be "sold" respecting the objectives of the census.

An official, a minister, or a denominational executive is elected to direct the census. A large representative committee works closely with the director, while subcommittees carry out the details. Subcommittees will be needed (1) to contact local pastors and secure commitment to the project, (2) to procure the required number of door-to-door census workers, (3) to prepare maps and assignments, (4) to tabulate data, (5) to distribute prospect cards (for evangelistic calling), and (6) to prepare a report of the findings. In a large city the various details can be delegated to subcommittees and where

68

financial resources permit, assistance be hired for the tabulation. In a smaller community several functions can be handled by a single subcommittee.

Subsequent sections of this chapter describe the work of the various subcommittees. Practical suggestions are made in the interest of a successful and comprehensive census project.

MAP PREPARATION AND WORKER ASSIGNMENTS

A subcommittee can prepare the map and make up the assignments for workers. Certain materials should be at hand in commencing the task—a clearly printed street map of the community, approximately three by four feet in size, can be procured in a bookstore or drugstore. In addition a bulletin of recent date, describing the community's population and housing characteristics,[1] is useful for reference purposes. Each such bulletin contains a small map showing the subdivisions of the community, and a copy may be examined in the reference room of the local public library or at the city engineer's office.

The personnel of the subcommittee should become acquainted with the various parts of the city, the location of important barriers and topographical features, and the sections where new homes are being erected. A knowledge of the location of depressed economic areas, apartment territory, and large-scale housing projects will prove useful also. A subcommittee should know its community.

Preparing the Map. Mark an outline of the census area on a regular street map of the community. If a canvass is contemplated for the entire city, the municipal limits may serve as outer boundaries of the census area also. If only a portion of the city is to be canvassed, it is desirable to have the boundaries of the survey area coincide with the outer boundary of a group of census tracts, wards, or precincts. The reason is obvious—population data are already available on such divisions of the community and may provide a check upon the completeness of the project. Often a boundary of the census tract or ward or precinct coincides with an important barrier or topographi-

---

[1] If a Housing Supplement Bulletin, Block Statistics, is available in the community, it will prove helpful in determining how many families reside in the various city blocks. Such supplements are available for many U. S. cities having a population of fifty thousand persons or more.

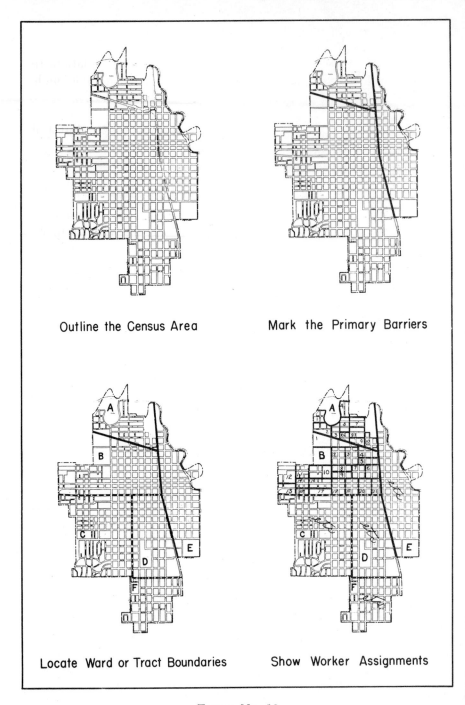

Outline the Census Area   Mark the Primary Barriers

Locate Ward or Tract Boundaries   Show Worker Assignments

Figure No. 10

MAP LAYOUT FOR A RELIGIOUS CENSUS

cal feature. This fact simplifies the work of the committee in laying out the community in preparation for the religious census.

However, such territories are still too large to serve as workable units in the religious census. Hence each census tract, ward, or precinct is subdivided into assignments. An assignment consists of a sufficient number of calls on households to keep the worker occupied for two hours. This averages about forty households. Only whole city blocks are placed in an assignment, and in areas of single family residences several blocks will be required to make up one assignment. In apartment areas a single block may contain as many as forty households. Since it is not possible to assign whole blocks and at the same time allocate exactly forty families to be contracted in the religious census, the committee must aim at placing from thirty to fifty families in each assignment.

The grouping of blocks into assignments must be carried out on the map for each census tract, ward, or precinct in the area to be covered by the religious census. Use a colored pencil or crayon in drawing assignment boundaries. A study of Figure No. 10, which illustrates the mapping required in the city-wide and in the neighborhood types of religious census, may be helpful to the committee. The three steps in the mapping process are (1) placing a boundary for the total area to be covered; (2) reproducing existing convenient divisions of the city, such as census tracts, wards, or precincts; and (3) plotting the assignments. Assignments are numbered in a serpentine fashion on the map with each number recorded later upon an assignment envelope. This map must be retained for reference in preparing a written report at the end of the project.

Assignments for Workers. The next step is to prepare each assignment with a hand-drawn sketch of the city blocks to be canvassed and a code number to identify its geographical location. Envelopes of ordinary letter size (approximately 3½″ by 6½″), normally used for this purpose, may be procured in quantity from a stationery store.

On the face of the envelope (Figure No. 11) is reproduced a free-hand sketch of the area to be covered in the assignment. This consists of from one to three city blocks. The sketch shows the street boundaries and is usually placed so that north is toward the top edge of the envelope. For identification purposes the face of the en-

71

velope also bears the census tract, ward, or precinct number plus the assignment number. For example, assignment twelve in Ward III would be written III-12. This numerical key makes it possible to trace each assignment to the geographical area canvassed as revealed on the master map. Notice that there is also a line upon which to record the name of the worker who accepts the assignment.

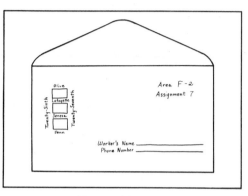

FIGURE No. 11

WORKER'S ASSIGNMENT ENVELOPE

Into the assignment envelope is placed the required number of blank religious census cards. One card is needed for each family canvassed, and a few extra cards are included in the event that the number of families in the assignment area is underestimated.

The Religious Census Card. The religious census card varies in size according to the purpose of the project and the personal preference of the originator, although usually it is three by five or four by six inches. Size is related to facility in handling, and either card referred to can be held in the hand easily while information is recorded. This is an important consideration since all data secured in a religious census are commonly procured in a few moments at the door of a home or apartment.

The committee must decide next what information is needed in the religious census. Ordinarily the following nine items are included: name; address; number of persons in the household; names of adults; names of children under eighteen years; church attended, church membership, or church preference; and race. Data for the entire household are recorded on a single card. A separate line is provided for information on each person. The sample religious census card presented in Figure No. 12 may be altered to suit the purposes of a local community. A local printer can reproduce the required number of cards at a modest cost. Denominational headquarters often stock religious census materials.

A religious canvass is conducted primarily to discover the religious

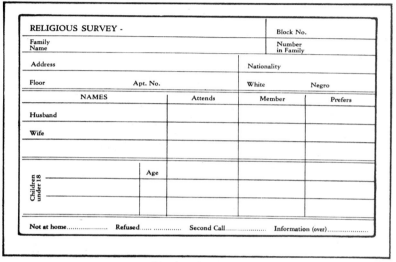

FIGURE No. 12

SAMPLE OF RELIGIOUS CENSUS CARD

characteristics of the population of a city or of a neighborhood. The census card is designed to place residents in one of three major religious categories with respect to faith: attenders, members, and preferences. The worker in conducting an interview with the householder will ascertain what church each member of the family attends and with which church he is affiliated. In instances where individuals neither attend nor belong to a church it will be necessary to discover religious preference. With respect to adults the classification is made after inquiring what clergyman performed the wedding ceremony or what religious background characterized childhood and youth. A preference should always be recorded in terms of a specific faith, denomination, and church. Such data are of great assistance in the tabulation process. Direct questions concerning race should be avoided.

73

In this section of the chapter an attempt was made to outline briefly the process of mapping the area to be covered in the contemplated religious census, to describe and illustrate the preparation of the assignment envelopes, and to present a sample census card. When the entire area covered in the canvass has been divided into assignments, the assignment envelopes prepared, the census cards printed or procured, then the committee is ready to launch the undertaking. Detailed and thorough preparation for the project contributes significantly to its prospects of success.

PROCUREMENT AND INSTRUCTION OF WORKERS

To determine the number of workers needed divide the number of families residing in the census area by forty. If some workers insist upon working in pairs, it will be necessary either to distribute two assignments per team or to recruit additional workers. This situation needs to be considered in planning the project.

With a generally accepted average of 3.4 persons per urban family in a community of 87,549 population, for example, there reside approximately 25,300 families. Applying the calculation described in the preceding paragraph, one finds that 632 workers will be needed. In an interdenominational project involving 30 local churches an average of 21 workers per church will be sufficient to carry the religious census to a successful completion. The reader may apply this principle to the local situation. For each 1,000 people in the general population seven workers are needed.

Recruitment of Workers. The local church can recruit volunteer workers from members and groups ranging from senior-high-school age up into adulthood. The co-operation of various church organizations for youth, young adults, men, and women should be solicited. When such groups show active interest in the undertaking, little difficulty will be encountered in recruiting a sufficient number of workers. The pastor is the key person at the local church level and of course may be expected to participate in this project.

The process of recruiting volunteer workers should be set in motion simultaneously with the preparation of mapping and assignment envelopes. A satisfactory estimate of the number of canvassers needed can be made early in the project. Experience shows that some

74

local churches will need a maximum amount of time to procure their quota of volunteers.

The Instructional Meeting. The next step is to arrange for a general meeting whereby canvassers are brought together for instruction. However, certain preparations need to be completed prior to this meeting. All the census assignments should be ready for distribution. A single mimeographed sheet summarizing key suggestions of procedure for religious census workers should be ready. These items are to be distributed at the meeting. Several large street maps of the city can be placed around the room. After the instructional meeting workers may wish to locate the city blocks referred to in their assignments. Several individuals may not know the city well enough to locate easily their assigned territory without the assistance of a reference map.

SUGGESTIONS FOR RELIGIOUS CENSUS WORKERS

I. General Instructions

1. Write address before ringing doorbell.
2. Secure information at the door! It takes more time to enter the home.
3. If no one is home, record hour and call back later.
4. Check racial information *after departing.*
5. Be sure assignment numbers are recorded on each census card.
6. Write legibly; get accurate information; record all answers.
7. When assignment is complete, return census envelope to survey office. Be sure that all cards are enclosed.

II. The Interview

1. The opening of the interview
   A. Introduce yourself.
   B. State purpose of your call.
   C. Proceed at once to questions. Be brief, businesslike, and friendly.

2. A suggested question sequence to follow
   A. How many persons live at this address?
   B. What is the family name?
   C. What is the husband's first name?
   D. What church do you attend? (Secure name of church and denomination.)
   E. Are you a member of that church? If not, where do you belong?
   F. What local church do you prefer (if person does not attend or belong to a church)?
   G. Are there other adults in the home? (Secure names and religious status.)
   H. Are there children? First name? Age. What Sunday school do they attend?

3. Closing the interview
   A. Glance over card to be sure all necessary items are filled out.
   B. Express appreciation of co-operation.
   C. Leave with verbal invitation to worship in the church of their choice.
   D. Move on!

The mimeographed page of key suggestions may be similar to the sample presented above. Note that suggestions for religious census workers are divided into two parts. Part I covers general procedure, emphasizing the nature of the worker's responsibility and encouraging him to keep on schedule by making brief census calls. Part II deals with the actual interview at the door of the household. Suggestions cover the opening of the interview, a series of questions to be used in the census,[2] and finally how to close the interview. The census worker is expected to conduct the interview at the door of the household.

A time and place should be fixed for the instructional meeting, which is normally held on a Sunday afternoon. Workers must attend this meeting, and each pastor is held responsible for the presence of his census workers at the agreed place on time. The meeting starts promptly and is usually a half-hour in duration. Several urgent items are on the agendum. Workers receive the assignments, register, hear the instructions, and start out immediately on the religious census. Many persons will be able to complete their assignments during the first afternoon and evening. Callers are expected to stay within the curbstones of the city blocks assigned to them.

Each worker receives the assignment envelope at the beginning of the meeting. It contains sufficient cards upon which to record the information needed from each household. The worker fills out a registration card upon which he writes his name, telephone, address, and assignment number. This card is taken up before the meeting is dismissed and is held as a record to trace assignments. Each worker receives a copy of the sheet of suggestions referred to above, and at the time of its distribution the leader stresses the key points in order that workers may apply the pertinent ideas to the door-to-door canvass. In giving instructions it should be emphasized that much time is wasted by entering homes and engaging in irrelevant con-

---

[2] The questions used in the interview should coincide with the information desired on the census card.

versation. Religious census information can be secured at the door of most homes. In short, homes should not be entered unless the weather is inclement.

Each worker is expected to complete his assignment. If a family is not at home at the time of the first visit, call-backs should be made. Usually a return call at a different hour of the same or the following day will catch the resident at home. One census card should be used for each household, and information should be secured directly from the head of the family or some other mature person. Small children and neighbors should not be consulted, however co-operative and well intentioned they appear to be. Commonly information procured from such sources is unreliable.

A sample interview should be given by the leader of the meeting, using one of the census workers to play the role of householder. The leader simulates the pattern of the interview at the door of the home. In response to questions the worker, posing as a householder, furnishes the information about himself and his family, while the leader writes the data on a card. This simple visual demonstration indicating how an interview may be conducted has proved very useful in instructing workers. Sometimes an interview with an unco-operative person is demonstrated also. Canvassers should be friendly and efficient.

Following the sample interview, a few moments should be set aside for workers' questions. Queries should deal with the religious census project but not with prolonged discussions by one or two individuals. These persons may be dealt with after the meeting is over. It is too late to raise the question of whether or not the project should be undertaken, and therefore such questions should be ruled out of order.

A time and a place should be announced for turning in the completed assignments. Usually Tuesday evening is designated as the time if the project has been launched on a Sunday afternoon. This interval is sufficient to get all calls completed. The place is usually the same room in which the workers received instructions. The person who is to be on duty Tuesday evening is introduced to the group at the instructional meeting so that all may have his name in mind. This is an indirect way of emphasizing the importance of completing the census on schedule.

Workers may wish to orient themselves and find the geographical location of assignments before starting out. Attention can be drawn to the maps of the community which have been posted around the room. Finally the meeting is dismissed with a prayer and workers dispersed immediately to the various portions of the census area. Persons with remote assignments are frequently transported to the areas by prearranged automobile facilities.

Completion of the Census. A word of caution needs to be said respecting the completion of the census. Every assignment must be given out. Each one must be cared for by some worker. Therefore if some assignments are left over following the Sunday afternoon general meeting, two alternative patterns of action are open for the committee. The hasty recruitment by telephone of additional workers may provide a solution. If this plan does not appear feasible, the balance of the assignments have to be distributed on Tuesday evening to workers who will give additional time to the project. It is not uncommon for a canvasser to accept and complete several assignments. There are always persons who find the canvass a thrilling experience. In instances where supplemental assignments are taken, reports should be turned in by Friday evening.

On Tuesday evening the person designated to receive assignments should make sure each worker has placed the census cards back into the envelope and that the assignment is complete. Workers with only a few call-backs remaining should be encouraged to keep the assignment one more day before turning it in. This may afford time in which to conclude the coverage of the remaining households. Since each worker filled out a registration card, it is relatively simple to check off each assignment as it is finished and turned in. Prior to Tuesday evening the registration cards should be alphabetized for speedy reference.

It is both unnecessary and undesirable to let the canvass of households consume more than one week of time. If each worker completes his assignment and turns it in on schedule, the project will not drag. Certain mop-up work is always necessary, but this can be reduced to a minimum if it is emphasized that every worker must conclude what he undertakes. Mop-up operations include the several assignments which need to be taken by ministers after canvassers have exhausted their spare time. The various steps of the project should be completed on a rigid time schedule if satisfactory results are to be procured. At the completion of the house-to-house canvass all assignments should be returned to local census headquarters. The religious census cards should remain intact in the original envelopes.

TABULATION OF THE RELIGIOUS CENSUS

Too frequently the project is conscientiously administered up to this point, and then the results are lost due to inadequate provision for systematizing and interpreting the results. Census data when properly tabulated have permanent value and can guide the judgment of denominational leaders and councils of churches for years ahead. Therefore it is essential that the information gathered in the religious canvass be organized into a significant report and the findings applied directly to churching problems.

Usefulness of a Tabulation.[3] In general a religious census may be tabulated for one or more of the following reasons: (1) Protestant leaders desire to apply the findings toward the solution of the problem or problems which originally called forth the undertaking. When the results are in summary form, prompt answers to critical difficulties may be found. (2) Tabulated results may indicate neighborhoods where new churches are needed and further point out which denominations have the greatest potential therein and hence should receive comity allocations from the local council or federation of churches. (3) Where overchurching is suspected to exist in urban neighborhoods, the extent of competition may be measured by the religious census and attention directed to the areas characterized by a dwindling margin of Protestant opportunity. The future outlook for individual churches may be estimated in accordance with census findings.

4) A general inventory of membership strengths and weaknesses by faiths and by denominations is revealed when a map is prepared showing the geography of the religious distributions. Neigh-

---

[3] In very large religious census projects or where sufficient funds are available, data may be transferred to Hollerith or Keysort cards which are punched, and tabulations are counted by machine. Possibility of error is reduced to a minimum, and a much wider range of tabular analysis is permitted due to the paucity of time required in handling the cards.

borhoods dominantly Hebrew or Catholic are likely to afford but a limited ministry for Protestantism. This limitation should be viewed against the fortunes of existing indigenous Protestant churches. (5) Results from a well-conducted religious census have permanent value and therefore need to be put in summary form for future reference. The numerical strengths of the faiths and denominations in a geographical pattern across the community should be shown. Successive censuses are likely to reveal which neighborhoods are changing and to what extent the alteration is occurring. Such information becomes essential background data for long-range denominational planning. Churches may be guided in relocation plans from information garnered from the current or previous religious censuses.

Selection of Enumerators. In the selection and recruitment of volunteer tabulators it is desirable to procure persons who will follow instructions. Young and middle-aged adults are commonly preferred although youth and older persons often prove satisfactory. Tabulation is a painstaking process which requires accuracy in details. For this reason particularly it is wise to train a small but competent corps of workers to handle the entire tabulation process.

The number of enumerators required depends upon the size of the population of the area surveyed and the number of items to be recorded in tables. With reference to the population a practical formula has been employed successfully in a number of communities. This formula was devised against a background of enumeration experience. Based upon the type of tabulation described in succeeding pages, it takes approximately four hours per one thousand population. Experienced volunteers, working under relatively ideal conditions, can reduce this average time.

If each enumerator proves willing to tabulate information on ten thousand population over a two-week period, one needs but to divide the gross community population by ten thousand to discover the number of enumerators needed. Volunteers working on the project several evenings a week plus a Sunday afternoon can quite easily do the necessary tabulation in a fortnight. Emphasis must be placed upon the procurement of a small but competent corps of workers.

Setting Up Tabulation Sheets.[4] The tabulation sheets should provide for a distribution of persons by faith—Hebrew, Protestant, and Roman Catholic—a distribution of Protestants by denomination; a distribution of all persons by vitality of institutional relationship—attenders, members, and preferences—within each faith and denomination; and finally a distribution of all persons by age groups—at least two categories, adults and children under eighteen years. While there are other possible breakdowns of the data which the local committee may desire, this simple tabulation sheet will prove useful in making a minimum tabulation. Scrutiny of a sample work sheet as shown in Figure No. 13 shows provision for recording the religious status of every person contacted in the census. Note that by placing a single tally mark the individual is properly classified. This arrangement saves many hours of work.

Occasionally a committee desires to tabulate additional information which has or may have particular significance in the local community. The sample work sheet, Figure No. 14, provides opportunity to tally two popular items—size of family (that is, number of children per household) and mixed marriages (interfaith or interdenominational). Procedure in enumeration follows the general line suggested above with one important exception: one tally is given for each household. This greatly reduces the work of tabulation and hence appeals to the local committee.

Both work sheets may be adapted to and mimeographed for use in the local community. One of each is required to tabulate completely an assignment in the religious census. This is the simplest and perhaps the most reliable means of tabulating a census where volunteer workers are used. An unelaborated procedure tends to reduce manual errors. Standardization of the process likewise facilitates the enumeration.

The Tabulation Process. When the tabulation sheets have been set up and mimeographed, there begins the routine process of in-

---

[4] Another type of tabulation sheet provides space for tallying the religious status of persons for an entire census tract, ward, or precinct. Regular analysis pads up to thirty columns in width are available at an office supply store. These pads are commonly used in the tabulation of a religious census by experts. Under circumstances where strict economy is an important consideration, several large sheets of heavyweight wrapping paper may be utilized. However, lines must be drawn manually with a yardstick or a straight edge to set up a homemade tally sheet.

RELIGIOUS CENSUS TABULATION SHEET

Area (Ward, Precinct, Census Tract, Enumeration District) Number——

ADULT TALLIES

	Attenders	Members	Preferences	Unclassified	TOTALS
Eastern Orthodox					
Hebrew					
Roman Catholic					
Protestant°-Adventist					
—Assembly of God					
—Baptist					
—Church of God					
—Cong.-Christian					
—Disciples of Christ					
—Episcopal, Protestant					
—Evang. & Reformed					
—Lutheran					
—Methodist					
—Nazarene					
—Presbyterian					
—Other Protestant					
Not Classified					
TOTALS					
Refused Information (by families)					
Not at Home (by families)					

° Add or omit denominations according to the requirements of the local religious census project.

FIGURE No. 13

specting each census card and entering one tally for each individual in the appropriate column and line on the work sheet (Figure No. 13). Each person in the household should be recorded. Occasionally census takers fail to procure all the desired data. In instances where information is not complete, a tally should be entered in a column set aside for this purpose under the heading "unclassified." Assignments should be handled one at a time and the code number on the outside of the envelope written in at the top of the tabulation sheet. In each case cards are replaced in the original envelope after tabulation. Later the cards will be dispersed to the ministers for evangelistic cultivation.

Use black lead pencil or ink for tabulating adults. Tally each adult according to religious faith and denomination, using the column which indicates the vitality of institutional relationship—attender, member, preference, or unclassified. Each adult in the household should be tallied before picking up the next census card. The enumerator should do all the adults in the assignment as the first step in the tabulation process. Let the tally marks accumulate where they will.

Next use a red pencil for recording children. Tally each person under eighteen years of age in the proper categories as described in the paragraph above. The faith and/or denomination of the mother is utilized in classifying children in religiously mixed families and in instances where the child's religious status is not given.

There may be instances where the local committee desires to tabulate minority population groups (Negro, Puerto Rican, Mexican, or Oriental) in separate categories. The enumeration process is no different from that described in the preceding paragraphs. Individuals may be tabulated either upon the work sheets referred to above or upon special sheets designed for the purpose. Tally marks of varying colors are a differentiating device which may commend itself in the local situation.

Tally households where people either were not at home or refused to give information in the special space provided at the bottom of the tabulation sheet. Each card should be examined carefully so that this information can be accurately reported.

Supplementary Tabulation Process. A second tabulation sheet

(Figure No. 14) provides facilities for tallying size of family and religiously mixed families. In both instances use one tally per family. (1) Consider, first of all, data by size of family. Space is provided for recording family groupings in separate categories by faith and by number of children. Tally only according to the religion of the wife, omitting households composed entirely of widowed and divorced persons. (2) With respect to religiously mixed families only the most obvious religious combinations are shown on the sample work sheet. Examine the religion of husband and wife in

Supplementary Tabulation Sheet

Area & Assignment Number _____

1. TABULATION OF FAMILIES BY SIZE

Faith	NUMBER OF CHILDREN IN HOUSEHOLD						
	none	one	two	three	four	five	six and more
HEBREW							
PROTESTANT							
ROMAN CATHOLIC							
Totals							

TABULATION OF RELIGIOUSLY MIXED FAMILIES

Combinations	Number of families
ROMAN CATHOLIC AND PROTESTANT	
ROMAN CATHOLIC AND HEBREW	
HEBREW AND PROTESTANT	
MIXED DENOMINATIONS	

FIGURE No. 14

making this classification. Tabulation of these data is relatively simple. The work sheet is designed to gather essential information very quickly. Time consumed in making this part of the total tabulation is small, thus commending itself to the local committee.

Hardly any community can afford not to tabulate properly the results of the house-to-house census. Interpretation of the findings is in the realm of guesswork without a proper systematization of the materials. The immediate usefulness of a properly tabulated census is great, and the long-range benefits become a continuing witness to the wisdom and pragmatic discernment of the committee in charge of the project.

Summary Tables. When the entire religious census has been tabulated, subtotals are made on each assignment tabulation work sheet. These subtotals are brought together for each census tract, ward, or precinct; and the materials are now ready to be placed in summary form.

Several summary tables will be useful to the committee: (1) number of persons who are Hebrew, Roman Catholic, and Protestant within each census tract, ward, or precinct plus the grand totals for the area covered by the religious census; (2) number of Protestants by denominations and by geographical territories (census tract, ward, or precinct); (3) number of unchurched persons by geographical territory; and (4) the number of adults and children in each of the preceding categories.

Further (5) the data by size of family and by religiously mixed families should be placed in tabular form in the patterns described under (1), (2), and (3). Understandably the practical needs of the committee will commend the preparation of certain additional summary tables.

The geographical factor in the tabulation of religious census data is of significant importance to church administrators and pastors. It furnishes insight respecting the religious composition of various neighborhoods and reveals where each denomination or faith is numerically dominant or weak. Vital information such as this should be available for administrative decisions.

Two suggested summary tables are shown on the following pages. Figure No. 15 presents a sample of a table showing the number of Protestants by denomination and by geographical territories. Figure

SUMMARY TABLE BY AREAS

	Area A	Area B	Area C	Area D	Area E	Area F	Area G	Area H	Area I	Area J	Totals
Eastern Orthodox											
Hebrew											
Roman Catholic											
Protestant°-Adventist											
—Assembly of God											
—Baptist											
—Church of God											
—Cong.-Christian											
—Disciples of Christ											
—Episcopal, Protestant											
—Evang. & Reformed											
—Lutheran											
—Methodist											
—Nazarene											
—Presbyterian											
—Other Protestant											
Not Classified											
TOTALS											
Refused Information (by families)											
Not at Home (by families)											

° Add or omit denominations according to the requirements of the local religious census project.

FIGURE No. 15

SUMMARY TABLE BY FAITHS

	Attenders	Members	Preferences	Unclassified	TOTALS
Eastern Orthodox					
Hebrew					
Roman Catholic					
Protestant					
Not Classified					
TOTALS					
Refused Information (by families)					
Not at Home (by families)					

FIGURE No. 16

No. 16 shows a community-wide summary by faiths and by vitality of institutional relationship. Undoubtedly the committee will prepare additional tables to match its special needs.

The purpose of summary tables is to sharpen the significance of the data with respect to several important focuses. This important analytical step advances the work of interpretation and prepares the way to check upon the validity of the information.

INTERPRETATION AND PRESENTATION OF MATERIALS

With the house-to-house canvass completed and the religious census arranged in tabular form, a subcommittee can turn now to the task of drafting a project report. Doubtless a few practical suggestions respecting the preparation of an oral and written report may prove instructive. Certainly sufficient detail should be included to permit a reasonable analysis of particular neighborhoods and other relatively small but significant areas. This geographical factor is frequently overlooked, thereby diminishing the pragmatic value of the project. "Accuracy in simplification" is the purpose of a written report, in whatever length it is prepared. Technical jargon and intricate tables and charts discourage religious leaders from an extensive use of the findings.

Ideally the report should include the following seven basic elements: (1) a description of the area surveyed (accompanied by a map), (2) a discussion of the type of geographical subdivisions utilized, (3) a statement of reliability, (4) a summary of the materials (in charts, tables, and text), (5) an interpretation of the data, (6) a brief list of the principal findings, and finally (7) a brief statement tracing the significance of the findings in terms of the problem to be explored or solved. Generally the report, ranging from five to twenty pages in length, is mimeographed or printed for distribution. Several copies should be placed on file in the public library, in the local college library, and in the offices of the local council of churches. Additional copies should be circulated among denominational leaders.

An *oral presentation of the findings* is made to two groups: a large general meeting comprised of representatives from co-operating churches and a relatively small committee which will work out in detail the practical implications of the report. In anticipation of these meetings several large charts which highlight and accurately summarize the principal findings should be prepared. Undoubtedly a good street map of the city, utilized as a base map, can show an outline of the geographical units (census tracts, wards, or precincts). These areas should be colored or hatched (with India ink or tempera) to show where faiths are numerically dominant and where denominations have their strengths and weaknesses. Such visual aids plus the use of a blackboard will greatly facilitate the speedy communication and assimilation of religious census facts. An experienced administrator or research person should be selected to conduct the meetings which afford the representatives opportunity for questions and discussion. Copies of the written report should be distributed for reference purposes.

Preparation of the Written Report. Let us turn now to a brief discussion of the seven basic elements in a good written report. An outline map of the area surveyed, plus a nontechnical description of the geographical subdivisions utilized, furnishes a necessary spatial orientation for the reader.

The reliability of the religious census depends upon the completeness of the canvass both in geographical extent and in intensive neighborhood coverage. To discover the relative completeness of the project one must compare the number of households (or dwelling units) in each census tract, ward, or precinct with the number of families of the same territory who were contacted in the religious census. Invariably the latter number will be smaller. Completeness of coverage in terms of percentage should be calculated and described for each census tract, ward, or precinct in the city. If 50 per cent or more of the residents within each geographical unit were contacted, then the findings may be regarded as reasonably trustworthy. Less than one-third coverage of the population in a unit presages the possibility that findings are likely to be somewhat skewed. Territories under consideration for new church work or suspected of debilitating competition should have a coverage of approximatley 75 per cent.

Here then is a suggestion for the committee in charge of the house-to-house canvass: the insistence upon the completion of every worker's assignment and the complete, legible, and accurate filling out of each card is one way of guaranteeing that the findings of the religious census will be representative. Thus the written report should contain a succinct statement describing the percentage of households contacted in each census tract, ward, or precinct. This reveals to the reader the reliability of the census.

Generally the charts and tables are accompanied by an interpretative commentary delineating the relative significance of the data. Toward the end of the report a list of eight or ten single-sentence high lights assists the reader in retaining a résumé of the leading facts presented.

Finally the conclusion should contain an application of the census findings to the critical churching problems of the community. What significance do the findings have for the church considering relocation, for the misplaced church, for competing churches, for the denomination interested in launching a new church? These and kindred practical considerations should be faced in drafting a conclusion. In short the written report must provide a background of facts against which intelligent decisions may be formulated and programs of action launched.

POSTCENSUS PATTERNS OF ACTION

Two principal courses of action stem from a religious census. The first deals with the administrative solution of churching problems. That this is an important consideration is hardly debatable. Less apparent perhaps is the need for an acceleration of programs of evangelistic outreach in the city. Multitudes languish in dire need of a vital spiritual ministry. Such persons should be sought out and served.

Administrative Decisions. The experienced urban minister has witnessed frequent mistakes in church location, relocation, merger, and program adjustments. Many such blunders can be avoided if at the time when a decision is under consideration the denominational administrator insists upon having access to an adequate body of facts upon which to draft an opinion. Such leaders are often compelled against their own better judgment to dispose of a churching problem about which they hold too limited information. The findings of a religious census therefore have considerable relevance to the critical situations confronting such harassed administrators.

Thus the project may quite properly be considered as an important functional tool in the repertoire of a wise Protestant executive. Certain decisions have to be postponed pending the findings of a religious census. This delay is warranted for the welfare of Protestantism.

Visitation Evangelism. A second pattern of action which appropriately follows a religious census is the visitation evangelism program. Each family or individual who is unchurched, as revealed by the canvass, should be contacted by callers from a near-by local church. This is an important consideration and therefore must not be overlooked in a follow-up program at the conclusion of the religious census.

Techniques for the visitation evangelism program are widely used with remarkable results. The follow-up of church prospects should take into account the fact that some persons are ready to join immediately, others will join after being cultivated over a period of time, and still others have been out of touch with organized religion for so long that only patient wooing will rewin them to the church. The extended use of laymen in evangelistic calling, the co-operation of local church organizations in broadening current friendship and participation circles, and the continual patience and industry of the pastor will issue in evangelistic growth. A visitation evangelism program should immediately follow the religious census.

TEN RELIGIOUS CENSUS SUGGESTIONS

1. A religious census aids in the solution of various critical churching problems and may be used also to take an inventory of the community.

2. Unchurched urban residents range from one fourth to one third of the population. These prospects for local church membership can be found by means of a religious census.

3. A successful census can be conducted by a local church, by a single denomination, or by a council of churches. The interdenominational project generally is more inclusive in scope and therefore commendably distributes the financial and functional burdens on a broad base. The economic consideration may be important to some communities.

4. A general committee, a volunteer director, and several subcommittees comprise the necessary organization of the project.

5. Seven house-to-house workers are required for each thousand people in the general population. A canvasser is expected to contact forty households.

6. Sample interviews should be given in the instructional meeting. Demonstrate how to conduct an interview with both a co-operative and an unco-operative householder.

7. Return visits or call-backs should be made where residents were not at home on the first call.

8. In the tabulation of data train a small but competent corps of workers to handle the entire process. On the average it requires four hours to tabulate information on one thousand population. A volunteer enumerator ordinarily can tabulate data on ten thousand persons in a fortnight, utilizing spare time during several evenings and a Sunday afternoon.

9. A written report should be prepared preserving the findings of the canvass. Representatives of all co-operating churches, plus other Protestant leaders, should receive copies.

10. A twofold follow-up action program involving both administrative decisions respecting critical churching problems and an evangelistic visitation project should climax the completion of the religious census. Thus findings of the canvass can point out the pathway to wise courses of action. When this type of outcome materializes, Protestant leaders place confidence in the project.

CHAPTER IV

Church Work in the Downtown Area

I N recent years American Protestantism has developed a profound concern over the problems which emerge from church work in the downtown portion of the city. Contrasting with the viewpoint of former days, it is now more realistic and objective. Accumulating insights derived from scientific studies add a new poignancy to the mounting anxiety in the minds of leaders. The importance of religious success downtown is evident when it is realized that no denomination can be effective without a strong church located among the secular institutions which clearly dominate the urban environment.

The larger the city, the more tangled and stubborn are the difficulties confronting the denominational executive. Yet all cities, regardless of size, have problems. In view of the new concern currently manifested, plus the acknowledged continuing importance of the field, a fresh analysis of downtown church work may be welcomed by harassed pastors and administrators. For better or for worse, organized religion is downtown to stay. Fortunately the eventuality is accepted since for many in the population this is the only ministry they will ever know.

DOWNTOWN—A PERMANENT URBAN FEATURE

Whether a city is large or small, the existence of a downtown territory to serve in a religious way appears inevitable. People require manifold material and cultural services, and the agencies for rendering such tend to cluster at the center of the community. Tardily Protestant leaders have come to acknowledge the omnipresence of the downtown district and the strong likelihood of its persistence during the foreseeable future. Even this belated admission may result in a fresh and pragmatic adjustment of denominational strategy to the urban situation. This possibility merits fulfillment.

The city in its evolution possessed a downtown section from the beginning. Its size is regulated principally by the commercial, cultural, and spatial needs of the population. Business is commonly centered in a constricted territory where a large number of the residents seek professional and business services, go shopping, pursue cultural and recreational interests, and perform other essential errands. For the convenience of all, the institutions are clustered into a single area which often centers the community life in various other ways. In New England conspicuously, and often in other regions of the United States, also, the downtown section of the community lies adjacent to what used to be called the village square or park. In former days town meetings were held upon the "green" (now a small park), and even today that place continues as the psychological center of the life of the city, although more recently developed residential neighborhoods fan out in various directions.

As cities gain in population size, the central business district expands. This expansion becomes a process of invading contiguous residential areas. In a word the city grows like a tree—from the center outward. Each inner circle crowds upon the adjacent outer one. Thus a very large city with a downtown area of corresponding size has undoubtedly invaded and altered the adjacent residential areas many times in order to make room for the increased commercial activity and multiple housing. According to prominent sociologists a city's structure can be described as a pattern of concentric circles, each with unique discernible characteristics. The innermost circle encompasses the downtown district. The band of territory which lies immediately adjacent, as one moves outward from the heart of the city, is an area in transition. It is in this area that changes brought about by the expanding central business district are commonly seen. Many of the oldest and grandest residential structures in the entire city are or were located here. Growth of a city usually means geographical expansion of the central business district, and consequently, as this enlargement occurs, many

94

fine homes are razed or converted to other uses. This is the price of progress.

There is no reason to believe that Protestantism will in the foreseeable future be stripped of the downtown church opportunity. Thousands of people continue to reside at the heart of the city, and where the population is, there should the church be also. Today, more than ever before, religious leaders should recognize the urgent need for the centrally located Protestant church, since multitudes of persons of many denominations reside there.

The central business district defies conventional church work patterns. Although the area provides a focus of transportation facilities which should facilitate a spiritual ministry and even furnishes a location of high visibility, nevertheless it is not an easy place in which to carry on religious activities. This is a fact attested to by scores of experienced pastors. Attempts to conduct downtown religious work in the pattern of a traditional neighborhood church have again and again resulted in failure. The situation is too volatile, too complex, too unique, too changing to respond to so naïve a treatment. Creative experimentation is demanded if the church is to be effective.

DESCRIPTION OF THE DOWNTOWN AREA

Nearly all cities, irrespective of size, possess similar characteristics with respect to the downtown area. This is a place of high land values and an area of prominent hotels and kindred facilities catering to the needs of transients. It is the focus of transportation facilities and the location of bus and railroad terminals. Traffic is more congested than in other parts of the city. It is the focal point of communication facilities, including radio, telephone, telegraph, and newspapers. Further, the city's leading stores situated here provide the largest and most extensive selection of merchandise. Manifold types of business and professional specialization are found also. It is the banking and financial center of the city. Is it any wonder that residents look downtown to find the psychological center of urban life? All else appears to be relative to it.

Anonymity is a featured pattern of human relationships. Speed and superficial contacts characterize the actions of pedestrians and commuters. To miss one section of a revolving door is intolerable. The tallest buildings, the narrowest streets, the main offices of commercial enterprises, are located downtown. Surprisingly enough, in spite of the extensive business and commercial activity referred to, a large population is housed in the central area. Great numbers of people take up residence in apartment buildings, in apartments above stores, and in other dwelling structures. Only relatively few are transients in the literal meaning of the word.

Clearly the downtown area focuses the life of a city. It centers the economic and cultural life of the urban community and properly should center its religious life. Therefore a downtown church is integral to the community's welfare, and for this reason major denominations are obligated to maintain work there.

A SIGNIFICANT RELIGIOUS OPPORTUNITY

Thus wherever people live, an opportunity for religious ministry exists; the more people, the more extensive the opportunity. The densest urban population is found downtown and in the territory immediately adjacent. More persons per square mile reside here than anywhere else in the city. Families as well as individuals are packed in like sardines.

This vital fact should not escape the attention of Protestant leaders. The situation in such cities as New York, Chicago, San Francisco, Los Angeles, Kansas City, St. Louis, Boston, and Atlanta illustrates the point. Approximately 12 per cent of the population reside in an area characterized by downtown urban conditions. What is apparent respecting huge cities is more obvious in urban places of medium and small size. Many people live at the heart of the city. Frankly speaking, it is highly erroneous to suppose that either no one or an insignificant population reside downtown merely because superficial observation reveals a concentration of stores, office buildings, and other large-scale nonresidential structures.

Protestantism must maintain a vital ministry at the heart of the city if it is to win America. In what other effective way will the influence of the great cultural and economic institutions clustered in the downtown area become spiritualized? How else will the ministries of religion be made available to this important segment of the population? None but an indigenous church can serve the thousands of downtown residents so completely out of reach of neighborhood religious institutions. These people need a house of worship at the heart of the city. Additional urban residents likewise look downtown for spiritual refreshment and guidance. If one denomination does not make an indigenous ministry available, other communions should.

Specifically there are at least four groups of persons who come under the ministry of the downtown church—hotel population, rooming-house residents, apartment dwellers, and downtown-minded people. From these sources are drawn the individuals who comprise the constituency of the centrally located urban church. No more heterogeneous nor challenging opportunity is presented to urban Protestantism. It is a difficult ministry.

Hotel Population. In numerous cities hotel population may be counted in the thousands. How likely it is that some guests are already interested in religion. All need to be. Since such people are transient (many of them remaining in the community from a day to several weeks during a business, social, or vacation trip), whatever relationship the church is to have to them must be quickly formed and intensely cultivated. Experienced pastors of downtown churches know the importance of this fact, for they discover many individuals standing in urgent need of a religious ministry. At this point the merits of spiritual service are clearly shown. Suicides have been averted; extramarital actions have come to light, and the broken homes were repaired; adult delinquency of manifold types has been discovered and the individuals redeemed from the depth of sin and trouble; and finally there are many instances of fresh appropriation of the resources of religion as a direct result of downtown church work among hotel residents.

However, not all instances of pastoral help are pathological in character or even urgent. Numerous individuals require the undramatic nurturing of personal faith and the freshening of social vision while away from home. This process so well undertaken and directed by the home-town church should be continued without interruption during travel. Seeking fulfillment of this commendable objective, individuals frequently drop in at public worship services incognito and slip out again without notice if possible. Thus un-

wittingly a vital ministry is being rendered in the downtown parish—
a service which will never be revealed in annual statistics. Protestantism should foster increasingly this brief but intensive religious
work among hotel residents. To people who travel the church is a
welcome spiritual oasis in a blatant urban world of brick, stone,
and steel. Who is willing to say that this is a trivial service?

Rooming-House Residents. Ministry of the downtown church to
occupants of rooming houses is a religious service of significant proportions in many communities, while in other cities single adults
are commonly overlooked or frankly neglected in a denomination's
program. The latter eventually is unfortunate, since bachelors of
both sexes respond generously to the call of religion and frequently
are desperately in need of association with persons of high ethical
standards and a Christian philosophy of life. Under church auspices
the proper kinds of friendship can be formed and nurtured. Even
among persons of varying age groups this constitutes a worth-while
ministry. Older people who are widowed, pensioned, or alone in
the world likewise merit more religious attention than they generally
receive. Christ wants to meet both the old and the young.

Frequently rooming houses provide but temporary quarters for
people who are newcomers to the city. Eventually some persons
will have improved their economic status and therefore will move
to sections of the community which offer more spacious or more
acceptable living facilities. This mobility is to be expected in as
much as many occupants of rooming houses marry local residents.
If a vital relationship is formed with the church during the period
of single status, it commonly results in worth-while religious participation later on. When individuals decide eventually to establish
permanent homes in the city, active affiliation with a local Protestant church becomes a matter of course. Thus the role of the downtown church grows in significance as one realizes the scope of its
possible ministry.

Apartment Dwellers.[1] Apartment structures are generally found
in or immediately adjacent to the downtown area. Residents are
often out of reach of any except the centrally located Protestant
church. Because apartments and rooming houses often serve as ports

[1] Consult Chapter V for a fuller treatment of the topic.

of entry for newcomers to a city, early contact with the residents is extremely important. This contact is facilitated by a favorable frame of mind toward religion which renders the newcomer especially susceptible to the friendly ministry of a church. The institution should plan to walk (figuratively speaking) beside the newcomer for a period of time, strengthening his religious habits and nurturing him in the alien place. He will need a balanced spiritual service during the perilous period of adjustment to life in the city. This relationship can become a major ministry, as alert pastors have discovered.

The principal difficulty encountered by pastors arises from the relatively short tenure of residence among apartment dwellers. People move frequently. Duration of stay varies from a few months to half a dozen years, and this mobility imposes abnormal limitations upon religious work. Hardly before adequate acquaintanceship is consummated, the family moves away to another part of the city or even out of town. Continuity of church relationship is retained under circumstances of extreme difficulty. Great distance often prevents people from returning to the original church for services.

This new problem thrust upon urban Protestantism is a source of considerable distress among leaders and has evoked experimentation with a short term but intensive religious ministry. One finding is clearly evident. No longer does the church have twenty to fifty years of temporal latitude in which to overtake the individual and confront him with the Christian gospel. Rather if the religious message is to be communicated at all, it must be imparted within a brief time span (a year or two) and mediated essentially to people on the move. Unless the downtown church reaches near-by apartment dwellers during early years of residence, it is unlikely that the newcomers will retain, much less acquire, vital habits of active religious participation by which faith is kept alive. To aid residents during this transitional period is a significant service to Protestantism. No denomination can afford to overlook so important an opportunity.

Downtown-minded People. Still a fourth group of individuals and families comes under the ministry of a church with a downtown location. When the religious institution is large and capably managed, it catches the attention of many professional and business people who are used to a superlative Protestant ministry. This is a natural development, for in many cities the centrally located church is the oldest organization of the denomination locally. Partly because of this fact and partly because of distinguished clergy who have served here, it has accumulated prestige throughout the years, and its history is a source of pride to the membership as well as to the community. Commonly persons of superior economic and/or cultural status are attracted to an older and stronger church which has grown up with the city.

It is urged by some Protestant leaders that downtown-mindedness is an acquired characteristic. Within reasonable limits this contention is true. Yet the development of such a viewpoint cannot be staged. Rather it evolves against an extensive background of experience in local churches. The preference develops as a fruit which ripens through the years and therefore tends to appear primarily among adults, who in turn expose their children to the ministry of the downtown church. It is a matter of taste and therefore does not necessarily reflect upon the important work of the neighborhood church.

Thus the religious opportunity of the downtown church is much more varied than that confronting the neighborhood institution. A wider range of ministry is demanded along with higher quality and flexibility in the program. In the preceding discussion it has been pointed out that transients, unmarried individuals, newcomers, and apartment dwellers, as well as downtown-minded persons, fall normally within the scope of its potential ministry. This is a unique as well as heterogeneous constituency. However, regardless of variations in age, sex, birthplace, economic status, educational achievement, occupation, or place of residence, the individual has religious needs which require the service of a local church. Beneath the distracting exterior of manifold socio-economic circumstances the needs of urban people are fundamentally similar. There are occasions of bereavement, success, frustration, disappointment, joy, failure, and sin. In all human experiences the ministries of religion must be proffered. For people who look to the downtown area for spiritual vision, help, and guidance an indigenous church should be provided. No denomination dare shirk this responsibility.

100

TYPES OF DOWNTOWN CHURCH WORK

A vast opportunity confronts Protestantism in the downtown area. Thousands of people harassed by gnawing spiritual and physical needs reside there and therefore require an indigenous ministry. To ameliorate these conditions churches throughout the years have been placed or kept in the central part of the city. This religious service has been a boon. More recently, however, considerable uncertainty has entered the minds of denominational executives respecting the wisdom of continuing a ministry to such areas. Therefore a succinct analysis of the current situation and its prospects may prove valuable, especially when regarded as an aid to the formulation of long-range urban church policies.

Experienced leaders discriminate between the problem of the downtown church and the downtown problem of religion. This pertinent distinction underscores a twofold insight: (1) a single church can scarcely cope with all the problems of the inner city, especially in large American communities; and (2) a broad strategy of intradenominational teamwork and Protestant co-operation is demanded by the situation. This dual consideration should be held in mind during the following discussion which treats the four leading types of downtown church work—traditional, transitional, institutional, and mission. Only the medium-sized and larger cities are likely to contain the full complement of varieties.

The Traditional Downtown Church. Nearly every urban community boasts of a popular church situated downtown. Its familiar tower or steeple stands on the green, across the street from a prominent public building, or perchance at some other conspicuous location within the geographical boundaries of the heart of the city. At best the edifice is likely to be a huge but older structure, well suited for the large congregations it attracts. Usually, however, it stands in need of a thorough remodeling and renovation.

As expected, a traditional type of ministry is featured here. Popularity depends upon it. Great emphasis is placed upon the ancient and relatively noncontroversial tenets of religion. This is evident in the extensive use of familiar hymns for public worship, in the reiteration of reliance upon a more or less literal interpretation of the Bible, and finally in sermons which promote "old-time religion."

Convictions which are clearly incompatible with "Bible religion" are scrupulously avoided. In hymnology, biblical exegesis, theology, social ethics, and churchmanship conservatism is the controlling viewpoint. That which is old is enshrined. For this reason the church's program and ministry appear to possess a degree of remoteness from the contemporary scene.

Further, teachings of the Bible and aspects of theology which stress personal religion are elevated to prominence and tend to dominate in sermon themes and public expressions of faith. The individual in a unilateral role is made the object of ministry. The application of religion to community, national, and world problems is limited often to attacks upon the liquor traffic, cosmetics, movies, dancing, and secularism in other churches. This program of social action is largely a vocal effort. Attention is but rarely turned to deeper rooted social issues such as race relations, industrial problems, and world brotherhood. In general, churchmanship conveys the impression of being on the defensive, valiantly holding the line against the alleged encroachments of secularism. Yet even here the dominant theme is personal religion. Let God worry about the social order.

A traditional downtown church follows the organizational pattern prescribed by the denomination and rarely supplements its ministries by special program elements demanded by the local situation. Conventional classes, societies, groups, and activities are sponsored. The preferences of older people are commonly solicited and respected, for what has been done in the past serves as a directive for the present day. Since the constituency is drawn from the entire city, a gangling form of parish organization is utilized to promote religious fellowship and to stimulate participation. This is a conspicuous feature of city-wide downtown church work.

Apparently these organizational patterns and emphases represent the religious fare which is preferred by numerous laymen who are business and professional leaders locally. Since the pulpit often is famous throughout the city, many people come to hear its eminent minister preach. This clergyman has a "voice" in the community. Supported by choral music of exceptional quality (commonly a paid quartet or soloists), such oral ministry attracts splendid attendance at Sunday worship services. Normally the larger congregation appears in the morning. Yet, surprisingly enough, three downtown churches out of four find enough interested people to hold successful Sunday evening services also, and midweek prayer meetings. Further, the large Bible classes for men and women so often featured undergird in a noteworthy manner the work of the traditional downtown church. Extensive activity on Sunday creates a favorable impression upon the community even though basic social problems remain relatively untouched. Some Protestant leaders are discovering that a vocal ministry even of a traditional type is not sufficient for the modern city. It but rarely penetrates the community.

The Transitional Downtown Church. In many American cities the traditional downtown church is evolving into a broader and more relevant institution—wider in the scope of its ministries and more directly responsive to the needs of the local situation. This adaptive transition has already progressed so far beyond the conventional pattern as to reveal a second discernible church type. Clearly the inexorable demands of a new day have failed to find the church altogether adamant and inflexible. Rather the means of communicating the gospel have yielded to necessary modification lest ancient customs become stumbling blocks hindering the rising generation from an adequate knowledge of the life and message of Jesus Christ. The Master has not been changed either in power or significance; only the methods by which He can become known to men have been improved. This longed-for improvement has been met charitably, yes, even welcomed, by Protestant leaders.

Thus among urban churches an increasing number seek to pioneer new patterns of churchmanship. Uniquely favored in opportunity to do so, the centrally located church is endowed with the imagination, leadership, resources, and physical facilities to carry the undertaking to a successful conclusion. Because of well-known difficulties endemic to religious work downtown, constituents often are in a mood to experiment and to accept creative modifications in church finance, Sunday school, choral music, counseling, recreation, public relations, radio programs, parish organization, and so forth. Apparently many Protestant laymen and leaders are not afraid to discard old patterns which have become irrelevant or perfunctory routine.

The church which pioneers new forms of churchmanship is interested in the practical implications for both the individual and society. Do the procedures produce conditions under which laymen may be induced to enter creatively, even joyously, into the life of the local church? Does the person actually grow and mature spiritually in the altered church environment? Further, under the aegis of the transitional downtown church do a responsible social-mindedness and social concern emerge along with an increasingly adequate personal faith? To what extent do constituents identify themselves intelligently with community problems and participate in the search for solutions? To find appropriate answers for these important considerations constitutes both a challenge and an embarrassment to Protestant leaders.

Naturally, transitional characteristics appear in downtown church life. Persons of such diverse economic, cultural, ethnic, and racial backgrounds come under its ministry that drastic change is often inevitably thrust upon the institution. Heterogeneity describes the group situation. Further, the individual's status is altered with the passing years—through marriage, income changes, improvement of cultural tastes, acquisition of social skills, and kindred circumstances. Alteration of church programs is not an option but a necessity. In view of this fact religious leaders welcome the insights furnished by frequent research studies and by the processes of religious education. Findings direct possible change into a broader application of Christianity to life's problems and a deeper cultivation of spiritual life in the individual. Alert Protestant leaders seek a strategy of work which matches urban change. In this development the transitional downtown church may play a dynamic and significant role.

The Institutional Church. A third type of downtown church is found in the economically depressed territory fringing the central business district, and its avowed purpose is to combine social service with a religious ministry. Organized assistance is proffered at the place of direst material and spiritual need. This approach is considered an effective way to counteract a negative environment, to combat personal and social disorganization, to reduce the shocking incidence of juvenile delinquency and adult crime, and to relieve human need among poor people of diverse racial and ethnic stock.

The hungry, the homeless, the outcast, the socially disinherited, the unemployed and the unemployable—all these merit the ministry of Christian succor and hope.

In an institutional church Protestant leaders desire to cope with both material and spiritual needs. A man is afforded not only a place to worship but also assistance in procuring a job or a place to live. This comprehensive ministry is made possible because the director of the institution is generally the pastor of the church, and he is surrounded by a staff comprised largely of trained and experienced social workers. A notable variation from this pattern is the dual program administered unilaterally—a clergyman in charge of religious services and a social worker directing the remainder of the program. In a given practical situation it is often difficult to know which is the better approach. Both procedures appear to obtain satisfactory results.

How to finance the work poses a complex problem. Rarely is the institutional church self-supporting: it operates on a deficit budget. A few projects are privately subsidized; many draw funds from the local Community Chest; nearly all receive some fiscal support from central denominational mission agencies. That the undertaking is embarrassed in nearly every city by the stringent policies set up by donating organizations such as the Community Chest is patent. Chest directors are fearful (perhaps properly so) lest religious work be done in the project, which in turn may bring criticism upon them.

Though the institutional church type is now definitely established in the city, there are some projects where a progressive de-emphasis upon religious ministry has reduced the work to scarcely more than a social-service center. Religion has been relegated to a remote corner of the program and rendered but a token effort. This development has become so widespread that it has engendered uneasiness in the minds of many denominational administrators and has provoked skepticism respecting the future of institutional church work. Undertakings dwindle and collapse soon after the spiritual de-emphasis stage is entered.

There are some leaders who urge that the yoking of church activity with social service has not been conspicuously successful in urban America. Social work has thrived in the arrangement while religious work has moved toward eclipse. Meanwhile tremendous sums of money, all out of proportion to the scale and importance of the undertaking subsidized, have been consumed. Whether or not the difficulty can be traced solely to project leadership is in part an academic question. The taproot of the trouble is elsewhere. Many institutions have been set up without adequate constitutional and administrative safeguards. As a result it is well-nigh impossible to keep the dual program integrated and functioning at an effective level. A swimming pool is scarcely a guarantee of a baptism of persons by the Holy Spirit. Sometimes only muscles are developed in the gymnasium. Too often the program of the institutional church is judged by its ideals rather than by its practical results.

No one doubts the difficulty of threading a wise path among the manifold perils and dangers which beset the institutional church. That some projects achieve remarkable success is evidence of the possibilities of the work. However, the fact remains that religion often loses its vitality in an uncontrolled and inundating welter of secular activities. Only an inexperienced person would deny this. When the religious orientation and motivation are lost, social work sinks to an embarrassingly low level. Jesus never failed to point out the spiritual significance of His activities and service. Without an adequate religious frame of reference the institution becomes a rather feeble effort, deficient in motivation and consequently in fiscal support.

In view of these facts it is not revolutionary to point out that the present patterns of institutional church work are due to undergo serious change during the next few years and, further, that the situation warrants serious study by Protestant leaders. Every aspect of the dual program should be adequately tested by appropriate criteria of religious effectiveness. Eventually, and in spite of the disturbing analysis given above, the institutional program must achieve recognition as a valid type of downtown church work. Even drastic and belated improvement can serve but to emphasize its unique ministry.

The Mission. The mission approach to downtown religious work occurs if at all chiefly in the slum areas, territory from which regular Protestant churches have long since fled. Basically the avowed objective is to bring an effective ministry to persons of severely limited economic and cultural status. To accomplish this purpose reliance is placed in the utilization of a relevant universe of discourse and a battery of techniques peculiarly suited to the environment. These methods often appear repugnant to the conventional church leader.

Because the leading denominations have turned away from the slums, religious organizations of the mission type spring up, although they are generally small, poorly led, and brief of tenure. A handful of individuals gather in a home, store front, or old hall to receive the "Words of Life." Rarely does the self-appointed leader possess adequate formal training either in Bible study or in general education to merit a following. Yet he gets one, and his charisma, though personal in character, derives from two sources—local residence and a flaming personal faith. Dominant emphasis is placed upon small midweek and/or Sunday services of an elementary sort. Little organization of the congregation beyond this point is either encouraged or achieved. Since the group is tiny, intense fellowship becomes a matter of course.

To understand the work of the mission one must realize that people prefer poor religion to none at all. This alternative is the only real option for multitudes of city dwellers. Since Protestantism commonly abandons work in deteriorated urban areas, the spurned residents are wont to quarry out religious salvation any way possible. The spontaneous mission therefore is a protest against having no religion at all. Thus self-appointed leaders arise and attempt to mediate a kind of religion to the people. Doubtless the outcome falls short of a seminary-level intellectual formulation of Christianity. Its crudities include such characteristics as street-corner theology, Horatio Alger economic philosophy, and stark Bible literalness. Yet this is probably the best level to which an untrained mind can ascend. If such a result is unsatisfactory, then an uneasy conscience should haunt the denominations which have "graduated" from poverty and now wish to forget the awkward rise to prestige and economic security. Abandonment of poor people is difficult to countenance in urban church work.

Regular churches can do something about the matter. An illustration may suffice to point out a practical remedy. I know of a community in which a slum mission outpost was opened and operated by the near-by downtown church. Arrangements were made to rent a store front in the heart of the needy area. Currently the pastor conducts religious services Tuesday, Thursday, and Saturday evenings. On Thursdays the program features youth and children. Adults are urged to remain away on that night. All services are comprised of familiar hymns, Bible reading, prayers, and a brief evangelistic sermon. Worship is simple, providing numerous opportunities for participation. Results have been astonishing, with people jamming the dingy store front beyond seating capacity. To attract people to the services has presented no problem. An indigenous location conveys the impression that the mission belongs to the residents of the neighborhood.

As residents became well acquainted with the pastor, individuals revealed how seemingly helpful were his ministries and then concluded wistfully that they surely would not feel at home in the big downtown church near by. To the surprise of everyone it was then discovered that the mission leader was likewise pastor of the "belittled" neighboring church. Because of the outpost mission arrangement and the evidence of friendly interest, a number of slum dwellers have made their way into the latter congregation and achieved religious satisfaction. Yet most important of all is the hearty response accorded an indigenous ministry. It is evident that people are reluctant to accept poor religion when better is available. This fact should be noted by Protestant leaders.

Here is an example of the extended ministry of a downtown church. Possibly the pattern merits study by pastors, executives, and administrators who may be concerned about religious work in slum areas. Practical programs should be formulated by many denominations and individual churches if residents of depressed areas are to be adequately served in the future. Although slight success has accompanied efforts to prepare people for life in a regular church, many slum dwellers never complete the precarious transition to it. The utilization of a special universe of discourse and special group-work techniques will continue to be required for them. Consequently discerning Protestant leaders regard the mission as a valid type of downtown church program. Spiritual needs persist in depressed urban areas no matter who lives there.

A brief discussion of the four leading types of downtown church work should suffice here. Administrative and program adaptation to cope with the special needs of the populations served appears inevitable if religious units are to survive. Beyond this a strident note of spiritual urgency is struck in all of the services. The auditor must no longer postpone procurement of an adequate personal response to religion. Decision day is every Sunday. This fitting emphasis applies especially where the downtown congregation turns over rapidly. Ordinarily from a third to three fourths of the congregation is new each Sunday. In view of this situation denominational leaders must not overlook the significant ministries of the traditional, transitional, institutional, and mission types of downtown church work.

PROBLEMS IN DOWNTOWN CHURCH WORK

Any noteworthy list of downtown church problems is likely to include the following six most common ones. Difficulties generally derive from the complex socio-economic situation. (1) The extreme heterogeneity of the congregation baffles pastors and administrators alike. (2) Adequate religious participation is often difficult to procure from members who travel abnormally long distances to church. (3) A disproportionate volume of personal counseling is thrust upon the downtown pastor. (4) Further, neighborhood churches become jealous of the apparent superior attracting power of the centrally located institution. (5) When financial difficulties harass the downtown church, a frantic search for solutions often ensues with the disastrous result that normal long-range stewardship training procedures are virtually abandoned. (6) Finally development of an adequate program is a complicated matter and a source of continuous difficulty. The problems endemic to downtown church work are among the fundamental concerns of alert leaders and merit serious consideration in the pages that follow. Workable solutions should be found if Protestantism is to be effective in the city.

The "Melting Pot" Church. More than any other urban religious institution the downtown church is a congregation of astonishing contrasts. Membership lists contain persons of subsistence income as well as persons of notable wealth, individuals of limited formal education as well as others who possess several university degrees. Cultural extremes are found to be just as great as the economic and educational ones. Recreational and vocational skills, preferences and leisure-time activities, differ widely also. Further, material differences produce psychological concomitants so significant that people are found to be widely separated in viewpoint as well as in general background. Certainly the dynamics of personal life vary considerably in the downtown church. Contrasts are both amazing and disturbing.

Can persons of divergent economic and cultural status meet at a common altar, or do such differences constitute an insurmountable obstacle to Christian fellowship? This question lays bare the fact that nowhere else in the world will these people be found together regularly in purposeful common assembly. Such heterogeneity conveys the impression that the congregation is less a fellowship of worshipers than it is a loose aggregation of individuals who separately seek God, and this phenomenon does not simplify the work and ministry of urban Christianity. Patterns of organizational work must be modified to procure results. Indeed the downtown Protestant church discovers in the situation a forthright challenge to bring about a working amalgamation of persons who derive from extreme cultural and economic circumstances. To this end the institution may not therefore specialize with one class of constituents at the expense of another, for a tangled ministry is thrust upon it. Its basic task is to achieve spiritual homogeneity out of economic and cultural heterogeneity. No one doubts the complexity of such a task nor regards it lightly, since institutional Christianity is severely tested under such adverse circumstances.

That there is no facile way to secure the desired amalgamation is patent. Yet a practical homogeneity infused with religious ideals must ultimately be found if the downtown church is to play a significant role in the religious life of the city. When excellent and extensive opportunities for Christian fellowship are provided by the church, a deep sense of community is likely to be discovered and developed. This accomplishment is within the reach of most congregations. If, however, the herculean task is shunned, the local church will either deteriorate into a country club or become a pseudo social-service agency. Neither eventuality is necessary or desirable.

The downtown church is tested as is no other in the urban environment. It is called upon to demonstrate not only that Christianity is relevant to any human situation however heterogeneous, but also that this spiritual force is the only adequate one in the world for the full amalgamation and true brotherhood of mankind. New Testament religion remains as the dynamic fashioner of human fellowship and mutuality. It alone makes mankind one within a lofty religious frame of reference. Through superlative fellowship opportunities the downtown church brings the pressure of Christ's life upon urban residents. Under spiritual tension and challenge amalgamation on a religious level may come to pass. Out of diversity can be fashioned a bond between men that no chance or happenstance can break. It is a bond of Christ, understood and applied in human relationships. Men become united not in common greed but by making common cause. They may become one in Christ rather than many in society.

A Bifocal Ministry. The downtown church combines the arduous task of serving people who reside in the suburbs at remarkably long distances from the church plant with a ministry to those who live near by. When the former, whether out of loyalty or spiritual curiosity, commute several miles to attend religious services downtown, a vital interest in Christianity may be inferred. An urban family I know drives twelve miles to church each Sunday. "I do not know how much longer my wife and I can keep it up," said the husband recently. "It means a round trip of twenty-four miles every week end." This amazing pilgrimage has been going on for ten years. Some constituents travel even greater distances. In contrast other members walk, drive, or ride mass transportation facilities from near by. To serve both the remote and near-by residents is the herculean task of the centrally located church.

Naturally then the downtown church comes by a widely dispersed membership. Parish maps reveal an extensive outreach in the pattern of a bifocal ministry. Although many individuals are drawn from the territory within one-mile radius of the church plant, an equal or often greater number are attracted from remoter parts of the city. An obvious result of the long outreach is a "skimming" type of ministry. This means that a single family or perhaps several families are served here and there, but nowhere is the city intensively cultivated. Scattered individuals and fractions of families are reached by the program. This far-flung parish pattern is typical of downtown Protestant church work.

The dispersed nature of the downtown parish produces special difficulties with respect to church fellowship. Distance compels limited participation. Too little participation is detrimental to personal religion. In Protestantism not only is the church affiliate expected to enter into close individual relationship with God, but also he must fraternize regularly with fellow members of the congregation. This latter emphasis is an essential part of the genius of our faith. Relationship with God is placed in a human setting to enable individuals of common religious persuasion to sustain one another in hours of temptation or distress. Unfortunately in the downtown church where the congregation is scattered to remote parts of the city in a bifocal pattern, it is difficult to assemble constituents frequently. Some pastors do not attempt it oftener than once a week—for Sunday morning worship. And this limitation becomes a spiritual handicap. Distance is now a recognized enemy of intimate Christian fellowship, since commutation hours are commonly charged off against the local church as an essential part of the individual's contribution to organized religion. Unfortunately, however, travel time has little value to the local church although it is a necessary concomitant of participation by remote residents. This is a minor ecclesiastical tragedy.

Limited participation complicates further the already laborious task of promoting a sense of community in the congregation. Therefore to cope with the baffling situation a parish organization plan is commonly used. This practical program divides the parish into fellowship cultivation units (based either upon chronological age or upon place of residence) and promotes human contacts. Some such arrangement is inevitable if membership cohesion is to be realized. The plan aids Protestantism in becoming a fellowship of persons making common cause. Significant fellowship opportunities do need to be multiplied. The spirit of the congregation must be kept high, relevant, and integrated so that worshipers may share regularly in the corporate life of the institution.

Further, a widely dispersed parish makes pastoral calling difficult with excessive time consumed in getting from one home to another. In cases of special need the minister must often spend half a day traveling to and from a parishioner's home. Thus it is understandable that the pastor of a downtown church frequently limits visitation work primarily to calls with a purpose. Every visit must count since an enormous investment of priceless time and energy goes into it. Casual visitation is reduced to a minimum. Yet even under justifiable restrictions the average downtown minister travels an astonishing number of miles in doing parish work each year and completes more than a thousand calls.

Still further, quality of preaching is inevitably stressed in the downtown church. People hesitate to come great distances for inferior sermons, and this eternal expectancy compels the pastor, whether he likes it or not, to devote more time and energy in preparation for pulpit work. Homiletical attention is usually directed along the lines of common personal problems and upon the religious resources available for everyday needs. This is a type of topical preaching.

Thus it is commonplace for the downtown church to encounter the distance factor in week-by-week religious activity. At best the bifocal ministry is a difficult one. Adaptation of approach is compelled by the realities of the parish situation in as much as this is the only church in the urban environment which cannot escape the spatial penalty. The lot of the pastor is not an easy one, but it is clearly one of the most challenging to be found in the city.

The Counseling Mecca. Many downtown churches maintain an extensive counseling program. If permitted, interview work would consume all of the pastor's time. Hardly a week end goes by but an additional covey of individuals in need of personal help seek appointments. An unending procession of youth, young adults, parents, and older people turns in here for guidance. This is a conspicuous feature of downtown religious work and properly lays claim to the pastor's time and energy.

Among the manifold problems brought to the minister are found domestic conflicts, vocational choice, sex difficulties, emotional disturbances, premarital and postmarital adjustments, juvenile delinquency, alcoholism, racial prejudice, labor-management troubles, unemployment, convalescence, bereavement, financial and educational problems. Obviously few clergymen are competent to handle wisely and well all such personal difficulties. They may lack training and breadth of experience. Therefore effective pastors tend to specialize in the problem areas for which they are specifically trained and to refer all other clients to proper experts or agencies.

Many critical problems growing out of marriage are normally handled by the minister. Among these are conflicts which develop as a result of mixed marriages. In some cities marriages between Protestants and Roman Catholics run as high as thirty-one families per thousand, and this situation is commonly an occasion for trouble. Further, conjugal friction develops frequently as a result of serious maladjustments in the realms of sex, finances, in-laws, and personality. Whatever the cause for domestic discord, a downtown minister is expected to initiate the process by which the resources of religion are utilized to salvage the happiness of the homemakers. To achieve this with regularity is to perform near miracles.

A recent development finds clergymen emphasizing a preventative type of counseling. In preparation for marriage a series of premarital interviews is given. Increasingly attitude inventory tests are utilized. This helps the persons to see themselves objectively. In some cases individuals are helped to avoid situations from which conflict is likely to emerge; in others aid is given to ameliorate the difficulties lest they spread and contaminate the entire love relationship. This is probably one of the most creative developments occurring in the field.

Preventative counseling is being carried on by clergymen in many other problem areas also. Personality disorders, vocational adjustments, and correction of unwholesome attitudes are anticipated and treated prior to the emergence of a crisis. This approach has proved successful with youth and young adults especially. And it has greatly broadened the possibilities for usefulness on the part of the downtown pastor. While people are often helped through sermons to endure bereavement and other forms of personal tragedy, troubled individuals have discovered additional values inherent in a more personalized approach. The sermon is frequently too general in its application. Thus in the personal interview Jesus revealed the possibilities of an important ministry to downtown church constituents. The approach makes everybody somebody and brings the resources of religion to bear directly upon personal problems. The need and the resource meet head on.

Relationship to Neighborhood Churches. That there is a ministry unique to the centrally located church is now apparent. Its public is comprised of hotel population, rooming-house residents, apartment dwellers, and downtown-minded people. This ample constituency evokes a ministry and program commensurate with the religious opportunity. Yet the downtown church does not work alone, but rather in co-operative association with sister institutions. This relationship is often endangered by developments outside the power of the former church to prevent.

Leaders in the neighborhood church encounter difficulty in understanding why urban residents go downtown to church and, further, why they continue to do so. Since apparently no one can prevent this eventuality, frustration is piled upon infuriating frustration. That it is a matter of viewpoint and personal preference appears as an inadequate explanation. Yet downtown-mindedness is a fact, and its origin probably lies in antecedent group experience. Persons accustomed to the downtown church approach and program will if necessary cross denominational lines to fulfill the desire to affiliate with a centrally located church. At first they drop in at worship services to size up the institution and its leadership. Perhaps they are attracted by the prospect of encountering a more experienced pastor, of hearing better preaching, and of mingling with community leaders. Undoubtedly the reason is less important than the fact that many urban residents actually travel great distances to worship and to participate downtown. To do so they pass by a number of excellent neighborhood churches. This action appears unwarranted, and worried neighborhood officials cannot accept it dispassionately.

The downtown church has a community-wide ministry whereas other churches serve relatively isolated neighborhoods. Therefore the former attracts people who are community-minded, sophisticated, and those whose formal ties with religion have become somewhat loosened and endeavors to bring to them the challenge of Christianity. This motley population makes up the congregation, and admirable unity in Christian fellowship is achieved by the inscrutable alchemy of the spirit.

But special difficulties have to be overcome. Secularism at its best flowers in the downtown church. The world's most polite people are there. The music lovers, the art devotees, the literati, the social climbers are present and articulate. This brings home forcibly the realization that secular ideals and manners are prominent among people who are successful in the everyday world. This puts a special burden upon the downtown church, for Christianity should be at its best likewise. Secular quality is superseded by spiritual quality. Men need to know that only in organized religion are found the "water of life," adequate salvation from failure and sin, and the victory which overcomes the world. If the downtown church did not exist, thousands of people would be without effective religious guidance. Clearly the centrally located institution has a broad program and ministry without which a denomination would indeed be weak.

In urban Protestantism it is normal, where a denomination is represented by two or more churches, to discover one situated in a downtown location. Both types of religious work are required in an effective and comprehensive strategy of the city. To the neighborhood church is given an indigenous ministry; to the downtown church, a community-wide service. However, the latter feeds its members into the neighborhood church life, sponsors new churches in the suburbs, launches missions in depressed areas, and serves as anchor church of the denomination. It is the mother institution, and no denomination can be effective in the city without a strong downtown church. Such is a basic fact in sound urban Protestant strategy.

Yet the downtown church is obligated to demonstrate at all times that its purposes and program are unselfish, co-operative, and noteworthy. It must work at a fourfold task: (1) to provide its motley constitutents with a complete religious and church experience, (2) to pioneer new patterns of effective churchmanship, (3) to make common cause with sister churches, and (4) to swing the general population's attention toward organized religion. The centrally located church which is conscientiously engaged in this valid task will undoubtedly serve the best interests of its sister churches also. A vital relationship between religious units situated in the neighborhood and in the downtown area is possible when pursued along the lines of teamwork and mutuality. Intelligent churchmanship requires the continued existence of both types of urban churches, and therefore leaders in each need to cultivate an adequate understanding of the other's problems. With the ebb and flow of religious fortunes in the urban community enlightened interdependence constitutes the chief hope of the future.

Financing Downtown Religious Work. How to finance downtown church work poses a difficult problem for urban religious leaders. The scattering of well-to-do families to remote suburbs undermines the downtown church's financial situation. An ever-present fear is that distance will eventually wean the people away. Besides, loyal supporters grow old and eventually retire from remunerative occupations. Younger members appear reticent to replace the persons who have so long and so faithfully carried the budget burden of the church. Though a stream of fresh prospects continue to join the church, old-timers tend to regard the incoming members as economic liabilities rather than as financial assets. Since many new affiliates actually do possess low or marginal income status, cynical observers say that those who need the church most are least able to finance it adequately. The wealthy move away; the poor remain.

Property in the downtown area often has a remarkably high real-estate value. Instances can be cited where a church location is valued in terms of hundreds of thousands of dollars. For this reason the downtown congregation is usually tempted to sell its desirable site for business, multiple housing, or other purposes and to transfer its ample equity to a suburban neighborhood where the institution would have smoother sailing financially speaking. The temptation to abandon the central city altogether is exceptionally attractive, and but few downtown churches have failed to consider this pleasing alternative at one time or another. Unfortunately on such occasions the dollar value of property appears to eclipse the religious value of a strategic site location. The interminable struggle to raise a budget while ministering from a site valued at a fabulous sum is one of the fierce anomalies of downtown church work.

Why then does Protestantism continue its religious work downtown? The reason is undoubtedly the most adequate in the world —people with unmet spiritual needs reside there. The extensive proportions of this opportunity are shouted by religious censuses which reveal that thousands of unchurched persons of Protestant background either take up residence downtown or return to it for spiritual guidance. Studies disclose that a cross section of humanity is found here. In addition to a notable ministry to entire families the church serves many unmarried adults and older people who commonly accumulate in a disproportionate ratio in the inner city. The latter specialization lifts the work of the downtown church to a new level of significance but introduces additional difficulties in raising a budget.

Consequently the tiny downtown church is almost always on the verge of insolvency. Smallness in the city means weakness. Where there are fewer than five hundred active members, the institution is commonly caught with a financial burden too heavy to bear. Allowing for the usual percentage of church "drones" (that is, persons who do not contribute), the budget problem falls upon the shoulders of a minority of the membership. These loyal persons in turn are caught between a desire to give generously and an awareness of the limits of personal income, and in the dilemma discover that they are unable to contribute beyond a full tithe to keep the project going. Discouragement and spiritual frustration are the ultimate fruit of the intolerable situation.

Three main solutions of the financial problem are in common use: endowments, mission subsidization, and self-support. As expected the relative effectiveness of the methods varies. (1) The establishment of endowments has in some cases proved a boon to the downtown church. Earnings from these monies supplement the normal financial sources. Trust funds and income-producing property (apartment buildings, stores, and hotels) have made it possible for a quality ministry to be continued long after the normal resources of the congregation have dwindled. Where funds have been needed on an incentive basis to spur congregations on to higher achievements, the endowment idea has clearly proved beneficial. But the benefits should be viewed against a background of the liabilities. When this examination is completed, one may arrive at a correct estimate of the matter.

Three perils are inherent in the endowment approach. First, where the local church should actually have abandoned a competitive or fruitless site, the presence of funds has prevented a frank facing of the facts. An intelligent decision was thereby postponed since the congregation was misled by a false notion that money alone makes the future secure. Second, shortsighted business methods have tripped numerous congregations. Some income-producing property was mortgaged beyond the point of safety so that not only was the title lost during depression years, but even the church itself barely escaped the sheriff's hammer. While attempting to guarantee the future, a local church may have mortgaged itself to the point where in general economic reverses its liabilities exceed its assets. Disgraceful foreclosure or equally distasteful bankruptcy proceedings mark the end of the church's misguided excursion into the business world. A third peril rises from an inordinate consciousness of the value of money and a diminishing awareness of the ideals of Jesus Christ. Instances are numerous in which mere solvency became the guiding local church objective, whereas the tendering of religious service became a matter of secondary importance. Churches should be financed but not hurt.

2. Mission Subsidization is regarded by some downtown churches as a last resort, for it often carries with it an intolerable stigma. By some it is considered a "kiss of death." Yet many congregations rely upon this type of outside assistance to maintain solvency. Funds procured from the local synod, presbytery, or conference often enable the downtown project to continue its ministry an additional span of years. National boards of missions usually furnish financial assistance to such troubled situations at the urgent behest of local leaders. Increasingly, however, the policy trend is turning away from subsidy. Scientific studies reveal that funds thus provided rarely save the situation. Too often the congregation becomes pauperized. What has seemed to be an easy way to deal with the downtown problem has turned out to be a dangerous and unwarranted solution or even no solution at all. The approach creates as many additional problems as seemingly are solved.

3. There are numerous instances of success where the method of complete self-support was utilized. In this approach a congregation accepts full responsibility for its budget. Plans are formulated and put into effect for raising the necessary money from indigenous sources. Almost universally an every-member-cavass approach is utilized since all practicable means of assuring financial support by persons who directly benefit from the work of the downtown church are applied. Members who are inclined to tithe are encouraged to do so. Proportionate giving is encouraged—that is, a person contributes weekly an amount equal to what he earns per hour in his vocation. Constituents who heretofore lacked personal habits of systematic support are trained to assume fiscal responsibility. Many

119

nonmember attenders at public worship respond generously to a special appeal made at regular intervals. No urban resident is too poor to contribute to a local church.

The most effective downtown local churches I know are totally self-supporting. This is the proper way to finance church work, and there are probably no urban congregations which cannot raise their own budget. An adequate financial potential exists. It becomes therefore a matter of adequate stewardship training and efficient local church administration. This task is a challenge to the downtown Protestant church. It can finance its own program. Complete solvency lies within reach. But the congregation must be made aware of this possibility and taught how to achieve it. Responsibility rests with local church leaders.

The Program Enigma. What considerations should be held in mind in setting up a program for the downtown church? Can effectiveness be achieved merely by reproducing the pattern of the neighborhood church? What special ministries appear to be required downtown? These and kindred questions press for attention, but first let us consider the nature of the public to be served.

Plans for an effective downtown church program should start with an adequate knowledge of the mind of the congregation. Since the constituents are a heterogeneous group, an attempt should be made to discover the dominant attitudes, preferences, viewpoints, clichés of thought, and religious habits of the people. To the centrally located church are attracted Catholics, Hebrews, the spiritually curious, prestige hunters, persons from various generations, newcomers to the community, individuals with critical personal problems, religious cranks and misfits, as well as a host of normal persons drawn from many denominations. A program has to be devised which will minister to this unique congregation. Recognition of shocking diversity, in mind as well as in cultural status, may prove a significant starting point. Somehow these people must be led step by step into an adequate experience of Christian fellowship and unity. To bring about this religious metamorphosis and to achieve Christian community is the dual purpose of the program. Mechanical arrangements serve well only if they nurture the process of Christian fellowship and personal growth.

The effective church is a complete church. Children, youth, and adults require a full range of ministries; and such should be available. A tragic lack of comprehensiveness is often found in smaller churches, and this situation compels the individual to look elsewhere for an adequate satisfaction of remaining religious needs. Therefore the function and administration of the program should be directed in a manner determined to guide persons into a full-rounded religious life. A complete ministry should be available not only to the individual but also to the entire family. In short, local church experience should prove a spiritual asset to the home and a boon to each constituent.

Quite apart from and beyond other benefits the downtown church program should communicate to its constituents the meaning of Christianity and train them in the appropriate habit systems whereby the experience of God is kept alive and thriving. At least four fundamental spiritual objectives underlie an adequate program: participation, prayer, leadership, and financial support. These serve as the marks of a healthy congregation, and each underlies an aspect of the individual's relationship to the church.

1. Participation of downtown church members means regular attendance by every person at public worship services, all church affairs, group gatherings, and special functions. It is as difficult to procure a religious viewpoint by proxy as it is to procure an education by proxy: in short it cannot be done. Thus a survey of the participation habits of a congregation may reveal a shocking current situation—one both spotty and unsatisfactory. Further, this investigation can disclose the congregation's reaction to the stated program of the local church. Program elements which are poorly attended reveal a negative vote. Regardless of whether low interest or an inappropriate meeting time accounts for lack of adequate participation, either the people should be re-educated to the importance of the element or eventually the activity ought to be dropped from the program. Officials can learn considerable from an analysis of member participation.

2. The prayer interests and habits of a congregation furnish an external clue to the religious pulse of the people. Here prayer is defined broadly to include the entire range of devotional activity by which the individual keeps a personal experience of God alive and developing. Grace at meals, bedtime prayers, daily meditations,

Bible reading, and kindred religious activity constitute a battery of primary devotional aids. Utilization of them may reveal mature acceptance of responsibility for one's own personal spiritual nurture, in which prayer, broadly conceived, is an essential ingredient. The history of one's prayer life is commonly the history of vital personal religion. Every church member requires experience regularly in private devotions, in a Bible class or prayer meeting where faith is wrought out and becomes articulate, and in a great worship service where the individual is borne up out of his provincialism into broad fellowship with God. This threefold devotional experience belongs to the Protestant discipline, and it supports the spiritual development of the individual. Ultimately Christianity must traverse the road from heaven down into the human heart via the local church program.

3. Leadership opportunity in a downtown church is often extensive. Without the contributed time and energy of lay members the religious program would collapse. Tasks performed by laymen range from Sunday-school teaching to regular ushering at worship services, and these reveal the amazing versatility of the congregation. There is probably no task too unusual or too difficult for members to perform. Underlying efficient church leadership is secular competence in administration, business, pedagogy, personnel work, and public relations; and such will always be needed and should be utilized in the downtown church.

Further, excellent leaders are needed in parish organization and visitation. With so many jobs to do is it unreasonable to expect every member to serve five years in leadership work at the local church level? Experiments in this direction by several denominations have met with surprising success. A rotation of officers and leaders may be instituted to make room for a turnover of officials. All may then secure varied church experiences and thus develop a rounded conception of the institution's task. People develop spiritually by working in religious programs.

The downtown church is too prone to turn over key leadership positions to paid personnel. Wherever it is done, fewer opportunities for participation remain open to the congregation. This practice applies especially to choral music. Soloists and paid quartets continue to be used although many local churches are procuring satis-

122

factory results from volunteer singers. Why pay laymen to sing and not pay them to teach or to usher? The presence of a large professional staff does not necessarily reveal that the institution is an effective downtown church. Very often the opposite is true. This contention points to the important discovery that only to the extent in which laymen conceive and administer the program does a church mobilize and use its indigenous leadership personnel. The church should be a training ground for developing Christians.

4. The practice of financial support among members underlies the church program and relates to its effectiveness. There are two facets to the problem. Can every member of the downtown church contribute? The answer is an unqualified "yes." Extensive investigation of the participation habits of urban church members in all parts of the United States renders this conclusion inescapable. No individual is too poor to contribute at least ten cents per week to the local church. Ability to participate financially is usually present where the desire to do so is lacking. This situation calls for the development of a new attitude. Apparently many individuals have become church members without learning to participate financially.

A second facet is this: how much can a member of a downtown church contribute? Obviously this question can be answered only by the individual. However, each person generally contributes according to the intensity of his personal religion, for a positive correlation exists between the relative amount contributed and the magnitude of one's faith. For example, in a congregation I know of a widowed domestic nurse tithes and thereby ranks as the second highest contributor in the church. Meanwhile a fellow member who is a prosperous businessman begrudges a few dollars per annum. Vital personal faith largely accounts for the difference in attitude and performance here. Many members fail to see that church support impinges not on fiscal ability but rather upon enthusiastic religious faith. That is why the local congregation needs to be re-educated. Vital religion is the thing.

The program of the local church depends upon the size of the budget that can be raised and the extent of lay member participation. If the institution has achieved success in communicating Christianity to its adherents through securing full participation, prayer, and leadership, then financial support will come almost as a matter of course. Persons without an adequate religious faith have difficulty in making generous contributions, but a Christian rarely knows when he is making a sacrifice. These four kinds of relationship underlie the program of an effective downtown church. The inclusion of specific elements depends upon the mind of the congregation and the requirements of achieving a complete church with an equitable ministry for all members of the family.

One starts with the mind of the downtown congregation. Program elements are selected and framed together to achieve comprehensive religious ends. Persons are pointed beyond the finiteness of the institution to God, and therefore the program is a religious means to a religious end. Thus its total impact upon the individual should be essentially spiritual. Members and constituents are trained to participate, to pray, to serve, and to support the local church. Unless this happens, the church works at but a small fraction of its true task. The desired outcome is to "feed" persons into the Protestant movement and thence into the Kingdom of God. This primary objective should never be lost sight of in program planning.

Over and beyond this ministry the downtown church may determine to provide prudently selected social services. The number and type included depend upon the needs of the neighborhood to be serviced. However, social work should be kept in an adequate religious frame of reference. People in cities need desperately to have the resources of religion applied to individual problems. Ultimately residents discover little religious salvation in recreational activity alone. Often social service diminishes a material crisis but leaves the spiritual crisis, equally important, untouched. If so it is a solution that does not solve, a social service that does not serve. No other agency or institution apart from the church can deal with the religious problem. Therefore any neglect of spiritual needs is criminal and unwarranted. The downtown church more than any other is tempted to be "off fixing the moon" rather than about the Father's business.

The preceding pages provide a brief description of six fundamental problems of the centrally located church. No doubt additional difficulties come to mind. These also merit consideration by the reader. However, the purpose of the present discussion is to point out some common problems and to evoke a thoroughgoing appreciation of the complex ministry undertaken by the downtown church.

THE EFFECTIVE DOWNTOWN CHURCH

An account of effectiveness in the downtown area focuses attention upon the regular church there. Treatment stresses the more common types—traditional and transitional—which prevail in most urban places. However, this primary orientation does not lessen the significance of specialized ministries available through institutional and mission types. Such work has already been dealt with in earlier paragraphs, and the task which remains is to set forth eight prominent characteristics of effective downtown church work: site, plant, membership size, staff, program, denominational teamwork, community relations, and ecumenical viewpoint. An exploration of these considerations may issue in a more prudent urban strategy and eventually may encourage additional efforts toward effective downtown religious work.

A Strategic Location. Is the church properly located? Experience indicates that the downtown church should be situated at a conspicuous accessible site in the heart of the city, and all efforts should be bent toward correcting a misplaced plant. To serve adequately the church has to be seen. Generally speaking, a location across from the post office, Y.M.C.A., Y.W.C.A., central bus terminal, subway entrance, city hall, or in proximity to a prominent hotel or department store fulfills this fundamental requirement. Such a site gains in strategic significance when it has the added advantage of being a point where bus or streetcar routes converge or originate. Conspicuous location is essentially a matter both of the prominence borrowed from a public building and of high visibility. This is of primary significance and is required by the church which desires to be effective. The ideal site is where cross the crowded ways of urban life.

An Adequate Church Plant. The local church plant should be of sufficient size and suitable architecture to match or excel the buildings in the territory. Ecclesiastical in appearance, the edifice merits good repair and fine landscaping. Adequate exterior lighting, a well-kept lawn, and an illuminated bulletin board attract the attention and admiration of passers-by. The building should be well lighted at night so that the corner upon which it is situated appears conspicuous and inviting. Within, the church should be modernized and equipped with comfortable pews, lounges, recreational quarters,

Sunday-school classrooms, and other physical facilities required in forward-looking religious work. Since downtown churches often have many older persons in the membership, the sanctuary should be easy of access. Elimination of long inside and outside stairways is desirable. The floor level of newer structures is placed hardly more than a step or two above the sidewalk. Further, offices for personal consultation should be easy to enter and to depart from inconspicuously and without embarrassment. Respecting all these details architectural counsel is available at the national headquarters of many denominations and at the National Council of Churches also. In a word the plant should have the appearance of a thriving church with all the facilities necessary to a vital program.

Effective Membership Size. Effective membership size for urban churches has been discussed in Chapter I. Here let us consider the significance of the factor in the downtown situation. A small centrally located church is likely to be ineffective or to have a premature demise. Almost insuperable obstacles appear in its path, and these prevent the institution from functioning properly. There are ominous difficulties which arise respecting finances, physical facilities, leadership, group work, Sunday school, lay participation, and other ecclesiastical obligations. A downtown church of less than one thousand members has noticeable difficulty in sustaining its ministry at the required quality level over a long period of time. A city church can be too small to function effectively.

Some downtown churches have huge memberships—ranging from two to ten thousand persons. In contrast, however, many are small, far below the required urban level of effective strength. By way of practical illustration let the reader consider the situation in his own community. An examination of the size of the membership, attendance of the Sunday-morning congregation, enrollment of the Sunday school, and both the quality and range of organizational activities can reveal some disturbing facts. If a particular church falls below the level of downtown urban effectiveness, for example, one thousand members, it should not be inferred that the church must go out of existence. Rather the general religious opportunity in the territory merits closer examination. Perhaps there are numerous unchurched residents near by, and a religious census can be utilized to locate them. An intelligent conclusion is that the church should thoroughly explore the current potential for achieving a membership strength which would assure adequate ministry to the downtown area. A city church can often be built up to and beyond the minimum level of effectiveness. This is a desirable eventuality and one within the reach of many congregations.

A Competent Church Staff. A downtown church commonly operates with a basic staff comprised of pastor, secretary, director of music and/or organist, and custodian. In addition some congregations employ a parish visitor, a director of religious education, and a social worker. A deaconess often serves in one or another of these roles. When the congregation grows beyond fifteen hundred members, two fully ordained ministers are ordinarily needed. For very large churches an additional pastor is required for each thousand members. All this indicates how common it is to find a basic professional staff in the downtown church.

Compatibility among staff members is of vital importance and is procured in part by the discriminating selection of competent personnel and in part by the cultivation of a Christian *esprit de corps.* Procurement of compatible ordained individuals has always been difficult. Recently a workable formula was accidentally discovered. A senior minister of middle age approaching the peak of his powers is teamed with an associate who is older in years and whose chief duties are to assist in church administration and to carry the major burden of pastoral calling. The former does the preaching and administers the work of the entire church; the latter carries out administrative decisions and handles details along with visitation work. Both share equitably in funerals, weddings, baptisms, and other special requests. Additional staff members are employed for specific tasks—namely, choral music, religious education, social work, and so forth. Care exercised in the selection of these persons plus the thoughtful definition of responsibilities will materially reduce friction and misunderstandings within the downtown church staff.

Unfortunately in the downtown church many professional services have to be purchased. This appears inevitable. In contrast the neighborhood church if necessary can get along with utilizing a volunteer choir director, a volunteer organist, a part-time custodian, and volunteer workers in the field of religious education; and this they commonly do. But the central church is virtually compelled to procure professional leaders. Often this requirement extends beyond an adequate staff to include singers, Sunday-school teachers, administrators, chefs, and social caterers. An obvious result is heavy overhead expense. Thus a disproportionately large budget appears as a necessary evil in downtown church projects. Yet it is agreed that money invested in trained leadership brings enormously satisfying dividends. A competent staff underlies the work of an effective church.

A Comprehensive Program. The hodgepodge of cultural and economic characteristics endemic to the downtown congregation reveals the need for a more diversified program than is commonly furnished by the strictly neighborhood church. The downtown situation demands a broader range of ministries, for more things have to be better done.

At the outset comprehensiveness in program means completeness. It must be a complete church. No member should find it necessary to seek another congregation to satisfy unmet religious needs. The program should be comprehensive in the range of its offerings to children, to youth, to adults, and to families. Yet withal the primary purpose of the program is to minister to spiritual needs. Additional ways of serving the individual, such as social, cultural, and recreational activities, may be regarded as important but secondary. Further, the illusion of effectiveness should be avoided. The gross number of participants is often submitted as evidence of an effective program, whereas the cumulative religious impact upon the individual is a more valid measure of ecclesiastical success. The depth to which Christianity penetrates a member's life and spreads its influence to mental processes and human behavior is a better test of the relevance of the church in the affairs of men. Indeed the downtown church program should minister to persons of all ages and circumstances but always on a superlative spiritual level.

The secondary program elements need to be assessed at their contributory value. Social, cultural, and recreational activities are primarily devices for finding persons who eventually may manifest an interest in the religious ministries of the church. The activity itself is a bridge over which persons may pass into a religious life. Were this not so, it would probably be difficult to justify prodigal expenditures of time and money in this direction. No one knows exactly how much it costs to win a person to God, but Protestant leaders are sure that it has to be done regardless of expense. Although the elements under discussion possess intrinsic secular value, it is naïve and dangerous to assign primary religious significance to them. They are not ends in themselves but pathways into the Christian fellowship. They help individuals find their way out of a vague easygoing life into one of disciplined spiritual endeavor. Finder organizations and finder activities provide opportunities for meeting church people, for looking over church facilities, and for forming friendships with persons who already belong to the church. Here is both an opportunity and a criterion. Unless a person is eventually fed into the larger Protestant movement, the program has failed to achieve its primary purpose. To serve all persons in a broad but spiritual way should constitute the local church's objective.

Denominational Teamwork. No downtown church, however strong, can truly stand alone, nor can it provide adequate ministry for an entire city. Religious work should be shared with other units in an enlightened pattern of denominational teamwork. This discussion certainly applies to cities above ten thousand population. When a downtown church becomes self-centered and/or develops a prima donna complex, the entire work of a denomination is impaired. In the city selfish congregations eventually fail. Survival depends upon teamwork. The combined ministries of all types of local churches are required to service the whole urban community.

Therefore abnormal self-interest, wherever it exists, should be cast out or transmuted into a deep concern for all the work of the denomination. Where a neighborhood church is weak, the enlightened downtown congregation should bolster the undertaking on a temporary basis with finances and leadership. In the suburbs, where a new church is urgently needed, again the downtown church should sponsor the project and walk beside the new congregation until it can walk alone. In some cities the old downtown church has an honorable record of participation in the establishment of numerous extension projects on the urban periphery.

This kind of denominational teamwork thrills the administrator and arouses confidence in the work of Protestantism. Properly the centrally located church must lead the way in strengthening the ministry of its denomination throughout the city. In numerous cities new churches ought to be established, others require relocation to desirable sites, and still others wait almost vainly for resolution of an intradenominational competitive situation. Thus a coveted opportunity for leadership is presented to the downtown church in a program of full co-operation for the denomination. By spending itself in such important tasks it saves its own life. In the city a denomination is no stronger than its weakest church.

Vital Community Relations. The effective downtown church needs a well-conceived and well-executed program of public relations. Experienced leaders say that no institution can thrive without systematic publicity and continuous noteworthy public service. The urban situation demands that every legitimate and permissible device for keeping the local church persistently before the mind of the community be utilized. An enlightened downtown church guards jealously its unique privilege of service and helpfulness to the community at large and to individuals who are out of touch with Protestant life. Yet the city needs to know that the church is engaged in its spiritual task. This story cannot be told often enough.

The centrally located church usually occupies a place of notable influence in the community. Its long history, succession of able ministers, imposing edifice, and impressive membership size contribute to the opinion that this institution is the leading church of the denomination in the city. Consequently the local radio station encourages the broadcast of worship services and sponsors occasional religious television programs. Of course the senior minister is expected to join one or more luncheon clubs, to serve on various community improvement committees, and to maintain an active interest in local affairs. These activities constitute a vital part of a systematic program of public relations. Service to the community through espousing causes, participating in social work, and promoting the general welfare is expected of the downtown church.

Further, publicity in the form of newspaper stories, display advertising, radio programs, city-wide functions (choir festivals, lectures, celebration of Reformation Day, and so on), and kindred activities aid in keeping the cause of religion before the minds of urban residents. The effective downtown church maintains a vital relationship to community life.

An Ecumenical Viewpoint. An opportunity is presented to the downtown church to guide prominent leaders of community life into full religious maturity. These individuals, equipped as they often are with superior education and splendid cultural background, are prone to feel that religion has little to offer them personally. With the achievement of reasonable financial security and a place of influence in business and/or the community, many appear to have settled back into a narrow complacency in lieu of a world-wide religious concern. Though giants in the business world, they are pygmies in the spiritual realm. This development constitutes a stubborn challenge to organized religion.

Thus the downtown church is called upon to redeem members from strict parochialism and arrested spiritual growth. It is challenged to bring constituents a Christian view of the world and a working knowledge of Protestantism. Spiritual horizons need to be extended beyond denominational boundaries, and the aspirations of a particular city church should be placed in a universal frame of religious reference. Among other considerations the local institution must discover what is occurring in the larger Protestant world and then mediate this knowledge to its membership. A worthy objective is the achievement of a thoroughgoing ecumenical point of view. Among urban churches the downtown unit is uniquely placed to speak and act adequately in the interest of world Christianity. It may become a dispersing center for grand ideas. In short the effective city church points the way beyond its own altar to the great world of Christian fellowship and activity. This is the road upon which all denominations mingle their loyalties and merge their aspirations.

Apparently a downtown church can achieve distinction with reference to physical facilities, staff personnel, program, and philosophy of work. In the foregoing discussion of eight essential considerations church leaders may find the urgent but unfinished task of urban Protantism.

WORKABLE IDEAS FOR THE DOWNTOWN CHURCH

Perhaps a selection of ideas bearing upon the solution of the downtown enigma will be appreciated by harassed leaders at the local church level. The problem as a whole is more than an administrative hardship; it is a parish embarrassment. Therefore a discussion of some concrete patterns of action may encourage new attacks upon persistent but common problems. Because of the limitation of space only essential details are given. Additional ideas might have been added, yet it seemed prudent to disclose the range of resourcefulness which alert pastors are bringing to the downtown situation rather than to attempt an exhaustive treatment.

Visitors' Minute. The visitors' minute is a brief period set aside in the morning worship service of a downtown church wherein the pastor extends a general welcome to strangers in the congregation. Newcomers are invited to tarry after service to receive a personal greeting from the minister, to meet the church staff, and to chat with church officials. Informal friendliness is featured in the situation. Does it get results? Here is a pastor who reports that sixty prospective families for membership were located in a single month. The visitors' minute is commonly broadened in practice to permit the entire congregation time enough to fill out a registration card upon which are reported name, place of residence, change of address, program interests, and other vital information.

In several downtown churches which I have visited the visitors' minute lasted five minutes and was diplomatically utilized to acquaint newcomers with the varieties of ministry available and the advantages of a prompt and friendly response to the local church program on the part of the visitor. In communities where congregations turn over rapidly it is important to utilize this inventory procedure for newcomers week after week despite the possible annoyance to persons who are permanent residents. To strangers the visitors' minute is the high light of the service. It constitutes gracious recognition of their presence and becomes a pleasant invitation to return.

Mimeographed Materials. Recently a downtown church was confronted with the problem of an inadequate budget and an urgent need for more promotional materials. Considerable money was being spent week after week on printed bulletins, but eventually leaders came to see that this budgetary item should be utilized in the purchase of a variatype typewriter and a stock of the more commonly used alphabets. Following the transaction it became possible to cut stencils, using printed format principles and emphasizing various program features by the use of varying sizes and fonts of type. This

132

economy measure permitted the production and circulation of additional publications. Although the machine has now been used for several years, it has proved increasingly satisfactory to the local church. Suggestions for improving mimeograph work are circulated free of charge by many stationery supply houses.

Promotional Materials. Many downtown churches have discovered the value of printed promotional materials, especially of the type where pictures are used. Postcard views of the church attract attention, and visitors like to mail them to out-of-town friends. Small pamphlets which list the stated meetings of the church may be illustrated with pictures of a chapel, a lighted tower, or some other ecclesiastical feature. Further, a brief history of the church may be condensed to a few hundred words and published in an attractive format. Commonly in printed materials downtown churches are inclined to use pictures of a prayer chapel, or a steeple, or a church window, or a set of doors, or a cornerstone inscription, or a religious verse, or several verses combined into an eye-catching, quickly read brochure. In a religious sense it pays to advertise. The distribution of attractive materials may encourage newcomers to look up the church.

Classified Directory of Membership. A few downtown churches have published a classified directory of members engaged in business and professional occupations. The directory, an annual publication, is designed to encourage the congregation to patronize fellow members. Ordinarily requests for this type of booklet originate among the people. Where necessary, latent interest may be stimulated to sponsor the project.

The name, address, and telephone number are furnished for each person included; and the material is arranged in topical categories similar to the classified portion of a telephone book. Vital information is thus made accessible to the congregation. In as much as no pressure is brought to bear upon affiliated persons to patronize fellow members, the church directory serves a useful purpose. Instances are not infrequent when individuals seek a Protestant lawyer, doctor, or business firm. Though religion may not be a determining factor, people often prefer to do business with persons of the same faith. The directory provides the newcomer with a list of trustworthy persons and firms.

Church Tower Amplifying System. A recent survey reveals that a score of downtown churches have installed tower amplifying systems connected with the church organ. Thus a quarter-hour program of hymns, boosted out into the street, is possible prior to the morning worship services each Sunday. Organ music that is pleasant and dignified is audible within a six-block radius. Little difficulty has been encountered in raising funds to purchase equipment. It is an attractive memorial idea.

A downtown church I know installed an automatic record player, connected to a timing device, so that on weekdays promptly at noon and again at 5:00 P.M. a five-minute program of hymns is played from the church tower. The appropriateness of this musical ministry is apparent when one realizes that a traffic light is located in front of the church. While motorists wait for the light to change from red to green, their attention is called pleasantly to the church on the corner. Hymn interludes are provided at the hours of peak traffic volume of vehicles. Scores of pedestrians and motorists have expressed surprise and satisfaction with this turntable ministry of organ music.

However, inquiry should be made of local authorities before purchases of equipment are made since some communities have regulations prohibiting or limiting the use of public amplifying systems. Where feasible this program turns the attention of the public churchward and supplements the gracious ministry of church bell or chimes.

A Weekday Noon Worship Service. Here is a downtown church which serves a cafeteria luncheon from a half-hour before noon to one o'clock one day a week (usually Thursday). Two meal seatings of thirty minutes each accommodate the patrons. Sandwiches, dessert, salad, and beverage are served at cost; and a person may eat all he desires. A freewill contribution covers the cost of the meal. Business people enjoy the homemade pies and cakes.

For five minutes before the noon worship service begins, a tower concert of familiar hymns is amplified out across the city from the steeple, pleasantly reminding pedestrians of the program. This music interlude is made possible by a connection to the organ. Further, the religious service is advertised in the previous day's newspaper, and all interested businessmen and shoppers in the downtown area are invited to attend.

Promptly at twelve o'clock, following the first luncheon sitting, a thirty-minute worship service is provided in the sanctuary. The minister opens the service each week with a theme hymn. The service consists of an appropriate poem, a sacred song by the soloist (usually male), a scripture lesson, a ten-minute meditation, and a brief closing prayer. What is the result? Men generally attend the service in greater numbers than do women, and for this reason the program is slanted to their interests and spiritual needs. The noon worship-service season extends from October through May and renders a significant ministry. It sustains men between Sundays.

Parish Fellowship Plan. The downtown local church is virtually compelled to organize its fellowship work under the supervision of individuals who live in various neighborhoods of the city. Whether or not, the plan of organization incorporates groups based upon chronological age, the underlying purpose appears to be that of keeping in close touch with all members and constituents. Regular contact is hereby actually made with every home of the parish in the hope of building up a Christian fellowship within the local church. Contacts are usually made by telephone, by personal visitation, and by general mailings sent out from the church office. Literature is occasionally left in the homes by the callers.

Effective fellowship plans at the local church level contain common elements. No program succeeds without careful organization. This is patent. At the outset a fellowship chairman is selected. He in turn selects enough divisional leaders to cover every neighborhood of the city. Then each divisional leader selects unit leaders sufficient in number to carry out the task in a given neighborhood. Each unit leader calls upon from six to eight families. Every church family receives six calls per year. Fellowship leaders are comprised of husband-and-wife teams, serve for one year only, and may be re-recruited. In larger churches the parish organization is under the close supervision of the associate pastor.

Families to be contacted in the fellowship program are placed upon a master list. However, families of church officers and of Sunday-school adult classes are omitted. When the master list has been divided among leaders, the work begins. If for any reason the fellow-ship caller is uncharitably received at a household, the family is turned over to the pastor to handle the situation. If the difficulty gets ironed out, the family is reassigned to another fellowship caller. Reports of all calls are made up through the organization, eventually reaching the church office. Further, if anything noteworthy happens to a member of any family between calls, the fellowship visitor is expected to inform the church office.

Larger city churches find it rather difficult to function effectively in terms of Christian fellowship and assimilation of members without a carefully developed parish fellowship plan. Success in this vital area of ministry depends upon comprehensive organization, close administration, high-minded leadership, and full co-operation of the membership. It takes several years to perfect the program, to train the workers, and to engender a supporting philosophy among members of the congregation. Thus studied patience is an essential ingredient in the process. Wherever the fellowship program has been undertaken with imagination, resourcefulness, and spiritual purpose, satisfactory results have come. The downtown church can scarcely escape the necessity of developing a program of Christian fellowship.

CHAPTER V

Church Work in Apartment Areas

P ROTESTANTISM can scarcely succeed in the urban environment today without an effective ministry to residents of the apartment areas. Already American cities have evolved to the point where multiple structures are an accepted and probably permanent form of housing, and however disconcerting this development may be, it thrusts itself upon religious leaders as an urgent problem which cannot be circumvented. The tremendous accumulation of population in a small area overwhelms some denominational executives and leads the naïve and inexperienced clergyman to assume that church work among apartment dwellers is easy. The exact opposite is frequently true. Obviously a ministry to the apartment area is primarily an urban church opportunity.

TRENDS IN MULTIPLE HOUSING

There has been a steady increase in the number of multiple-housing structures erected in United States urban places since 1900. In larger cities especially the trend has been conspicuously accelerated. Large-scale redevelopment projects have resulted in the rehousing to apartments of thousands of families. The apartment trend in small and medium-sized urban communities has also been greatly quickened since the beginning of the current decade. As much as one half of the population of some neighborhoods in cities of this population class reside in apartment structures. This has significance for urban church work.

The fact that large cities are gaining in population and that medium-sized communities are growing rapidly may indicate that multiple housing of some type is bound to persist into the foreseeable future. The enormous in-migration of rural and small-town residents

137

to urban places during the war years has produced a serious shortage of housing which still continues. A majority of the newcomers are in the cities to stay. Apparently for many communities multiple structures afford the best solution of the acute housing problem.

Examination of a large urban community reveals how predominant is the apartment pattern of living. New York's borough of Manhattan reports more than 337,000 families residing in large-scale housing structures. From 20 to 100 families live in a single apartment building. More than 80 per cent of all residence buildings in Manhattan contain 10 or more families. These phenomena may indicate that for decades to come the borough will be prominently characterized by multiple-housing structures rather than by buildings of single or two-family type. To a significant though somewhat lesser degree is this true of many other large American cities.

The apartment type of housing seems to commend itself to contemporary American city living. It fits in with the general desire of the urban population to produce smaller families, to reduce the task of housekeeping, and to remain relatively near the downtown area. There appears to be an increasing tendency for newly married women to continue in employment for several years after taking marital vows. Homemakers have discovered that both husband and wife may work and yet maintain a satisfactory home life in the compact modern apartment. Childless couples and nonfamily groupings often continue residence in apartments for decades. The apartment with its compactness and many conveniences constitutes an attractive type of housing. With no snow to shovel, no lawns to mow, no furnaces to fire, no ashes to carry out, no screens or storm sash to put on, and limited homemaking responsibilities the suite winsomely commends itself to practical-minded adults. Proximity to shopping facilities, accessibility to places of employment by facile transportation, privacy, and anonymity—these are some of the conspicuous advantages which appeal to the modern urban dweller. Some residents point out that it is more economical to maintain an apartment than to own a home.

During the recent war period thousands of additional families took up occupancy in multiple-housing structures for the first time. Surprisingly enough many such residents have been won over to apartment living by the apparent reduction of household duties and other advantages. Further, during the war years thousands of housewives discovered that under apartment conditions they could be gainfully employed and concurrently maintain a home. Obviously many such persons accustomed to a higher standard of income and habituated to the reduced tasks of housekeeping are convinced of the advantages of the apartment pattern of living. Rural in-migrants are unlikely to return to modest or substandard circumstances previously known now that they have had this urban experience. For better or for worse they are in the city to stay. It is the church's responsibility to make the duration of their stay for better.

LOCATION OF APARTMENT AREAS

Multiple housing is predominantly an urban phenomenon. The term has minor significance to rural America. Structures are large, multistoried, and conspicuous; and they contrast sharply with the average person's conception of what a home should look like. Even an inexperienced observer detects the difference between the massive apartment structure and the conventional single-family residence. Some individuals are awed by the contrast while others are repelled. Nearly all are impressed.

Although ministry to apartment residents is primarily an urban religious opportunity, not all city churches are strategically located to provide adequate religious services. This is due to no fault of Protestant leaders but rather to the fact that apartment buildings are restricted to certain parts of the city, and location is a matter of zoning. However, it is the responsibility of leaders to discover where these areas are and which local churches should provide the required ministries.

The precise location of apartments should be spotted on an up-to-date zoning map commonly procurable at the city engineer's office. Zoning regulations which govern the use of land are in force in nearly every American city. These municipal regulations designate certain territories (Figure No. 17) within the incorporation limits of the city for multiple-housing use. Such areas are relatively small and are clearly indicated on a zoning map. Usually apart-

139

ments are found in the territory within or immediately adjacent to the central business district. In very large cities multiple housing is more widely scattered.

Slum clearance projects are usually a type of low-cost multiple housing. Here nearly always an apartment structure supplants old substandard and condemned residence facilities. The area is

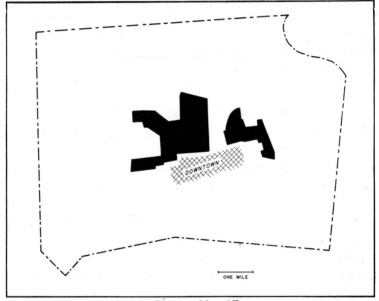

FIGURE NO. 17

APARTMENT TERRITORY IN A MIDWESTERN CITY

"redeveloped" in order that it may be recovered to healthful urban living. A recent examination of such projects in a number of cities reveals that more people than ever before now reside in the blocks razed for the redevelopment project. More families, rather than fewer, thus may now need to receive the ministries of religion. This is a sharp and continuing challenge to urban Protestantism.

Apartment structures are situated in urban areas of transition. Certain streets near the central business district formerly were lined with the finest homes of the city. Today many of yesterday's mansions are in poor state of repair. Others have long since been razed and replaced by modern apartment structures, for as the city grows, a more intensive use of land near the center is often necessitated.

In as much as land values (and therefore taxes) are high, owners find it a measure of economy to move to the suburbs and eventually to convert the old mansions into income-producing property. The erection of an apartment building usually results in a more intensive use of urban land and yields additional revenue to the owner, thus enabling him to pay the inevitable higher taxes and higher maintenance expenses. Families taking up residence in apartments are often compressed into smaller quarters than those in which they have been accustomed to live. However, the sacrifice of space is frequently exchanged willingly for a modest rental and/or an increase in the number of conveniences.

In some communities private capital has been invested in large-scale apartment projects. After the purchase of a large tract of land builders have erected a cluster of apartment buildings, producing a compact community of many thousands of residents. A shopping center is included within the acreage, and currently public transportation facilities provide access to places of employment. I know of a project which houses forty thousand people. It is the largest one of its type in the world. Such apartment developments financed by private capital tend to be located near the periphery of the city. Some are actually situated outside the municipal boundary. Since most of them are large-scale and contrast sharply with the housing in adjacent territory, no difficulty will be encountered in detecting geographical locations. Mute and often magnificent, they shout their presence.

The location of the principal apartment structures should be recorded on a map of the city and outlined with a colored pencil. Add also the number of dwelling units and the average rental in each project. The same map can be used to show the locations of near-by Protestant churches. These data will help Protestant leaders to discover and to assign responsibility for religious ministry to apartment residents. Churches less than a mile distant can serve this population group.

For purposes of the present discussion an apartment building may be defined as a housing structure in which six or more families are accommodated. Some apartments are in smaller structures. However, difficulty of church work among residents increases directly in proportion to the size of the apartment building. Persons who

141

live in modest-sized structures (which may be made up of flats or apartments) are relatively accessible to the urban pastor. On the contrary, however, when apartment structures are large, outer doors are kept locked; and a caller must gain admittance by permission of a doorman or hostess. This is especially apparent in apartment buildings where rentals are high and accommodations exclusive. While access to the population from the church viewpoint is not nearly so much of a problem in low-rental apartments, other difficulties hamper the provision of the normal religious ministries. It is all too easy for apartment residents to get out of touch and remain out of touch with organized religion. Faith dies under such circumstances.

CHARACTERISTICS OF APARTMENT RESIDENTS

Apartment dwellers are human beings living under apartment conditions. The annoyances, disappointments, frustrations, tragedies, hopes, ambitions, and successes which characterize common humanity likewise constitute the diurnal texture of apartment life. Perhaps the most striking fact about this segment of urban population is residence in a multistoried building. Protestant leaders frequently overlook the fact that here are people who yearn for and require the regular ministries of the church.

However, apartment residents do possess characteristics which set them apart as a distinct urban public. Sorting processes which function in other phases of city life operate in this connection also. As a result people with common traits and viewpoints are "piled up" or grouped together. Individuals possessed of common domicile needs are attracted to a multiple type of housing. A cumulative outcome consists in the emergence of a segment of urban population which contrasts clearly with the remaining residents of the community. The city sorts its people into relatively homogeneous groups.

To be effective the Protestant clergyman must achieve an understanding of the apartment resident. Experienced leaders emphasize the importance of the ten traits briefly described below, recognizing of course that all characteristics would not necessarily be found in every apartment district. However, it is doubtful if there exists a multiple-housing area in an American city which does not possess several of the traits named. Perhaps the discussion will shed some light upon the difficult problem of ministering to apartment residents. Understanding may provide an important preliminary step toward effective action on the part of the conscientious pastor.

Economic Status. Persons of varying income and from many walks of life take up residence in multiple-housing structures. Indeed the apartment buildings themselves represent a wide range in average rentals and in quality of accommodations. Suites rent for more than two thousand dollars per annum in some cities. Other apartments are so modestly priced that persons of subsistence income may live there. Geographical location in the urban community and size and quality of quarters are important factors related to the amount of rent paid. This would indicate a range of rentals which corresponds with the full gamut of urban incomes. One gets what he pays for in housing. Thus low rental apartments are principally located in deteriorated sections of the city, medium rental facilities in more desirable neighborhoods, and expensive suites in exclusive territory where prestige elements and restrictions are conspicuously present. For this reason a study of the multiple-housing structures in a particular neighborhood of the urban community can reveal the approximate economic status of the residents. Such information may enable Protestant leaders to be realistic in local church work. In the field of religion all persons regardless of income level may avail themselves of the ministries of the church. The economics of Christianity are the economics of spiritual need.

Inaccessibility. Pastoral calls cannot be made with facility upon persons who live in multiple-housing structures. This is especially true of the larger apartment buildings. Not only is it difficult to gain entrance to the building, but frequently residents are not at home. The common complaint made by clergymen and laymen who do church visitation work in apartment areas is that much time is lost in trying to make contact with residents. This is a new problem in American Protestantism, for ministers are used to finding someone at home, though it may be only a child. The church's awareness of the situation has been stubbornly slow in development. Additional years will be required to hammer out a solution, and therefore local church leaders should be encouraged to make experiments.

In general the apartment resident rather enjoys the fact that he cannot be contacted too readily. The bother of solicitors and the nuisance of salesmen have thus been obviated. No one is more inaccessible in the urban community than the resident of an exclusive apartment house. However, the application is even broader, for most multiple-housing population are hard to contact. The annoyance of not finding persons at home is a conspicuous difficulty for pastors serving any type of apartment. Urban people utilize the residence less as a place to live than do suburban and rural dwellers. Thus the minister cannot just happen by and expect to find someone in. If people cannot be contacted, they cannot be won to God.

"Come and Get Me." Although studies reveal clearly that apartment residents are interested in religion and will respond to pastoral calls and cultivation, yet only 2 per cent of the multiple-housing residents voluntarily take the initiative in finding a church. This is a prominent characteristic of the apartment dweller. The local church is compelled to go to the residents via a program of cultivation and personal visitation. Initiative should be taken and held in providing participation opportunities in the life of the local congregation. The institution should let the apartment resident know he is wanted, needed, and will be used. In spite of the fact that findings accumulated from religious censuses reveal that most residents are interested in the church and religion, fellowship cultivation is needed to galvanize people into participation action. The church is expected to come and get them. Residents expect to be found and asked to participate, yet they will do little to hasten or facilitate the process. A city church gets the people it persistently cultivates.

Small Families. Several types of small families reside in apartments. Here is an elderly couple whose children have reached maturity and have established homes elsewhere. Here is a childless older couple who choose to pass the declining years with a maximum of comfort and a minimum of homemaking and property responsibility. Sometimes chronic illness makes apartment life a more convenient pattern of living. Here are a young husband and wife who possess little furniture and have a limited income. For them a temporary solution of the problem is provided by the furnished apartment. Residence in modest quarters becomes an ad interim instrument of economy until savings are accumulated in an amount which will permit the purchase of a home or the rental of larger

144

quarters. When children are born to the couple, the compactness of the apartment is further emphasized. The growing family size compels a search for more adequate housing elsewhere. Thus a dominant characteristic of the apartment area is small families. Religious needs vary according to the domicile under consideration, but all individuals should be placed under the aegis of the Christian church.

Nonfamily Households. There are various types of nonfamily households in apartment areas. Most common is that of bachelor girls. In rarer instances one finds bachelor men living together. Two or more individuals will rent a suite for light housekeeping. Such persons commonly are found in cities where ample opportunity is afforded for employment in the white-collar occupations. Cities which are political capitals or which house the main offices of the large insurance companies and kindred business enterprises attract many unmarried individuals to the community. Divorced persons and widows often take up residence in apartments. There are also quasi families, that is, a daughter or son residing with an aged parent, or sisters sharing an apartment. Often the nonfamily household is but a temporary or transitional status.

Compact quarters and convenient facilities require a minimum of housework and furnish the added advantage of anonymity so often cherished by unmarried adults. Older persons covet the quietness and absence of confusion which are largely impossible in accommodations where many children are growing up. The relevance of religious ideals to persons living in nonfamily households must not be overlooked. Often moral standards loosen under such dwelling conditions. For this reason Protestantism should maintain a vigorous ministry in multiple-housing areas.

Preponderance of Adults. The predominant population of the apartment is adult. Approximately 80 per cent of the residents are over twenty-one years of age, and this includes persons varying widely in marital status and chronological age. Young single adults are present, especially females. Widowed and divorced persons constitute another important segment. Further, older and younger married couples reside in apartments in great numbers. Few teen-age and younger children are present except in low-cost redevelopment projects and "garden-type" facilities. Therefore a local church's fundamental relationship to apartment residents is a relationship with adults, and its ministry should be so conceived if reasonable effectiveness is to be achieved. Employment conditions, state of health, and psychological emancipation are among the factors which condition church work with adults in apartment territory. Few institutions are more competent in this field than the Christian church. Mainly it needs to mobilize its resources and experience to bear upon this unsolved urban problem.

Anonymity. Many apartment residents cherish the anonymity which is made possible under such living conditions. The person may come and go as he pleases with minimum concern for those who live about him. He may secrete himself from relatives and from unpleasant public contacts. He may live in isolation, or he may cultivate a small coterie of acquaintances. The size and personnel of his friendship circle is his own business. No one is much concerned about the next-door neighbor, who also goes and comes in his own insular way. The privilege of not being intruded upon by other people is a protection coveted by some apartment dwellers. Many have lost the art of being friendly and the skills of approaching a stranger. Privacy is wanted at almost any price. The advantages of anonymity are sought not with a conscious intent to eliminate religion from life, but rather with a desire to avoid the annoyances of gossip, of persistent salesmen, of inquisitive neighbors, and of unsavory human contacts.

Habitation in such close physical contiguity, however, provides a number of opportunities to make casual contact with other residents. In some apartment situations the women meet in the basement laundry, in walks with the dog, or as the baby is wheeled out for an airing. Confrontations occur in hallways, in elevators, in the manager's office. Where individuals find themselves *en rapport,* the relation is likely to develop into a permanent friendship. However, where a desire for isolation continues, one may reduce personal contacts to a minimum. Anonymity is secured by delimiting one's contacts with humanity. Such is the antithesis of Christianity, for the church emphasizes personal worth and social interaction. Thus a basic principle of the Christian fellowship is challenged in the apartment situation. Residents should be encouraged to explore the sanative possibilities of personal growth in religious group life. This is a task of the church.

Density of Population. No other territory in the city is more densely populated than the apartment area. Often several hundred families live in a single city block. By contrast blocks of one-family residences may average as few as twenty households. Population is often ten times more numerous in multiple-housing territory. Obviously the Protestant church adjacent to apartments is situated in a densely populated area. People in great numbers thus may reside within easy access of a neighborhood church.

Mobility. In some cities one fourth to one third of the families change residence every several years. I know a family who moved eleven times in fourteen years. Though this illustration may appear exceptional, it emphasizes the fact that population shifts do occur in the city. Mobility is particularly noticeable among apartment residents where the housing accommodations are overpriced and/or unsatisfactory in location. When buildings are substandard as is often the case in low and medium rental territory, turnover of population is a foregone conclusion. In high-grade and exclusive apartments duration of residence is much longer. This is a result, in part, of the more satisfactory pricing of accommodations in terms of value received by the tenants. Additional sources of mobility include changes in marital status, in family life, in economic circumstances, in vocation, and in domicile preference. The search for a desirable neighborhood underlies mobility.

Since population shifts are endemic to the urban environment, the church does not have an interminable period in which to cultivate apartment residents. Time is short, and cultivation should start almost immediately upon receiving the prospect's name and address. Because of possible brevity of residence the apartment dweller should be encouraged to commence participation in the local church program before another change of residence occurs. Mobility emphasizes the importance of prompt and relevant local church action.

Port of Entry. Apartments situated in medium-priced and low rental areas frequently afford a port of entry for newcomers to the community. Strangers tend to locate in or near the central business district. Until well established economically newcomers often procure housing which is inferior to that which they are accustomed to and thus make a temporary home while becoming acquainted with the city. Prior to the war port-of-entry areas had a relatively complete turnover of population every five years. Many families moved within a year.

Apartment areas which come under this description afford short-term housing for bachelor girls, newly married persons, and couples who have started their families. Such residents do not look upon the present housing facilities as permanent. Eventually acquaintanceship with the city and improvement of economic status prepare the erstwhile newcomers for home ownership or a change of residence to better rental property.

One would expect that in many cities because of extreme shortage of housing the rate of mobility has greatly declined. However, pastors who are serving port-of-entry territory report that they are confronted currently with problems of mobility which match prewar conditions. Effective religious work with transient apartment residents or shifting population groups may strengthen the work of the denomination in other parts of the city as well as render significant service to the persons involved. A major denomination should furnish a vigorous religious ministry to the entire urban community.

CHURCHES SERVING APARTMENT AREAS

Several types of churches are advantageously situated to serve residents of apartment areas. Physical proximity of less than one mile may be regarded as essential. A shorter distance is preferable for projects exceeding three hundred dwelling units. The church within the denomination which is situated geographically nearest should undertake responsibility for serving the apartments. An extensive study of many cities reveals that at least three types of urban churches are located in or near apartment areas: (1) the neighborhood church, (2) the downtown church, and (3) the institutional church.

The Neighborhood Church. Often a neighborhood church finds itself in an urban area of transition. Large, once prosperous homes have depreciated in appearance and lack modern bath and toilet facilities. Some actually are in dire need of drastic structural

148

repairs. Others have been razed and replaced by modern apartment buildings.

The local church in the neighborhood commonly views these changes with alarm. It seems as though something precious is passing, and the inclination is to cling to the old rather than to adapt to the new. Religious leaders grow apprehensive about reaching the incoming apartment dwellers who are so numerous. Yet the future of some neighborhood churches impinges upon success in ministering to these very residents of multiple structures. Older affiliated families which have moved away and currently return to the area for worship eventually die off or transfer membership to churches nearer to their remote places of residence. Diminishing membership must be replenished from the only remaining source— residents of the neighborhood.

An accessible reservoir from which to recruit member replacements is the adjacent apartments. To succeed in making the transition from an outmoded pattern of church work to one better adapted to the current situation requires a thorough working knowledge of the apartment opportunity. Cognizance of the economic status of the multiple-housing population is essential. The effective local church must go out of its way to offer special ministries and to provide program elements which challenge the attention and interest of apartment residents. Ideally a confluence of apartment dwellers with home owners and other residents should be achieved. This suggestion is practical since it is rare for a neighborhood church to be located in the center of an apartment area. Commonly the church is presented a dual opportunity—ministry to apartment residents and to persons in other types of housing. To furnish a significant ministry to both should constitute the spiritual goal of the Protestant church.

The Downtown Church. In some cities the downtown church accepts responsibility for ministering to persons who reside in centrally located or adjacent apartment areas. What a unique opportunity is presented by the situation! If the downtown church is large, well led, and has a good plant, it may dominate the central city area sufficiently by its strength, prestige and high quality program to attract persons who otherwise might remain indifferent to the work of organized religion. The viewpoint with which people commence their institutional relationship is not nearly as important as the religious goals to which they are eventually led.

Residents of apartment structures where an above average rental prevails are likely to respond to the ministry of a great downtown church. However, sheer institutional size and prestige elements alone will not suffice. A carefully organized program of cultivation must be set up and utilized. The parish unit plan has been found to be effective. In many communities the downtown church is advantageously situated to undertake a share of the important ministry to apartment residents.

The Institutional Church. This religious organization in addition to the normal ministry of a church provides a manifold program of social services. Normally its staff includes professional workers trained and experienced in the social field. This setup is the occasion for a special entree to modest rental apartments which is often unavailable to churches of the conventional type. The institutional church in some cities is situated in close proximity to apartment structures. Possibly rentals are modest since the institution is most frequently placed in a quasi-depressed area. An opportunity for ministry to multiple-housing residents is thus often thrust upon the institutional church. Effective response to the religious opportunity is urgently necessary.

Three principal types of urban churches therefore are likely to be accessible for residents of apartments. The church plant must be less than a mile distant to assure optimum effectiveness. The responsible local church regardless of type must be strong enough to swing the attention of the community its way. It must use publicity appropriate to its ministry. And it must thoroughly cultivate the residents of the neighborhood and make fellowship on the religious level a successful undertaking. Experimentation with a wide range of ministries may be required in apartment districts of the city. Thus may Protestantism adapt itself to another need of the modern urban community.

HOW TO LOCATE AND CONTACT APARTMENT RESIDENTS

There exists no simple single device by which apartment residents may be located and effectively contacted. Churches which succeed in ministering to multiple-housing residents utilize a battery of

150

procedures. Reliance upon a single organizational device or program element is the surest path to failure. Since apartment dwellers do not take the trouble to locate a near-by church, the religious organization must search for them. Basically a dual approach is required: indirect—residents must be attracted out of the apartment buildings into a church, and direct—the local church must reach into the apartment suites and find the dwellers one by one.

The Indirect Approach. A well-conceived and continuous program of publicity should be set in motion. Stimulation of a city-wide "go-to-church" campaign, week-by-week advertising in the newspaper and busses, the establishment of community forums and lecture series, feature radio programs, newspaper articles about the local church—these are several means by which the attention of the community may be swung toward the local church. Other attention-getting devices include a bulletin board which has its message changed several times weekly, a rose window or well-designed lancet in the church illuminated at night, a set of chimes or an amplifying record player for the church tower, a well-kept lawn, and an imposing church plant. Spotlights may direct attention to the church tower. A minister of vivid personality is essential. Though the church may specialize in doing unusual things to gain attention, publicity action should be kept within the bounds of good taste and subordinated to the objective of reaching people for Jesus Christ.

The apartment resident's attention must be directed toward the local church. This is of fundamental importance. People who do not search for a church must find themselves encountering it in the pursuance of day-by-day secular affairs. A visual reminder of the religious institution is secured by passing the plant and by reading advertisements and articles in the daily papers. If the building is attractive, it will be noticed on shopping tours. An audio reminder is furnished by tower chimes, a bell, or amplified organ music. People still associate bells and the organ with churches. It is a traditional response.

Under such circumstances the winsomeness and relevance of the local church may contrast pleasantly and attractively with the brash impersonal life of the city. Situated in the midst of hurry and frustration, the church may appear as a haven from life's troubles, a rest beside the weary way, a shadow in the hot desert of urban affairs.

The ancient refuge from secular confusion may be rediscovered in the church around the corner. There are many frictions and frustrations that attend life in apartments. Through the indirect approach people are reminded that the church stands ready to serve. Its ancient ministries are still accessible and are as near as the telephone. Thus a careful check of the appearance of the church plant and its relations to the community is prelude to effective work in apartment areas.

The Direct Approach. In spite of a well-conceived program of publicity and public relations designed to attract the attention of residents of apartment structures, the response is frequently quite discouraging. Less than 2 per cent of the dwellers generally respond. Thus it becomes necessary to supplement the publicity program by one of direct action.

Residents should be sought out in their living quarters by personal visitation. The direct approach consists in finding and contacting the residents one by one. The initiative is taken by the local church, utilizing fully the experience and time of both minister and parish workers. Residents of the apartment area are cultivated by personal visitation, by friendships, by telephone, by mail, and by personal religious ministries. In short every effort is made to draw each resident into a vital relationship with the local church. The friendliness, vitality, and relevance of religion are stressed.

Several direct approach techniques have proved effective at the local church level. (1) *Religious Census of Apartments.* To secure a prompt and complete knowledge of the religious affiliation or preference of apartment residents a periodic census should be taken. The project can be part of a community-wide undertaking. Apartment managers or agents normally co-operate in granting consent to canvass buildings under their jurisdiction. The detailed procedure for conducting a religious census is given in Chapter III, and the reader may find helpful suggestions there. A complete census should be conducted every two years in apartment areas of the city.

2. *Registration Cards at Worship Services.* To secure the names and addresses of strangers many urban pastors distribute registration cards regularly at worship services. Usually everyone in attendance furnishes the desired information in order to protect

strangers from the embarrassment of being made conspicuous. Cards gathered up on Sunday are sorted and assigned to workers who will visit the strangers during the ensuing week. Some pastors take a registration once a month, others three or four times a year. The frequency of the registration depends upon the type of the local church and the nature of the apartment area adjacent to it. Downtown churches tend to poll the congregation monthly. Where residents move often, a registration of church attenders is required more frequently. A local church should experiment in order to discover a pattern which produces acceptable results.

3. *Persons Contacted Through Church Organizations.* Frequent examination of the list of persons who attend Sunday school, women's groups, men's clubs, young adult programs, and youth organizations may reveal the names of individuals who reside in apartment structures and in other adjacent housing facilities. Church organizations serve in part as "finder" groups, locating persons who may be cultivated later for membership. In many communities pastors regard this group function as an excellent source of prospects for church affiliation. Commonly apartment families are often discovered through visitation to the homes of Sunday-school children and of persons who participate in religious organizations. Further, names of unchurched apartment families may be procured from neighbors who reside in the multiple structure. Obviously the latter have already found their way into the life of the local church, and many prove valuable workers in contacting persons out of touch with religion.

4. *Prospects from Sick Calls and Funerals.* In times of trouble and bereavement apartment residents often turn to the pastor of a near-by church. On such occasions the minister should accept and conscientiously follow up every request made. Personal problems are of major significance to the troubled individual. A clergyman's willing and ready response will be remembered to the advantage of the local church. Response to human need, however, should be the underlying purpose. Continuous pastoral ministry of this type over a period of years will develop a constituency among apartment residents. It is the pastor's duty and opportunity to stand beside individuals in need of personal help and under the circumstances

to mediate the required Christian ministries. People remember those who graciously walked beside them in hours of crisis.

5. *Names of Newcomers.* There are several sources of names and addresses of newcomers to a city. One may subscribe to a local version of the *Professional and Businessman's County and Legal Record* which is published weekly at a modest rate. This contains an up-to-date list of newcomers to the city. The local church follow-up is by personal visitation and/or by a letter which welcomes the new residents to the community. Advertising agencies such as the Welcome Wagon and kindred organizations generally make available to the minister a list of new residents who are of his particular denomination. Occasionally a realtor who owns or manages apartment houses will provide the downtown pastor with a list of newly moved Protestant families. Some insurance agencies have been co-operative in a similar manner. The council of religious education or the federation of churches in some cities provides a service of this type to local ministers. All available sources of names of newcomers should be listed and utilized.

6. *Trained Apartment Visitors.* A number of persons may be recruited from the local church to make regular visits upon apartment residents. Satisfactory results have been procured with laymen when the pastor instructs the callers in the principles of an efficient interview and friendly visitation. The interview should be planned in a manner to secure desired objectives. A visitor will need to know how to gain entrance to the building. In many cases this may be arranged by the pastor's contacting the owner, agent, hostess, or janitor. However, some apartment buildings are never locked, and thus the visitor merely walks in.

The apartment visit should culminate in a friendly personal contact. Something should be left at each household—a devotional pamphlet, a Sunday worship bulletin, a historical brochure, a printed sermon, a religious picture, or a program of organizational activities. An oral invitation to attend church services may be extended. Where families are not at home, a "doorknob" greeting card is left.

Apartment visitors should report back to the church office all situations needing pastoral attention. Illness, counseling opportunities, domestic difficulties, and crisis situations may require prompt action. Friendliness and service characterize the trained visitor. Normally from five to ten calls per month are assigned. A local church can begin working upon its apartment opportunity as soon as it becomes aware of a religious need.

PRINCIPLES OF AN EFFECTIVE APARTMENT MINISTRY

Protestantism in the city is confronted by both opportunity and challenge. Many apartment dwellers eventually move out to the periphery of the city and purchase homes. Often they become the "pillars" of a church. Thus prompt and effective contact with the apartment family should be made during the interim of multiple-housing residence. This important ministry rounds out the work of a denomination in the city. The local church is under spiritual obligations to make an efficient effort to handle its opportunity.

The secret of successful church work among apartment residents lies in a combination of the indirect and direct approaches described earlier in the chapter. A many-sided attack upon the problem will secure results. Reliance upon a single program element commonly issues in failure. When the clergyman tries but one method, and it proves ineffective, he is likely to conclude that the people are of another faith or are disinterested in religion. This is a *non sequitur,* for neither conclusion follows from the facts in the situation. Obviously the minister attacked the apartment problem in a naïve fashion. An effective approach is many-sided and sustained over a long period of time. Resourcefulness and perseverance are virtues contributory to success.

In order to sharpen the message of the present chapter six practical suggestions relative to a strategy of religious outreach will be described. These have been gleaned from a study of church work in apartment areas in cities across America and therefore are valuable as a battery of practical procedures.

1. *Attract the Attention of Apartment Residents.* Every effort should be bent to swing the attention of the community toward the church. The use of dignified publicity, of advertising, of public relations activity, of audio-visual reminders, of radio programs, of timely program elements, and of an attractive plant may help turn the attention of apartment residents churchward. People need to

know that a Protestant church is in the neighborhood and that it is accessible to them.

2. *Establish an Annual Program Feature.* Apartment residents and other unchurched persons should be provided occasions for looking over the church and meeting some members of the congregation. These occasions are nonreligious in nature. A drama program, a choir festival, an annual fair, a high-grade rummage sale, a Christmas party, a clam bake, a turkey supper, or some other recurring significant annual function may achieve for the local church a reputation for friendliness and service in the neighborhood. During the annual feature pastor and key laymen should be conspicuously present and generally mingle with the patrons. The occasion may attract many unchurched persons. Friendliness may encourage such individuals to visit the worship service in the near future.

3. *Furnish Close and Continual Pastoral Care.* Apartment residents are won to the local church one by one. If the pastor appears friendly and accessible, he will be called upon for ministries to strangers in times of illness, bereavement, weddings, baptisms, and special problems. A minister I know secures a list of all persons in attendance at each funeral of nonmembers. The funeral director makes the information available. Scores of Protestant prospects have been found and eventually drawn into the local church in this manner. To render effective pastoral service at a time of crisis will do much to attract apartment dwellers to the church. Therefore no request should be deemed too casual or too demanding to elicit a wholehearted response. Each random contact by the minister should be carefully followed up by personal visitation. Eventually individuals who have been served by religion tell the story of the relevance of the church to the community.

4. *Launch an Efficient Visitation Program.* The task of making effective contact with newly located apartment residents is facilitated by a carefully organized visitation program in the local church. Selected teams of visitors, husband and wife if possible, make weekly or monthly calls in the interest of the church. The completion of several calls by each team month after month during the year (eight months) will have cumulative beneficial results. In apartment territory it is necessary to call promptly after receiving an address. Relationship to the church should be intense since of

necessity it is often short in duration. Apartment residents must receive personal attention and personal visitation if satisfactory results are to be procured. It is personal contact with friendly members that convinces the unchurched that a local church is interested in them. People desire to unite with a friendly church.

5. *Provide Extraordinary Worship Services.* Superior preaching and superior choral music should characterize the Sunday worship services. No matter what pattern of worship has been used in the past, a critical examination of the current elements in the service should be made. A practical outcome of the survey may conceivably be a higher quality of vocal music and preaching. Apartment residents expect the best, for many have come from large churches. It is desirable to have a volunteer choir recruited in part from apartment dwellers. The entire experience of worship should be satisfying and significant. From the time the person enters the church building until he departs, there should be an atmosphere of friendliness and a sense of being wanted. Ushers can do much to impress strangers positively with the true spirit of the church. In some communities ushers are trained specifically for their duties in the Sunday worship services. Great religious worship will be remembered for years.

6. *Maintain a Strong Local Church.* There is need to dominate the neighborhood in a religious manner. Ordinarily the city church should be above five hundred persons in active member strength, but in an apartment area effective size is approximately a thousand members. Sheer greatness in size may guarantee other benefits. Urban effectiveness in religion calls for a broadened organizational structure which provides many persons an opportunity to participate in the life of the institution. The local church must be large and strong. Strength in numbers, in organization, in program elements, in leadership, in finances, in evangelism, is mandatory.

The opportunity for Protestant work in multiple-housing areas has enormously increased since the turn of the century. Because the situation calls for new patterns of churchmanship and specialized techniques, the denominations have been slow in making an effective response. Today Protestant local churches which are in proximity to apartment areas need not postpone an immediate extension of religious ministries. Preliminary guidance is provided in the present chapter to enable the local church to make practical response to its larger opportunity. Imagination and resourcefulness yoked with persistent hard work can procure success in dealing with the apartment situation. Apartment dwellers are human beings living under multiple-housing conditions, and as such they require the regular ministries of the Christian church.

CHAPTER VI

The Neighborhood Local Church

OST city churches are neighborhood in type, attracting members, constituents, and Sunday-school persons who reside in the territory adjacent to the church plant. The ministry is local and intimate. Extensive studies reveal that approximately nine tenths of the urban Protestant churches belong in this classification. This fact alone, even if no other reasons were forthcoming, should emphasize the relevance of the present discussion.

WHY THERE ARE NEIGHBORHOOD CHURCHES

Two fundamental considerations merit exploration at the outset— the structure of the city and the practical service radius of an urban church. Let us consider first of all how the physical structure of the city appears to be causally related to the relatively compact neighborhood parish phenomena. Normally a city is comprised of a single central business district (referred to as downtown) surrounded by a cluster of residential territories. The spatial extent and general configuration of each neighborhood territory are commonly determined by the location of primary barriers. Topographical features, such as steep hillsides, ravines, bodies of water, and large parcels of land in nonresidential use (that is, parks, cemeteries, railroads, and industrial properties), tend to separate municipal territory into residential neighborhoods and also to impede the free movement of population. These physical barriers have to be reckoned with, for they divide the city into neighborhoods, thereby imposing special difficulties upon Protestant church work.

Thus semi-isolated residential areas or neighborhoods are formed (Figure No. 18) which eventually achieve relative economic and institutional self-sufficiency. Situated within area boundaries are vari-

159

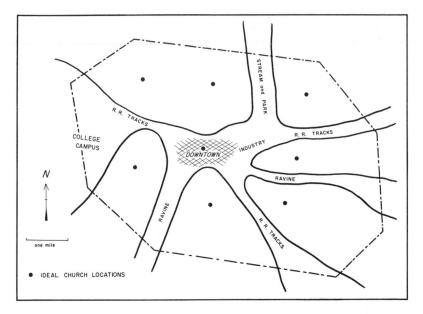

FIGURE No. 18

NEIGHBORHOOD STRUCTURE OF A MEDIUM-SIZED CITY

ous commercial establishments—food markets, drugstores, dry-cleaning places, and kindred local service businesses. They are for convenience purchases. Here also may be found an elementary public school, a branch library, a theater, and several churches among the institutions serving the specific neighborhood. In larger cities manifold additional services are available. This situation has meaning for organized Christianity in that effective religious work today requires a detailed and accurate knowledge of urban neighborhood phenomena.

Pockets of residential territory usually vary in size, in dominant type of housing, in economic quality, in remoteness from the downtown business district, in population density, and occasionally in the racial or ethnic background of the inhabitants. Consult the sample shown in Figure No. 18. Such differences are significant to Protestant church leaders and constitute clues indicating the types of religious work and ministry which may be required by any specific neighborhood. Wise denominational and interdenominational planning is, or should be, based upon an adequate knowledge of neighborhood variance. How otherwise may the work be expected to prosper?

A minister, administrator, or layman may profitably investigate the neighborhood pattern of his own local community. A local survey can start with the procurement of an up-to-date street map. Such materials are available generally at a bookstore or the city engineer's office. To the map must be added the location and extent of primary barriers. Utilization of vivid colors (pencil, show-card colors or India ink) in marking the location of rivers, lakes, ravines, cliffs, bluffs, parks, cemeteries, golf courses, airports, public institutions, sewerage disposal plants, railroad sidings, factories, industrial properties, and kindred phenomena will assist in delineating the boundaries of the various residential neighborhoods. Groups of homes will eventually be noted lying between the primary barriers. In larger communities the local city planning commission and the college department of sociology should be consulted for assistance in preparing the map. When the survey has been completed, data should be thoroughly studied by religious leaders until the significance for church work becomes apparent. Barriers reveal the community's neighborhood structure, and this knowledge properly underlies sound urban church strategy.

A second major consideration is the practical service radius of an urban church. The findings of a scientific investigation recently concluded on several thousand city churches are instructive at this point. Data were assembled and analyzed respecting the place of residence of members in relation to the location of the church plant. The analysis was broadened by a parallel study of Sunday-school enrollees. What was discovered? Surprisingly the practical service radius for nine city churches out of ten is one mile. Within this distance reside from two thirds to nine tenths of the active members and Sunday-school enrollees of a local church. The idea is generalized in Figure No. 19. This finding applies to the work of many denominations and probably to all belonging in the evangelical tradition. Beyond the known service radius city churches practice a "skimming" ministry, at best attracting but scattered families and individuals. A thoroughgoing penetration is achieved only in near-by territory.

If Protestant leaders possessed and properly evaluated this knowledge, undoubtedly fewer churches would be placed off center in

161

neighborhood and/or close against primary barriers. Fewer churches would be located on dead-end streets, in the middle of the block, and out of sight. Rather locations at least one mile away from barriers and sites adjacent to an elementary school or in the heart of the shopping center would be chosen. Effective religious work depends upon strategic plant location. There is scarcely any

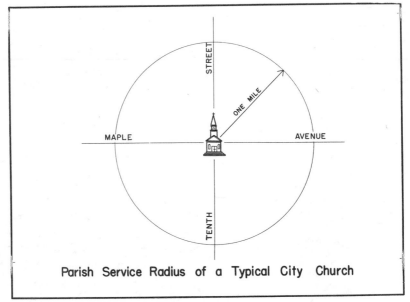

Parish Service Radius of a Typical City Church

Figure No. 19

MAXIMUM PARISH OF A NEIGHBORHOOD CHURCH

justification for mislocating a congregation when it is known that few city residents circumvent a primary barrier to participate in a church. On the contrary it is prudent to recognize frankly that many people will cross denominational lines rather than affiliate with a congregation outside of the local neighborhood. They would rather cross denominational lines than railroad tracks.

Consider the problem from another vantage point. Can the unstrategically placed local church make up its loss of service radius by attracting persons a greater distance in the opposite direction from the cramping influences of a contiguous barrier? Unfortunately this is a vain and fruitless hope. Extensive field research discloses that such deprivation is rarely compensated for by abnormal outreach in another direction, regardless of the distance to the perimeter of the neighborhood or the density of the population. In fact a sacrifice of any portion of the urban church's normal service radius results in an irretrievable loss of growth opportunity. The religious institution is compelled to make the most out of what remains. To overcome this handicap where the situation is extremely circumscribed and to assure the congregation of a hopeful future, a relocation of the plant may be required. Recognition of this stubborn fact is essential preparation for effective church work in the city.

In as much as cities are permanently structuralized into discernible neighborhoods by the location of primary barriers, and since most urban churches are unable to conduct a significant ministry beyond a one-mile service radius, the religious leader confronts at last the inevitableness of the neighborhood church. Recognition of this normal eventuality opens the way for a realistic approach to urban religious work.

As the city increases in geographical size, contiguous suburban housing developments which are potential neighborhoods become annexed. Thus the municipal boundary moves outward, ever invading the adjacent countryside. Villages and budding communities are engulfed by the movement. Rapid urban growth in recent years has produced many new or enlarged neighborhoods which currently may lack adequate religious facilities. Since churches are properly placed where concentrations of people reside, most religious institutions are neighborhood in type. This implicit spatial strategy results in a scattering of Protestant congregations across the entire city. It makes the neighborhood church endemic to the urban community. How can there be a more effective ministry than an indigenous one?

THE EFFECT OF PRIMARY BARRIERS

Thus it may be affirmed that in the urban community the typical Protestant church is neighborhood in character and function. Numerically dominant in places above 25,000 population and outnumbering other types of city churches in a ratio as high as nine to one, the neighborhood church challenges the imagination of Protestant leaders. Attention should now be turned to a serious analysis of the situation.

Urban church typicality may be approached with reference to such diverse factors as geographical dispersion of members, elaborateness of worship forms, theological beliefs, race and ethnic background of the constituents, and range of program elements. Obviously discussions are bound to differ widely from one another, depending upon the particular frame of reference utilized. Yet each may properly serve the purposes of the investigator. It is beyond the intent of the present chapter to detail the respective merits of the several possible approaches, and therefore attention shall be focused only upon the parish dispersion factor which has gained a vast new significance lately.

Recent research in the geographical dispersion of urban church members and Sunday-school enrollees has stimulated Protestant leaders to re-examine this particular frame of reference. Patient analysis of fresh data has yielded pragmatic insights and in turn has encouraged additional investigative activity. Proximity of residence to the church plant among members furnishes a convenient starting point for the present discussion. Considerable data of this sort have been gathered, covering churches situated in more than a hundred American cities. The reader's attention is directed to the negative effect of near-by barriers upon local church outreach as illustrated in Figure No. 20. When several thousand parish dispersion maps[1] were analyzed, it was found that most urban churches are neighborhood in type. To some religious leaders this discovery comes as a surprise: they had not expected the species to be so prevalent. Here then is a noteworthy finding—in a neighborhood church the majority of the constituents are attracted from residences situated within the parish service radius (one mile) of the church plant. This fact underlies the present discussion of the typical urban church.

Just as downtown churches of various denominations are prone to gather in the city's central business district, so in a similar fashion neighborhood churches tend to cluster at or near a secondary shopping center in residential territory. Like birds of a kind Protestant churches flock together. Such focusing of church locations into a relatively small area is a common urban Protestant pattern and yet one which is frequently misunderstood. Failure to comprehend its universality and its intrinsic advantages has resulted in

[1] Consult pp. 43-45 for directions to prepare a parish map.

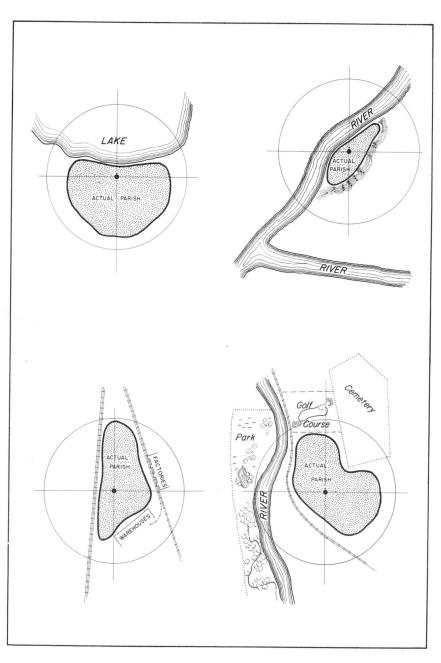

FIGURE No. 20

INFLUENCE OF BARRIERS ON PARISH OUTREACH

fruitless debates in ministerial groups and the passing of bizarre comity regulations in councils of churches.

Church clustering is common because neighborhood territory is normally bounded by primary barriers and desirable church sites are scarce. Acceptable corner properties which lie adjacent to an elementary public school or a shopping center are few in number. Further, features which commend a site to one denomination appeal with undiminished attractiveness as a strategic location for another communion. Therefore churches of various denominations tend to cluster within neighborhoods throughout the city and at the psychological center of the residential territory, but this does not necessarily result in a situation that is competitive. Protestant competition derives from overchurching not from church clustering. However, clustering should never be countenanced within a denomination.

It can be said that the neighborhood church is a natural product of the physical structure of the city. Primary barriers tend to isolate pockets of residential territory from the ministry of a downtown church. Ultimately, as cities grow, the number of neighborhoods increases, with the result that many additional people live remotely from the central business district. Few of these residents can longer be served adequately by the downtown church. Therefore new congregations need to be organized in order to bring all parts of the expanding city under the ministry of the Christian church. This means that the city eventually requires the combined ministry of the downtown and neighborhood churches united in a pattern of teamwork. It emphasizes the important role in urban religious life occupied by the neighborhood church and reveals its appropriate specialization in an intensive indigenous ministry. Without this essential and often unheralded parish work Protestantism could scarcely handle its city-wide opportunity. Thousands of persons would reside outside the effective reach of a church.

FEATURES OF A NEIGHBORHOOD MINISTRY

To press the analysis further let us consider some of the leading features of neighborhood church work. Of particular interest are the following: (1) a congregation of neighbors, (2) a short parish service radius, (3) neighborhood variance, (4) neighborhood specialization, and (5) scattered constituents. In turn the relative significance of each feature will be treated briefly, describing the practical implications for Protestantism in the city.

A Congregation of Neighbors. Constituents of the church are neighbors who reside along adjacent streets in a natural neighborhood. Many make common cause in local fraternal orders, parent-teacher associations, social clubs, and kindred organizations, thereby acquiring personal contacts and developing acquaintanceships which may ripen into enduring friendships. This intermingling social process underlies and in part produces an emerging neighborhood consciousness. Street and lighting improvements, preservation of shade trees and protection of children at play—these also are among the local interests which bring fellow residents together and stimulate neighborhood-mindedness. Further, common patronage of near-by grocery stores and drugstores as well as other mercantile establishments strengthens the sense of community. If the territory bears a name (for example, Woodlawn, Lawndale, East Side, Highland Park, Jones Hill, and so on) and possesses a notable history, local loyalty reaches the potent level of emotional attachment and pride. The appearance of a community spirit therefore is a normal eventuality in neighborhood life, and it aids in the work of the church.

That the local church is comprised dominantly of neighbors, that is, of persons who reside in a common territory and whose interests are relatively kindred, is natural. Urban neighborhood structure compels such an indigenous ministry. Just as adults are drawn together in making common cause, so children establish friendships among classmates at the local public school. Eventually residents are caught securely in a web of indigenous personal relationships. A part of that web is provided by the local church itself. Research studies disclose that from two thirds to nine tenths of the persons affiliated with the type of church under discussion reside within the service radius (one mile) of the church plant. Without question the typical neighborhood parish is overtly compact, with members concentrated in a limited geographical area set off by primary barriers. Similarly the parish configuration for Sunday-school enrollees reveals an even more closely focused dispersion pattern. That participants congregate from short distances in a discernible configuration is one of the most important and most obvious facts about the neighborhood church. The effective institution is likely to attract many people who know each other from secular contacts.

To put the matter another way, the institution is identified with the neighborhood in which it is situated and learns to "fish in its own pool." Here its primary and only significant religious penetration is made. To be healthy therefore the church must possess a notable local neighborhood anchorage of members. This achievement is necessary whether the population is wealthy, middle class, or poor; for the healthy institution becomes identified sociologically, economically, and culturally with the residents of its territory. Yet identification is rarely complete. In extremely heterogeneous neighborhoods the lack of total identification is embarrassingly evident, and the problem harasses the local church almost beyond endurance.

Finally Protestant congregations are recruited normally with reference to population accessibility, residential stability, and potential for religious participation. The people who live nearest, who are most stable, and who are most interested are sought out. This is apparent in the well-nigh universal use of recruitment patterns which tend strongly toward economic and cultural homogeneity. A selective process of this type may be quite unintentional though one of its fruits is to produce an urban congregation comprised dominantly of neighbors. This discovery furnishes a useful clue to program planning.

A Short Parish Service Radius. The local church is limited by the number of persons who reside within its practical service radius. This is not surprising. Just as public elementary schools are established at strategic points across a city according to a known service radius (one-half mile), and just as mass transportation lines (streetcars, busses, and so on) are laid down by engineers according to a known service outreach (one-fourth mile), so also Protestant churches should be placed according to known ability to function. The actual service radius of a neighborhood church is one mile. This means that the site of the church should be centrally located within a territory, permitting a ministry to a maximum number of constituents distributed in all four directions—north, east, south, and west. This area constitutes a normal circle of parish service.

Too close proximity to primary barriers wastes part of the service radius, reduces the possible number of residents within effective parish outreach, and imposes debilitating limitation upon the local congregation. A diagrammatic illustration of this point is revealed by the figures in Figure No. 20. It is interesting to note that primary barriers (topographical and industrial) as well as large tracts of land not in residential use (parks, airports, cemeteries, schools, and so on) reduce significantly the number of families within service reach of the local church. The fact that persons do not commonly cross primary barriers for church participation discloses the severe potential penalty imposed upon the mislocated church in a neighborhood ministry. Because of this, primary barriers seriously affect the shape of parish configurations, distorting the membership concentration into irregular patterns. This is evident from a study of the chart. Poor location yokes the church to an unpromising future. To recognize that even the most virile local church rarely overcomes such handicaps is essential to sound urban religious strategy.

Thus to be effective a local church should be situated not nearer than one mile to primary barriers in any direction. This precaution has the advantage of assuring a maximum number of residents within the practical service radius of the plant. It guarantees an adequate future congregation in a regular neighborhood. Respecting narrow elongated residential areas (provided a Protestant church should enter the territory at all) a site in the shopping center or near an elementary school should be selected. The main object is to seek a location from which an effective ministry to the largest number of people can be provided.

A short parish service radius has an additional pragmatic inplication, for locational health is determined in part by reasonable remoteness from another church of the same denomination. The minimum distance separating sister churches should be one and three-fourths miles. This is approximately double the normal service radius of a single church, and therefore competition can be avoided. No exceptions from this guiding principle should be allowed. Foresight exercised in intradenominational strategy assures each congregation of the reasonable prospect of reaching at least minimum effective size (five hundred members). To reach this goal each church should

169

have a neighborhood of its own in which to work. With respect to sparsely settled territory or areas comprised principally of single-family homes the pinch of religious competition is acutely felt, and the struggle for institutional survival is keen and often ruthless. This eventually is unwarranted and can be avoided through adequate recognition of the church's relatively short service radius in parish work.

Neighborhood Variance. That differences do exist among urban neighborhoods is common knowledge. Well aware of such disparities is the experienced city pastor. It is interesting to discover that differences range from housing through economic status, from race and ethnic background through religious composition. Further, differentiating characteristics come not singly but in clusters, aiding the perceptive observer in identifying any particular type of urban neighborhood. This may become evident to the reader from a brief survey of the situation.

Neighborhoods vary according to population density. Semi-isolated territories may possess a population of as few as several hundred persons. Access to adjacent areas is commonly blocked off by industrial installations, topographical features, and other types of primary barriers. This important fact needs to be regarded when church extension and general planning are under consideration. On the other hand urban neighborhoods may be heavily populated, counting the residents in tens of thousands. Dense population means multitudes of people living within the service radius of the church, and a religious census is normally required to discover the extent of Protestant opportunity. Churches within the same denomination, however, should not be placed closer than one and three-fourths miles from each other regardless of how extensive may appear the Protestant population.

In geographic outline and spatial extent neighborhoods also vary perceptibly. From a score to several hundred acres may be enclosed by the perimeter of the territory. Distortions in neighborhood configurations are caused by the location of primary barriers.

The polyglot neighborhood is made up of persons of diverse ethnic and racial stock. Often the area affords a place of residence for Negroes, Orientals, Latin Americans, and foreign-born Cau-

casians (especially natives of Italy, Poland, Austria, and other traditionally Roman Catholic countries). The composition varies from
city to city as well as from neighborhood to neighborhood. Among
the characteristics of polyglot territory are dense population, substandard housing, and unsavory health conditions. Circumstances of
crowding and inferior living quarters complicate even further
the already difficult task of the local church. Often people who
have low incomes and who lack the opportunity or ability to improve their economic status are compelled to dwell here. So
with the accumulation of frustration and without adequate skills
for group living the law of the jungle prevails. It is a rough and
tough existence, characterized by frequent recourse to force and
primitive patterns of action. In large cities where the accumulation
of nonwhite and foreign-born persons aggregates hundreds of thousands, distinct neighborhoods for various races and ethic groups
are common, and such territory may retain its peculiar identity for
generations. Protestantism has much to learn in ministering to such
areas.

Further, amount of effective income sorts urban population into
differing neighborhoods and elevates the importance of economic
status. Large and expensive homes tend to cluster in definite sections of the city, and these dwellings, set upon ample lots amid
spacious lawns, are relatively easy to discover. Only persons of superior income can afford residence here. What city does not have its
area of splendid domiciles? By way of contrast one may note the
neighborhood of middle-class homes near by. Residence structures
and land plots are smaller by comparison, yet they likewise appear
in large concentrations, typing the area conspicuously. The external
differences provide trustworthy clues revealing inner economic and
cultural disparities of signal importance. Salary and material pos-
sessions here are relatively modest. Finally one finds neighborhoods
composed of workingmen's homes. It is here that persons engaged
in the manual occupations generally reside. Homes are small and/or
found in multifamily structures. Dwellings are modest in appointment and often show evidences of deterioration, lacking paint,
needing structural repairs, and possessing antiquated plumbing
facilities. Some are situated in areas unfit for human habitation, ad-

jacent to industries which emit smoke, gas, and noise—a nuisance and hazard to healthful living. Older areas of the city may have been converted to cheap apartments and rooming houses. Thus this brief discussion points out that the amount one is able and willing to pay for rent or home ownership constitutes a prominent basis for the distribution of residents to the various economic neighborhoods. Effective income is a determining factor in the urban sorting process. A majority of city dwellers are caught in its iron grasp and yield to its inexorable demands. What affects city residents affects Protestant church work also.

Finally portions of the urban community are likely to vary in religious composition. The distribution by faiths in the city is always differential, indicating why a church prospers more readily in one neighborhood than another. The inner city is customarily thought of as a Roman Catholic stronghold if the population is Caucasian. This is particularly evident in communities housing numerous foreign-born residents, though there are many midwestern and southern cities which prove exceptions. Hebrews tend to colonize both on the edges of Negro districts and in better residential territory, including apartment areas. Protestants live everywhere in the city but are more numerous in some neighborhoods. Degree in religious composition is important and should be explored objectively by means of a community religious census. Since impressions are embarrassingly untrustworthy, adjustment of churching problems should always. be based upon religious facts. The manifold neighborhood differences should be regarded in the development of a city-wide religious strategy.

Neighborhood Specialization. Along with the Roman Catholic and Hebrew faiths Protestantism encounters difficulty in reaching extensively persons of extreme wealth and of extreme poverty. In fact some denominations provide no ministry for poor people; others offer none to the wealthy. Communions which endeavor to serve the entire range of the economic scale are rare indeed. This complete ministry is easier described than done. Apparently it is thought prudent to specialize—to concentrate upon the residents of one neighborhood or another, one class or another, with the unwarranted hope that some other denomination will serve the omitted population groups. In this manner the primary problems of social and economic hetereogeneity have time and again been adroitly side-stepped. Such an approach is unworthy of Protestantism.

In depressed urban areas techniques for doing religious work have been painfully slow to evolve. Even excellent pilot experiments purporting to test new procedures, however meritorious, fail to attract widespread attention or to modify the traditional approach. As a result polyglot neighborhoods remain an enigma to Protestantism, although the church has proved more successful with some racial and ethnic groups than with others. The fact remains that when conventional programs fail, leaders are baffled and ultimately turn aside in quest of greener pastures. Further, as expected, wherever the margin of Protestant population shrinks to a few scattered families, great difficulty is encountered. Boundless sentiment runs head on into the stone wall of reality. Thus the limited or declining opportunity appears an aggravating adjustment for most denominations. Yet in many coastal cities and among older industrial communities inevitable change thrusts this single alternative upon the local church. As a result denominations are prone to neglect or abandon low-income and/or depressed urban territories, since church work proves too difficult or too unrewarding.

Actual identification then of the Protestant church with a particular neighborhood appears to be related to the economic status of the population and to the race or ethnic background of the residents. Few denominations serve all peoples. However, it should be remembered that there is scarcely a neighborhood without some kind of Protestant church, store front, or rescue mission. Persons of extreme wealth or extreme poverty appear equally difficult of access via the conventional techniques of Protestant church work. Although scattered individuals in both classifications are drawn into local church affiliation by some denominations, the rank and file of these economic classes are left without an adequate ministry. Apparently Protestantism lacks a current strategy of work broad enough and sufficiently relevant to encompass all city neighborhoods. This is an unwarranted deficiency.

Between the economic extremes Protestantism manages a reasonably effective ministry. Identification is significant and conspicuous in neighborhoods where income runs above subsistence level and yet below great affluence. It is here that Protestant churches register a smashing success by featuring program elements and a viewpoint which are attractive to white-collar and skilled manual workers. Persons in the professions and in the managerial vocations are pleased to find the churches interested in them. As a whole the denominations are most successful in reaching middle-class residents. This is not surprising since it is the group aimed for. Such is the story of specialization in urban places. Unfortunately the economic and/or cultural status of the population influences Protestantism largely in its identification with neighborhoods. Denominations specialize where it is relatively easy to maintain self-supporting work. It is a pay-as-you-go plan.

Scattered Constituents. Virtually every urban church claims that some members and Sunday-school enrollees travel distances of more than one mile in order to participate, and the facts support this contention. How to account for this exceptional loyalty poses a problem which tests the perspicacity of the wisest city pastor. Previous residence within the service radius of the neighborhood church plus friendship ties and general religious loyalty are among the reasons cited by active remote members themselves. Further, this exceptional attracting power is aided by the individual's strong emotional attachment to the building wherein noteworthy personal religious experiences (for example, formation of churchgoing habits, deepening of faith, conversion, and so on) occurred and/or satisfying friendships were generated which now fused together conspire to draw the erstwhile residents back. Whatever may be the reason, surveys indicate that even the tiniest urban church reports scattered constituents and that the phenomenon is relatively universal. Only newly established congregations appears as an exception.

However, because of the unusual loyalty of these persons there is a tendency to exaggerate their numerical significance. This is patent. If the individuals are church officers and/or generous in financial support, this propensity throws off all reasonable restraint. What is overlooked is that officers and contributors ordinarily have high visibility no matter where they reside. Other affiliated persons vanish into the group. Thus an officer may appear to outrank many run-of-the-mill church members. In a similar fashion systematic contributors may be overranked. Therefore false estimates of the numerical significance of scattered members start with value judgments

174

rather than with head-count statistics. For this reason a word of caution is in order.

Another misapprehension urges that scattered constituents are comprised principally of officers and contributors. Quite the opposite is true. Only a small percentage occupy leadership positions and/or support the budget. While one finds a few cases of exceptional loyalty, the majority of remote members drift into inactive status and ultimately are lost between churches. Unless the remote member remains rather active, he will soon be lost sight of because of the notorious carelessness with which local church records are kept. In some neighborhood congregations as many as one third of the persons who affiliate are lost track of through poor record keeping. Further, membership in a remote institution is frequently utilized by the individual as an excuse for avoiding active relationship with the local church near by. Here then is the heart of the matter: poor participation habits generally characterize the majority of scattered constituents.

Indeed the attitude of many scattered constituents furnishes an additional source of deep concern. Distant members tend to regard attendance, financial support, and other forms of participation as a favor which is bestowed upon an ever-grateful neighborhood church. This viewpoint stems from an attitude which blindly delights in interfering with the work of the church and in issuing ultimatums. Certain administrative policies are favored, and these must be pursued in the local church organization or else personal support will be withdrawn. This threat, spoken or implied, reveals the paralyzing ultimatum complex at work. Because ties to the local church are often sentimental and unprogressive, nonresident constituents frequently prevent the church from making a normal though radical adjustment of program as dictated by the current needs of the neighborhood. In short, scattered constituents may prove to be spiritual assets or liabilities, depending upon the genuineness of personal religion and the accuracy of perception of the religious task. Therefore loyalty and support should be accepted, even encouraged, though never at the sacrifice of a worth-while indigenous ministry. Persons who maintain distant memberships run the risk of joining the ranks of the inactive. This is not a heartening eventuality.

To achieve a healthy viewpoint involves among other considera-

175

tions but tentative reliance upon scattered constituents. Eventually the church should make a significant penetration of its own neighborhood and should focus its ministry chiefly upon persons residing within the practical parish service radius (one mile). If the local institution cannot achieve a strong neighborhood anchorage of members, one may doubt whether its long-range work among scattered constituents can ever be very significant. Without a dependable indigenous ministry a single change of pastors may reduce the church to a state of spiritual and financial insolvency. This has proved a hard urban lesson for denominations to learn.

THE PROMINENCE OF LAYMEN

In a unique way the neighborhood church belongs to the people. No other urban congregation affords more extensive lay opportunity for participation, and at the same time none depends so completely upon volunteer assistance. Here is where the layman increasingly shapes the policies and speaks his mind. As a consequence all-out lay participation is directly solicited and given high priority in the corporate life of the institution. Encouraged both by the residence proximity of affiliated persons and by manifest religious interest, the local church relates a host of volunteer workers to appropriate tasks. This yoking process offers no insurmountable difficulty since opportunities are so numerous and so varied that every individual may find a task which matches his interest or talent. Thus the layman is lifted to prominence in this ministry and only too gladly acknowledges the church in which he works as his favorite one. Be it ever so humble, there is no place like the neighborhood church.

Why Laymen Are Needed. The typical Protestant church in the city leans heavily upon laymen to carry out the program because there is no other acceptable alternative. The congregation is virtually staffless apart from the services of a full-time minister. This severely limited professional staff consists of the minister, a part-time janitor, a part-time director of vocal music and/or organist. Fortunate indeed is the neighborhood church which in addition has secretarial assistance for such is exceptional. Whether he wills or no, the pastor is compelled to rely upon the contributed time and energy of laymen to accomplish the religious task. Thus to become an able administrator and hard-working parish shepherd are the twin goals thrust upon him. A staff of volunteer workers just has to be recruited. This is patent.

Yet the recruitment problem is not unsolvable. Because of the church's relatively small membership size (normally ranging from fifty to five hundred families) the minister may presumably call upon each family in the constituency several times per year. Informality, friendliness, and close pastoral care are possible in the situation; and there is time for the aggressive mobilization of lay workers. Consider, however, the plight of the pastor who fails to perceive his task in this essential fashion; for he cannot do the job alone, nor will he raise up indigenous leaders to accomplish it. No matter what else may appear to be achieved in the parish, only the delegation of responsibility to properly consecrated and oriented laymen will gain the objectives of the congregation. Careless administration and erratic pastoral work bear but the bitter fruit of ecclesiastical failure and spiritual frustration. This is a needless eventuality since a realistic knowledge of the neighborhood church reveals clearly the need for incessant and large-scale recruitment of laymen to compensate for the missing professional staff.

The large understaffed city church presents a problem. With limited personnel how may the processes of religious discovery, decision, and development be generated and adequately guided in the life of individuals? One notes that in the field of public education a measure of effective administration is to be found in the ratio of pupils per teacher. Certain important educational objectives appear difficult of realization if the "pupil load" per teacher becomes too large numerically. This would seem to indicate that there exists an optimum pupil-teacher ratio for achieving desired results. Similarly in the religious field a measure of effectiveness may be discovered in the member-minister ratio, that is, number of members per pastor. In fact who does not know of certain churches which achieve the odious reputation of "pastor killers" because the pastoral working burden is too heavy? The multitude of funerals, weddings, baptisms, sick calls, stated meetings, speaking engagements, and public worship services piled on top of administrative responsibilities and religious counseling is a burden beyond the strength of one pastor; yet no additional staff assistance appears forthcoming. Obviously the result is a condition of extreme overwork and mounting institutional inefficiency. Many important tasks remain undone because the routine demands upon the minister's time crowd out consideration of them.

This observation applies particularly to the larger neighborhood church which has outgrown its previous status but which has thus far failed to achieve administrative reorganization at the new size level and with an adequate staff. The lag in adjustment produces an intolerable situation in neighborhood church life and yet one which needs not persist indefinitely. To secure relief, experts propose a ratio ranging from six hundred to one thousand members per individual minister. Additional clergymen may be added in this ratio as the church grows. This proposal is not novel in church application, for we are told that Roman Catholicism provides staff personnel on the basis of one priest for each thousand souls in the parish. A comparable approach merits consideration among Protestants.

However, the majority of neighborhood churches are small and eventually reconcile themselves to a minimum professional staff, since a modest budget and limited religious opportunity warrant no other. What then can be done?' At the outset it is acknowledged that the neighborhood church affords an excellent opportunity for intense pastoral work of the traditional type. Here the urban minister should complete at least a thousand pastoral calls per year in order to contact all the homes of the parish and to recruit people who are able and willing to take responsibility for the manifold aspects of church life. Further, he is impelled to nurture spiritual growth among consecrated laymen who teach Sunday-school classes, sing in the choir, or engage in other aspects of the institution's life. This is by no means a minor service. Without constant parish cultivation and persistent recruitment of leaders it is unlikely that the neighborhood church can carry out its essential urban ministry. The absence of an adequate professional staff elevates the layman to enviable prominence in the city church. He counts because he is needed.

The Accessibility of Laymen. To participate regularly in the life of a local Protestant church requires reasonable proximity of residence to the church plant. It has been pointed out already that most of the members and Sunday-school enrollees live within one-mile radius of the plant, revealing an outstanding neighborhood church

178

characteristic—compactness of parish. The implication is that lay-men live near enough to the church to serve in it.

Recall the relation of this finding to other related phenomena. Specialists tell us that the universal optimum distance allowed for boarding transportation facilities (bus, streetcar, and subway) is one-fourth mile, for walking to elementary schools is one-half mile, and for neighborhood shopping is one mile. Since the environment for the church coincides closely with that of the secular in many important respects, it is reasonable to expect that mobility patterns of population carry over and undergird religious activity. What facilitates the transfer of action patterns is that many of the same people are involved in both spheres. This is a dynamic fact. Is it not plausible that church members use regular transportation facilities, go on shopping tours, and send their children to the public schools? Parish research discloses that most constituents reside within one mile of the church with which they are affiliated. This confirms our normal expectation.

Oddly enough this distance factor plays a positive role in the frequency of lay participation. When homes are near by, volunteer workers can carry out assumed or assigned responsibilities with a minimum of personal inconvenience in as much as transportation time and expense are negligible. People do not mind traveling a short distance to help in church affairs. Daytime and evening meetings may be attended and business transacted without haste, permitting adjournment at a reasonable hour. In fact some laymen practically "live" at the church during a busy period in religious activities. From the viewpoint of membership proximity the neighborhood church enjoys a definite advantage over other city churches and therefore should learn to capitalize upon it. Nearness means accessibility.

Many constituents of the neighborhood church have leisure time, a portion of which can be placed at the disposal of the local church. Recent attempts to tap this reservoir have produced among other pragmatic approaches time-tithing clubs whereby men and women contribute one tenth of their total leisure time to religious service. Stressing the volunteer motif and worked out on a weekly basis, the program has gained rapidly in favor among pastors and parish leaders. It provides a reasonable action pattern for church participation as well as one set in a spiritual frame of reference. Scarcely anyone would have surmised that such a large number of service hours per person were available for local church purposes.

It should be added that laymen do demonstrate all-around competence adequate to any task entrusted to them by the church. With respect to formal education, native ability, and experience covering the management of group affairs who among the residents of the neighborhood are better qualified for leadership? Once oriented, these volunteers successfully handle the manifold affairs of the church. Thus in conclusion it may be said that constituents reside near by, have leisure time, and possess both the desire and the ability to contribute to the cause of local Protestantism. This is a boon to the neighborhood church.

Participation Opportunities. The layman participates in numerous ways and performs manifold tasks. He has to, or else the neighborhood church would close its doors. Even a superficial analysis of its functional life discloses a jumbled web of organizations, committees, and administrative machinery. Clearly an institution which has under its custody children enough to comprise a small elementary school, youth sufficient to populate a high school of modest size, adults numerous enough to form several fraternal orders, elderly people enough for a home of the aged, fiscal affairs to rival a thriving small business, counseling problems sufficient to occupy a professional psychologist full time—not to mention the manifold administrative and spiritual tasks of the pastor—is bound to be a complicated project. When comparisons are made, one soon discovers a range of activity and work which makes the local church the most underrated institution in the city. What other voluntary association ministers to so many persons in so many circumstances?

To regulate this institution, to accomplish religious purposes, and to feature relevant program activities require the contributed time and energy of every able-bodied member. Lacking a professional staff, the neighborhood church is compelled to recruit volunteer assistance on a large scale.

Let us consider the general situation by means of an example. In the following table are grouped the manifold tasks which a city church of 500 members finds essential to carry out its ministry to the community. It will be noted that there are 475 tasks for laymen.

180

These leadership responsibilities are distributed among 18 basic categories, ranging from administration to group work activity. Classifications affording the more numerous opportunities are placed at the beginning. At the time of this writing 103 tasks or 22 per cent await to be claimed by laymen. Meanwhile the functioning of the church at an effective level is being hindered. Ministry remains on

VOLUNTEER TASKS OF A CITY CHURCH

Task Category	LEADERSHIP TASKS		
	Appropriated	Unclaimed	Totals
Administration	49	18	67
Sacred Music	42	14	56
Visitation of Constituency	23	27	50
Meals and Refreshments	26	16	42
Public Relations	35	1	36
Teaching of Religion	27	8	35
Committee Work	30	—	30
Financial Matters	29	—	29
Dramatics and Entertainment	24	1	25
Office Work	12	9	21
Property and Buildings	19	—	19
Worship Arrangements	13	1	14
Sports and Hobbies	9	4	13
Missionary Promotion	9	—	9
Public Speaking and Discussion	7	2	9
Religious Literature	9	—	9
Record Keeping	9	—	9
Group Work Activity	—	2	2
TOTALS	372	103	475

a skeletal basis in a number of vital areas. Yet an examination of the active membership of the church disclosed that 316 persons do not participate in the local church at the level of task responsibility. Laymen themselves should arouse fellow members to positive action.

Perhaps this concrete illustration can demonstrate the vast opportunity for laymen to share in the life of the neighborhood church. If the institution succeeds at all, success is due primarily to lay efforts; but if it fails, failure stems from the reluctance of laymen to take responsibility at a meaningful level. Though local church success or failure rests in the hands of consecrated laymen, there is no doubt about the myriad opportunities for participation which are open to members. This is both a boon and a handicap.

Mecca of Volunteer Workers. The neighborhood church may well be described as a mecca of volunteer workers. Although its members are mustered into service whether or not requisite training and relevant experience are evident, yet these laymen are soon metamorphosed into volunteer choirs, Sunday-school staff, functioning committees, organizational personnel, and a wide variety of church officials. This minor miracle goes on year after year. Indeed mobilization of available talent and energy is required if the ongoing programs of worship, Christian education, group work, and parish cultivation are to be maintained. Even such highly specialized functions as dramatics, musicals, hobby shows, and landscaping are competently managed through volunteer service. All this brings out the striking feature of contributed time and labor which, though not novel in evangelical Protestantism, has gained fresh prominence in recent years. This rediscovery promises to restore vitality in the urban church.

Many organizational leaders, parish choir members, singers, and Sunday-school teachers contribute individually more than a hundred hours of free service per annum. That this service is proffered willingly as a form of self-expression and religious loyalty needs to be lifted up since most of the actual work of the neighborhood church is achieved by and through laymen. This willingness to serve emerges as an important by-product of the relatively close identification of the local church with the residential neighborhood in which members live. A sense of camaraderie is often generated among the corps of workers which is marked by banter, good-natured rivalry, and spiritual earnestness. How like a fellowship of kindred minds the group becomes.

Participation loyalty is definite, intense, and relatively easy to muster, since to help in the church is like working for the improvement of one's own neighborhood. The secular and religious spheres are drawn very close together. Thus heavy reliance upon volunteer workers is endemic to the neighborhood church, for constituents relish the experience, develop spiritually from it, and contribute importantly to Protestantism in this manner. One wonders what other institution on earth commands so extensive, so constant, and so valued service. "Like a mighty army moves the church of God." In its vanguard, unnumbered as the sands, march a host of dedicated laymen.

NEIGHBORHOOD CHURCH HANDICAPS

Realism in urban religious work demands unhesitating confrontation with neighborhood church problems. That handicaps do exist is well known to informed pastors and laymen. Even a brief analysis can open the topic for further exploration by the reader. Experienced leaders acknowledge that difficulties generally derive from five fundamental sources: (1) an inadequate church plant, (2) a staffless church, (3) neighborhood limitations, (4) ineffective membership size, and (5) an inconspicuous pulpit. One or more of these handicaps harass most neighborhood churches.

Inadequate Church Plant. It is upon an inferior physical plant that religious leaders focus their most frequent complaint. An inspection of thousands of city churches reveals that many congregations do lack adequate facilities with which to carry out a normal ministry to the community. Possibly one half of Protestantism's neighborhood church buildings are unsuited to their current ministry.

In what sense is this so? Innumerable edifices are old, antique in appearance, unsafe in construction, misplaced on the site, potential fire traps and health hazards, ill suited to the Sunday-school requirements of the present day, and generally lacking in recreational and social facilities. Additional plants are but basements, temporary structures, or crudely remodeled buildings. Many lack modern and adequate lighting facilities, proper means of heating or ventilation, even decent toilet accommodations; while others have no outdoor bulletin boards or visible means of church identification. Thousands lack stained-glass windows, attractive landscaping, even a recent coat of paint. Often the sanctuary is on the second floor, necessitating a hazardous stair climb for pregnant women and elderly persons. In short an inadequate church plant repels people from participation. It discourages an active relationship.

The point of the discussion is essentially this: no matter how oblivious to these manifold physical limitations appear the devoted men and women who worship regularly among them, the stranger and alert leader note them immediately. For in the city no Protestant church thrives without showing semblance of being a going concern. One wonders why intelligent laymen countenance such intolerable conditions year after year when they would not put up with kindred handicaps a fortnight at home or in business. In appearance and in appointment the neighborhood church should match the finest homes in the territory. This is a practical ideal.

A Staffless Church. Further, the neighborhood church lacks a complete professional staff, and it is common for the pastor and a part-time janitor to comprise the entire paid personnel. Occasionally an amateur musician receives a token gratuity for part-time employment directing the choir and/or playing the organ (or piano), though seldom are singers compensated. Virtually all of the work of religious education is entrusted to volunteers, whose qualifications sometimes scarcely go beyond an overt willingness to help. Somehow the local church muddles through.

Ostensible staff limitation forces the neighborhood church to place great reliance upon volunteer lay workers. Thus the congregation appears to have turned its very handicap into a recipe for success. It has found a significant ministry in the development and utilization of volunteers. No thoughtful person would wish to underrate this vast host of unpaid lay workers which has been raised up to mediate the church's ministry to the community. Nor should one overlook the fact that these loyal persons have limitations with respect to time, experience, and ability. Consequently when ineptness in performance comes and inefficiency appears, such conditions must be tolerated if there is to be a program at all. Contributions of spare time are made by people who are willing but who lack either experience or ability. This deficiency causes breakdowns in the local church program which prove annoying to the general membership and quite intolerable to the stranger. The staffless nature of the neighborhood church constitutes a handicap difficult to surmount.

Neighborhood Limitations. A residential neighborhood contains a definite number of people and has a known geographical extent which derives from indigenous housing and the relative position of primary barriers. Further, an apartment or multiple-housing territory is likely to have more persons per city block than an area built up principally of single-family dwellings, and yet both are probably

184

bounded by a rim of primary barriers which limits the outreach of the neighborhood church. How many Protestants are in residence is readily ascertainable by means of a religious census. Whether the local institution prefers the given situation or not begs the question since its very fortune and future impinge upon the available Protestant population within its service radius. Ordinarily twenty-five hundred are needed as a minimum reserve from which to develop an effective local church.

Strangely enough no one ever needs to speculate respecting the religious composition of a neighborhood. How many unchurched persons reside within the service radius of the local church, and of what faith and denomination, may be determined at any time by means of a house-to-house survey. By this process the Protestant potential of a neighborhood is measured in the kind of objective terms which point to an intelligent course of action. No church should be started, relocated, or closed without a religious census of the area under consideration.

Limitations of the territory are also the limitations of the local church. There are only so many peaches in a peck basket, likewise in a bushel. A small neighborhood imposes a modest religious ministry upon the congregation, whereas the medium and larger territories offer relatively greater opportunity for church membership and Sunday-school extension. Yet in any case the church cannot serve more Protestants than reside in the neighborhood. The distance penalty renders unwise the exclusive or extensive cultivation of non-residents. With this fact in mind one should recognize that the presence of other indigenous Protestant churches constitutes an additional limitation of the neighborhood, both actual and potential. Severe competition may derive from this source and generate a sense of frustration among church members.

Regardless of the environing conditions, a local church should strive for a full ministry within the possibilities of the neighborhood territory. This requires an intense cultivation of opportunity until the very last unchurched person is found. To find and win all such persons can yield a growth pattern with respect to membership and Sunday school—even in an unpromising neighborhood. This vital ministry can be had.

Ineffective Membership Size. A church can be too small for effective religious work in the city. Gauged by the accepted urban standard (five hundred active members), many Protestant units are so diminutive that membership size itself is actually a label of weakness. Thoughtful leaders find in this condition a depressing handicap since impaired religious effectiveness in numerous communities can be traced to this source. Virtually all tiny urban congregations are of the neighborhood type.

In the city smallness of membership itself constitutes weakness. Consider some of the facts. There are just not enough people to go around among the various church groups and organizations. Identical persons are listed upon committee after committee, provoking program breakdowns due to participation duplication and leadership weariness. When a meager number of individuals comprise the membership and officiary of many societies and clubs, the result is an excessive accumulation of offices upon a few persons. A tiny church I know of has the problem of seven persons holding forty-two major leadership positions. Yet two positions represent the maximum which a layman has time to handle adequately. Any attempt to redistribute these offices to procure functioning committees will be met with suspicion and regarded as a personal affront. Some persons collect offices as a philatelist gathers stamps—it is an interesting hobby. Such a condition is more common than is acknowledged. Further, some children's and youth organizations may not even exist on account of the scarcity of individuals of the necessary age. Or worse still, children of all ages are thrust together into a catch-all association with the vain hope that some obscure religious objective may be accomplished. Under these subideal conditions it is apparent that a boy or girl will encounter difficulty in obtaining an adequate religious fellowship experience. Obviously the church is too small to furnish one.

When diminutiveness is combined with other factors such as disproportionate dominance of females and aged constituents, paucity of employed members, meager budget, and inadequate church plant, one may readily surmise the calamitous outcome. In contrast a certain robustness of size and balance of age and sex groups are essential to urban church success. Unfortunately the smaller a church becomes in membership size, the more antisurvival factors multiply. It is difficult for a small church to combat the vast forces of sin in the city and to swing the attention of the community toward New Testament Christianity. Its puny efforts are swallowed up in rampant secularism.

An Inconspicuous Pulpit. Few neighborhood church pulpits are sufficiently outstanding to attract Protestants in large numbers from throughout the city. This is reluctantly but generally acknowledged since it is rare for a person to seek out a particular neighborhood church for its preaching. The interested layman looks for other values, such as friendliness, modest size, and need of his services. This observation need not imply that sermons are incompetently prepared or poorly presented, though there may be instances of shoddy homiletical work in the city. Rather it points out patently that the neighborhood church is often outclassed in this respect by the downtown institution where pulpit effectivenes is the conspicuous specialty. Because of its city-wide reputation, central location, high visibility, long history, trained staff, and significant size the downtown church holds a unique advantage in the homiletical field. Normally only clergymen of exceptional platform competence are brought to its pulpit. Therefore the neighborhood church is misguided if it aspires to rival the downtown unit in sermonic effectiveness. On the other hand the importance of good preaching need not be de-emphasized here, for the man in the pew knows an efficacious sermon when he hears one.

Part of the handicap derives from pastoral leadership. Neighborhood local churches are commonly served by ministers who are relatively young (and commonly inexperienced) or who are approaching retirement. Laymen say the pastor is either too young or old. Exceptions exist of course. Yet who among us does not know that smaller urban churches are most frequently handicapped with respect to inexperienced or inept clergy? How can it be otherwise? Salaries are relatively low, parsonages are poor or nonexistent, and church facilities are often ridiculously inadequate. This accumulation of negative circumstances combines to prevent the congregation from securing a wide range of choice among clergymen. Conditions force the pulpit committee to take what it can get. Is it surprising then that members come to accept the plight of the neighborhood church in a mood of frustrated resignation? Consequently the very urban church which stands in urgent need of superior pastoral lead-

187

ership often fails to procure it. This is the dilemma which underlies the inconspicuous pulpit—if youth knew, if age could.

Further, the public worship service often contains substandard choral music. The mark of the poor amateur is indelibly upon anthems. Persons whose best days of voice production are in the past commonly continue as choir members, and along with the limited number of voices, the dearth of males, the untrained and weak voices, add to the apparent difficulty of blending the vocal efforts into an adequate production. Frequently instrumental music for public services is hardly on a higher plane. As a whole the church music, both vocal and instrumental, scarcely proves an attractive feature to persons looking for inspiration after a hard week in office or factory.

Other aspects of the public worship services contribute limitedly in terms of public relations. Poorly mimeographed bulletins, careless ushering, friendship cliques which ignore strangers and convey the impression of a "closed corporation," plus the added handicap of a small congregation total up to an unsatisfactory experience for many discriminating urban dwellers. Such negative conditions are important and therefore merit the deep concern of church leaders. Inferior facilities and mediocre performance should never be mistaken for informality. These rarely can substitute for an ordered and adequate religious setting. God is a spirit, not a chaos.

The wonder is not that the neighborhood church falls short of ecclesiastical perfection at some points but that it succeeds in bringing the ministries of Christianity significantly into so many lives. In spite of acknowledged handicaps a vast and remarkable religious work goes on. Thousands upon thousands of Protestants are destined to find God if at all under the aegis of a neighborhood church. This is a notable ministry, and therefore the unpretentious work of a modest urban church merits increasing administrative recognition and sympathetic oversight. Fortunately most urban church handicaps are superable when proper remedial and/or compensating measures are launched in time.

SPECIALTIES OF A NEIGHBORHOOD MINISTRY

The neighborhood church has valuable assets which, if properly capitalized upon, may redeem its ministry from whatever frustration stems from its acknowledged handicaps. Above and beyond the regular spiritual services characteristic of a Protestant church religious specialization not only is possible but even necessary in the neighborhood situation. Apparently certain aspects of the work demand direct attention and administrative concern if the institution is to be effective. A clarification of this point is in order, and this will be found in the subsequent pages which treat five important specialties describing the church's responsibility to its own fellowship, to the rising generation, to the community, to the church at large, and to its potential leadership. This ministry of specialization needs focusing and additional administrative emphasis. Eventually it may prove an effective antidote to urban secularism.

Stimulation of Friendliness. The neighborhood church has a natural opportunity for encouraging the development of amicable relations within its constituency. Here is a congregation of neighbors and acquaintances who possess intrinsic interrelationships and patterns of activity which may support the proposed endeavor. People live along the same streets, send their children to the same schools, shop in the same stores, participate in many of the same organizations, thereby disclosing an underlying secular pattern which may be utilized in developing church friendships. This basic process of intermingling becomes religion's starting point.

The well-nigh universal appearance of the phrase "a friendly church" on Sunday bulletins may be more the expression of a hope than the description of a reality. Therefore the neighborhood church should strive to turn hope into reality. To accomplish this common interests, common relations, and common tasks normally must be discovered and transmuted into centers of group action which may yield satisfying personal relationships. In this matter the neighborhood church needs only to capitalize upon its own unique advantages. Since its very location is tantamount to approximate identification with the residents of a natural urban territory, specialization in getting friendships started is warranted. This is the best antidote for the loneliness of the city.

Action rather than words is needed. Do not talk about it. Instead the church should furnish opportunities for intermingling, for getting acquainted, and for having people do things together. The creation of the appropriate atmosphere and the provision of occasions in which friendship has a chance to germinate are necessary. The generation of friendliness within the congregation is a natural and significant opportunity for the neighborhood church. Recent researches disclose that a friendly layman is the most important single reason why people embrace Protestantism and even choose a particular local church. In a practical sense friendliness is next to Godliness.

Cultivation of the Sunday School. Currently the work of the Sunday school is suffering from an administrative de-emphasis which probably is unintentional. This is unwarranted since one third of the city's population is comprised of children and youth under eighteen years of age, and more people live in the city today than at any previous time in American history. If there is an urban opportunity for a ministry to the rising generation, it is surely dominantly localized in the neighborhood church. The presence of an elementary school near by and the predominance of family units combine to underscore this reasonable contention. Within the service radius (one mile) of the local church children reside in great numbers. How numerous they actually are may be ascertained at any time by a door-to-door canvass. The city church never needs to guess about the extent of its opportunity.

There can be no future where the children remain unserviced. How important this emphasis is may be seen from the fact that from 50 to 100 per cent of the "new" Christians (first decision for Jesus Christ) derive from the Sunday school. Thus the close and continual cultivation of a ministry to children and youth yields great benefit to the local church and its denomination. This task is tremendous in scope and properly calls forth the energies of every parent and Sunday-school teacher. How can the pastor escape primary responsibility in the process?

As go the fortunes of the near-by elementary schools, so go the fortunes of the neighborhood Sunday school. Vigilance in watching the trends there, as well as observance of changes in the community's faith and racial composition, may guide the local church in its program and prepare it for expansion or reduction of religious opportunity. No city church needs ever to close its doors as long as there are children and youth to serve. Out of this constituency will come the church of tomorrow, and therefore Protestantism should take larger responsibility for guiding the young into religious maturity.

190

Promotion of Community Improvement. Supplementing its normal spiritual ministry the local church should serve as an agency for community betterment. Ways need to be found by which the influence of rampant secularism is met and eventually annulled. Two important aspects of this consideration are worthy of attention. First clearly religion should have a broad application to life, and its exacting ideals should be applied to the various forces (liquor, gambling, prostitution, and so on) which interfere with the high fulfillment of human life. To some people this challenge is too lofty and too likely to lead into controversial issues. That this ministry of reform is needed in many cities has been adequately demonstrated by recent crime investigations. Evil has spread like a green bay tree throughout municipal life. Religion alone can launch counterforces.

Second the neighborhood church should ally itself with good causes—cultural, moral, and social improvement programs which do not require compromise with its basic ideals. The wide diffusion of religious teachings has proved a benefit to society. Consider the important work of the Red Cross, boy and girl scouts, social agencies, health departments, park and recreational commissions, service clubs, the public library, and other groups which seek to reduce personal and social disorganization by attacking the root causes. The neighborhood church can hardly ignore the other forces working for righteousness in the community. In fact it should give encouragement and freely promote such desirable developments. This is a ministry of alliance.

As a matter of fact the neighborhood church will encounter difficulty in seeking to thrive if it does not work for community improvement. Most of its members are involved in the city's fortunes, and therefore its constituency must come to know that its spiritual objectives are not "pie in the sky, when you die," but rather the progressive infiltration of contemporary society with religious ideals until all may feel the pressure of Christ's life upon their own.

Attraction to Christian Vocations. A traditional ministry of the urban church consists in recruiting persons for full-time Christian service. The current shortage of ministers, missionaries, deaconesses, and religious workers of many types lends a new note of urgency to this specialty. Personnel is the great need of both home and foreign mission fields.

191

The recruitment of individuals for Christian vocations comes naturally to the neighborhood church. Through the years it has engaged in this work. But there is another important reason. It is said that approximately three fourths of the members of urban Protestantism find God first under the auspices of the neighborhood institution. Because so many persons are converted here, religious idealism is in flood and the desire to serve is most intense. This tender spiritual beginning eventually gives way to a dominant vocational purpose which is neither blunted by contact with the secular world nor superseded by the educational experience. It survives because it is genuine.

The initial orientation to God's purposes is nurtured jointly by continuing religious experience and by the challenging companionship of a thoughtful pastor. The latter opens the way for numerous opportunities for leadership experience in Sunday school, youth activities, religious witnessing, and adult worship services. Practice in teaching, in preaching, and in conducting worship aids the maturation process and progressively orients the person to the requirements of full-time work in the religious field. Further, participation in personal work, program planning, and general administration edges the individual along toward the eventual crystallization of vocational choice.

Central in the process is the deepening of one's life with God. Steady companionship with the pastor and regular association with other mature Christians provide the novice with examples of flaming faith—so important to young life. The influence of a good home, attendance at youth camps and institutes, and summer-work experience in home mission projects will complete the metamorphosis. As expected, formal education and professional training must be regarded as important in the process.

An advantage possessed by the neighborhood church consists in being at the very source of supply of "new" Christians, and hence it can accelerate the work of recruiting persons for full-time Christian service until the current need has been met. Concentration upon this normal specialty can yield not only a worker from every local church but also an additional one for each five hundred members or fraction thereof reported on the rolls. Teachers of children and youth, parents, and the pastor may unite their efforts to procure workers in the ratio indicated above. In this manner Protestantism may make a creditable response to the present emergency.

Nurture of Religious Leaders. Many laymen are experienced in types of secular activity which prepare them for responsibility in the local church. Because of the peculiar vocational requirements, they have achieved a basic mastery of techniques with which to get things done through other people. They know how to plan their work, how to delegate responsibility, and how to check up periodically upon the execution of duties. Further, individuals who have held offices in fraternal orders, in school or community organizations, and in other churches likewise possess executive ability which fit them to take up administrative or teaching duties in the church immediately. Thus experienced leaders require only a brief orientation. Every able-bodied layman qualifying for this category should be mustered into service promptly. This procedure affords the quickest and most effective way to solve leadership problems, and it provides a dependable inner core of workers around whom the administration of the local church may be planned. Here is where most churches should begin.

Providentially perhaps there are not enough persons with adequate previous leadership experience to meet the exigencies of the hour. Consequently the neighborhood church is forced to "grow" additional leaders, that is, to recruit relatively inexperienced persons and train them for officeholding and other types of religious service. Utilizing a lead and learn approach, the pastor may patiently groom individuals until they achieve skills and reach a level of usefulness.

Normally an apprenticeship in minor offices and on secondary committees can develop a person's potentialities and establish self-confidence. Close personal guidance provided during the extended learning process underlies the development of all capable leaders. Clearly the neighborhood church has a responsibility and an opportunity to produce its own leadership. This specialty is a normal but often neglected function. Perhaps a score or more of new leaders can be produced yearly by patient cultivation. Nothing that the pastor gives his attention to will bear greater dividends in personality development and in general help to the local congregation. The nurture of religious leaders is a great single need of urban Protestantism.

Several paths lead into local church leadership, and along them

193

lie pedagogic processes through which the novice must pass. The most common route taken is that of special tasks. The pastor asks an individual to take responsibility for a specific task. The church lawn needs grading, a shrub needs to be planted, a room needs to be painted, a special fund must be raised, an anniversary is to be celebrated, a religious census is necessary—to one or another of these special tasks a person's attention is directed and responsibility assigned. According to the interest and talents of the untried member this affords a door through which he may pass into larger service. Big decisions for service often turn on small hinges. The apparent trivial task by which a layman gets started in church work must not be underrated. Here is where the wise pastor teaches the people to assume responsibility toward the religious institution.

A second path leads into local church leadership—administrative appointment. Persons ready for advancement or larger responsibility are named by the local church nominating committee to fill out terms of office vacated by death or other reasons. Also when special committees are named within an organization, the chairman may select persons who need such experience or who can make a contribution.

Finally a third path consists of the democratic elective process whereby popularity and apparent competence combine to elevate a person to office. Through normal local organizational channels persons of all ages have an opportunity to be honored in this fashion. The widespread use of a rotation plan respecting church officers opens the way for the eventual utilization of all competent persons in the congregation. Tenure in office is shortened from life to several years, and no one can succeed himself in office without an interval of a year. Broad participation in church life is encouraged among laymen when offices and leadership positions are passed around, and this arrangement works to the advantage of the church no matter how small the congregation.

Thus to nurture religious leaders the neighborhood church may utilize all three paths in a unified ongoing process. Not only should individuals learn the nature of the church's task, but also they should achieve a mastery of general principles of group work, namely, simple parliamentary procedure, planned division of labor, delegation of responsibility, techniques of getting along with people, and methods of follow-up on details. These skills and the church experience itself are important and enduring contributions to the religious life of the individual.

WAYS TO STRENGTHEN THE NEIGHBORHOOD CHURCH

Throughout the discussion above emphasis has been given to the importance of pastor-laymen co-operation in coping with local church difficulties. Many informed leaders are aware of the task and urge that a joint discovery of the needs of a particular congregation can sharpen personal concern over existing limitations and eventually pave the way for the accomplishment of urgent improvements. This exploration raises the important question of how leaders may ameliorate the current situation. Thus we come to a consideration of five practical ways by which the concerned religious leader may strengthen the neighborhood church.

1. *Procure growth trends in the local church.* Select a period ranging from fifteen to fifty years in duration, terminating with the most recent year for which data are available. Using the statistical yearbooks of the denomination, obtain figures for membership, accessions to membership, Sunday-school enrollment, local church finances and benevolences per annum during the trend period. Occasionally data for trend studies are assembled year by year, but it is more common to gather such materials for five- or ten-year intervals, utilizing years ending in five or zero.

Divide the data into two parts. (a) Take the long period—the remote past—back as far as the trend material permits, usually thirty to fifty years. This will allow an overview of the recent history of the local church. (b) The near past is generally regarded as the chronological division covering the latest fifteen- or twenty-year period. In processing these materials data are placed first of all in tabular form. Then percentages for both trend periods are calculated. Usually trends by decades are also included in the analysis, but decennial findings are not highlighted unless a significant aspect appears.

Next analyze and discuss the trend patterns of the local church with attention given to both the longer and shorter periods of time. Prepare a set of findings with recommendations for action. In all this research a lay committee should share and co-operate with the minister in preparing a report. The educational significance of this process is vital to the local church. A valuable way to learn is found in participation. Laymen as well as clergy need to discover the trend situation. Participation in the study allows time for insights to ripen and fresh truth to appear. Proper courses of action are likely to become clearer and reveal themselves sooner when religious trends have been discovered for what they actually are and have been carefully analyzed. A neighborhood church can start changing its trend situation in a single year by aggressive and intelligent action. Conspicuous growth should normally characterize its ministry.

2. *Cultivate unchurched persons within one-mile radius.* There is hardly a neighborhood church which does not have numerous prospective members residing within its service radius. Who these people are and where they live should be ascertained by means of a religious census. It is hazardous to trust impressions of the religious composition of the territory. Community knowledge understandably is not amenable even to so-called scientific conjecture. Only a house-to-house canvass can provide access to the kind of facts upon which an intelligent answer can be formulated.

Prelude then to an evangelistic cultivation of the neighborhood is the religious census. In the latter project call-backs and complete coverage of the territory are featured. This means that every family in every city block is contacted. Religious affiliation or preference is procured on each person of the household and is recorded upon a card for subsequent perusal and analysis. The reader may wish to consult Chapter III for details of the procedure.

It is natural and desirable to follow up the religious census with a visitation evangelism program. Cards bearing the names of prospects should be divided into three basic groups: (a) persons ready to join the local church immediately, (b) persons who may require a series of visits to secure a decision, and (c) persons who will be won if at all only after long, patient, and skillful cultivation. This pragmatic sorting process assists visitation workers to distinguish prospects according to religious readiness. Unchurched Protestants normally fall into these pragmatic categories.

Next set up a permanent visitation program committee within the neighborhood church even if the minister himself must train the callers one by one. In most cases the program makes an inauspicious beginning and gathers momentum only gradually. It takes a year or even longer to put the visitation program upon a relatively permanent basis. The proper follow-up of the religious census is by a systematic evangelistic visitation program which develops into an ongoing feature of the effective neighborhood church. Thus persons found by the census may be won to Protestantism as quickly as possible.

The significance of this continuous outreach program cannot be exaggerated. Recent studies reveal overwhelmingly that the primary source of adult religious decisions is personal visitation on the part of laymen. A friendly member is a boon to Protestantism. Many people affiliate with a church because an acquaintance or friend personalizes the significance of that religious relationship. Social intermingling is a unique characteristic of life within Protestantism, and therefore personal contacts and witnessing loom important in the recruitment of new members. Out of the reservoir of unchurched persons in the neighborhood many urban churches may increase in member strength up to 50 per cent or more. To maintain continuity of growth the territory around the neighborhood church should be thoroughly investigated every three to five years by means of a religious census. Many new prospects will be found, and ultimately significant trends of Protestant opportunity may be detected. For the local church this inventory may make the difference between success and failure in the city.

3. *Improve the participation pattern of members.* Adequate knowledge may be lacking respecting membership participation patterns within the local church. Such vital information reveals local church strong points and weaknesses. These data can be procured quite readily and analyzed with reference to their important bearing upon program planning for a neighborhood ministry.

To explore participation patterns the reader should write or type out a complete list of local church members, placing the names in alphabetical order down the left margin of a sheet of typing paper. Place but one column of names on a sheet. Next a committee should record the number of times each individual was present at public worship services during the past year. A shorter period than twelve months is likely to contain bias, since the summer months and special religious seasons provide great fluctuation in frequency of attendance. What shall be done if no attendance records exist? Simply choose the coming twelve-month period and have the attendance record taken during the year, thus procuring factual information useful in the proposed inventory.

Further, indicate after each name the number of times a member was in attendance at Sunday school, at meetings and functions of the various women's organizations, men's groups, youth activities, and children's program, as the question applies. Use code letters to retain identity of the entry. Records of the individual organizations should be scrutinized since attendance is often revealed through payment of dues, voting on motions, reports of committee work, responsibility for the program, and kindred activity. Information should be assembled on all the church members who reside in the city and adjacent suburbs.

The next step is analysis. Persons who are very active, those who are moderately so, and those who rarely or never participate in the life of the local church are placed into separate groupings. Count up the number of persons recorded in each category. Consider whether the persons are youthful, middle aged, or elderly. Account should be taken of special home circumstances and conditions of personal health. Mothers of small children, persons harassed by chronic illness or precarious health, and individuals who have vocational travel requirements find it nearly impossible to attend church regularly. Of course these and kindred conditions merit sympathetic consideration on the part of the committee, but alibis should be detected and exposed. Accurate notes including all relevant information should be written upon the membership work sheet. Through follow-up interviews let each layman account for failure to acquire the habit of significant church activity.

A set of findings should be drafted by the study committee. Such materials not only merit thorough examination by all church officers but also deserve close scrutiny by the entire congregation. Democratic discussion of current conditions may prepare the way for constructive change. Mimeographed copies of the findings accompanied by simple charts will enable the general membership to grasp the gist of the report. Intelligent action and change are among the desired goals of local church research.

Persons who are not adequately entering into the life of the church can be interviewed and tactfully acquainted with their participation status. Every reasonable effort should be expended to discover what circumstances appear to stand in the way of reconciliation and full participation. Wherever possible remedial measures can be utilized to correct alleged injustices or misunderstandings. Definite tasks and church chores should be offered to inactive members in order that they may have a clear opportunity to be reactivated. To discover that one is wanted and needed will strengthen considerably the influence of the .local church in the neighborhood.

4. *Intensify the ministry to persons.* In city church work the great unanswered question is the forlorn wail of the urban resident —who will minister to my condition? Unnumbered individuals, who are not necessarily psychopathic, are distressed by experiences of overwork, fatigue, insecurity, irritation, unemployment, confusion, frustration, domestic unhappiness, and bereavement. What precisely does the neighborhood church have to offer? Is there a ministry to the people who may never enter a mental institution or come under the care of a psychiatrist? Experienced observers insist that this is a common spiritual service desperately needed in American cities.

It is unlikely that these troubled persons will be helped much by a mimeographed form letter sent out from the church office. What may be required is a large scale recovery of a plain pastoral ministry, unadorned by the ministerial ambition to work with "unusual cases" or to build up a grand clientele for formal interviews. Perhaps only in the neighborhood church ultimately may be retained the semblance of an intensive parish ministry wherein the pastor goes from house to house bringing the mercies of God to persons buffeted by the winds of life and harassed by wavering personal fortunes. Regular companionship and spiritual assurance are traditional fruits of pastoral work. A generation is poorer without them.

Of course the Protestant counseling function is bound to grow and to develop specializations unknown to former generations. Instances of technical need beyond the capacity and resources of the average pastor are common, and many channels of referral have opened recently to aid him. Under such circumstances the alert minister will send needy individuals to the proper social agencies, doctors, or clinics as the case requires. Clergymen with exceptional technical training are inclined to co-operate closely with psychiatrists and other specialists. This is an expected and understandable development.

However, it will be unfortunate if this proliferation comes by way of neglect of general pastoral cultivation. An intensification of ministry to persons is called for. Neither the mimeograph machine nor display advertisements, in spite of their acknowledged merits, can truly supplant the devoted pastor who loves his people. Somehow every church constituent must come to feel the pressure of Christ's life upon his own and learn to appropriate the resources of religion in terms of ordinary human problems. In this process the minister ranks supreme. As a man of God he can walk beside and counsel with the busy harassed city resident. This need not be a trivial ministry.

5. *Make physical improvements regularly.* Because the neighborhood church commonly lacks an adequate plant and/or facilities, attention may be drawn to possible physical improvements. Progress in this sphere is necessary if the morale of the congregation is to be maintained at a high level. An easy-to-notice change should be made at regular intervals—perhaps every six months.

What can be done ought to be done. Improvement may mean various things to different congregations. It may mean painting the exterior of the church plant, laying a new concrete sidewalk, renovation of the sanctuary, replacement of noisy theater seats with secondhand or new pews, making of Sunday-school equipment by hand, repair of the outdoor bulletin board, gowning of the choir, replacement of a worn-out organ or piano, regrading and seeding of the church lawn, preparation of a room for nursery children, and so on. No needed change should be regarded as trivial or beyond the capacity of the congregation. Men of faith always find a way to do what has to be done.

These improvements should reveal to the congregation that in spite of straitened financial circumstances progress in the proper direction can still be made. It is likely that many of the improvements will have to be made by means of volunteer labor and donated materials. When church funds are scarce, businessmen often will donate a limited amount of materials for this worthy cause. Then members of the congregation furnish the labor without compensation. It would be rare to find a city church that cannot make some of its necessary improvements during the next several months, even in spite of its present financial situation. Time tithing offers immense possibilities in that it involves the contributing of one tenth of a member's leisure hours. Members and constituents work out the tithe by investing energies and time to bring noticeable improvements to the church at regular intervals. Many urban congregations are discovering this resource.

A committee of officials should check over the building, grounds, and facilities in order to discover where improvements ought to be made. Obviously construction involving contractors requires careful planning and fund raising. This also fits into the step-by-step program of physical improvements, for the church's ultimate goal is to procure a plant and facilities adequate to the needs of a neighborhood ministry. This is an objective around which all interested members may rally. Who does not wish to see the neighborhood church looking its best and functioning at the peak of effectiveness? If laymen become fully aroused, they can change the world.

CHAPTER VII

New Church Work in the City and Suburbs

ILLIONS of Americans who emigrated from the farm, the village, the town, and the city during the war years have by now largely established themselves in a new environment. As a result many urban communities have grown enormously. This population increment has thrust a heavy burden upon existing Protestant churches which find it increasingly difficult to provide an adequate religious ministry for all the newcomers. Protestant opportunity has been greatly enlarged in most cities and towns. Consequently alert pastors and denominational administrators have determined to extend their work by the establishment of additional new churches, especially in the suburbs.

A Need for Guiding Principles. The proper site for a new church may be located as scientifically as one for a business establishment or a school. To accomplish this, objective information related to the sociological nature of religious institutions should be gathered and utilized intelligently to reduce the number of misplaced churches. Guesswork in the religious field has been found to be as expensive and unwarranted as it is in any other sphere of human affairs. Altogether too often the selection of a church site is made in terms of factors but remotely related to the problem.

One needs only to look about his own community to observe churches that are badly placed. In fact the history of Protestantism in many cities is an account of succesive plant relocations made with the often forlorn hope of discovering a site more advantageous than the last from which to do effective religious work. Church locations have been made largely on a "topsy" basis. Denominational administrators and trained pastors are becoming increasingly aware of the need for a set of clearly formulated principles to guide leaders in selecting new church sites. Obviously no pragmatic formula can be devised by which all mistakes in church location could be eliminated, yet it is evident that many errors in judgment can be avoided.

Problems Related to Site Location. Where · are new Protestant churches needed? Where do concentrations of unchurched people exist? To what extent do such population aggregates constitute a Protestant opportunity? What characteristics do they possess which indicate a type of church required? In what specific ways does housing have an important bearing upon church extension opportunity? To what extent are local comity agreements involved in the problem? What denominational fortunes are involved? What pragmatic considerations should be held in mind in the selection of a site? What provision for ministry ought to be reviewed before starting the new church project? Should a Sunday-school structure be erected first and a church plant later or vice versa? When is it likely the new church may become self-supporting? How may the congregation be reasonably sure that the extension project will succeed? These may be some of the questions going through the mind of the reader at this point in the discussion.

SIX FUNDAMENTAL GUIDING PRINCIPLES

There are at least six fundamental guiding principles which may be utilized in determining the establishment of a new church. Seek for (1) a concentration of unchurched Protestant people; (2) freedom from physical and psychological barriers; (3) freedom from unwholesome or hobbling competition; (4) a conspicuous, accessible site; (5) an adequate plant; and (6) an effective ministry.

These guiding principles should be regarded as a minimum rather than a maximum list of success factors in church extension planning. Common sense may call for some adjustment of the principles in a particular local situation. To secure best results the six suggestions need to be thought of as a battery of guide lines within which the wisest decision possible is made.

A constant hazard to the proper establishment of a new church is the Judaslike influence of relatively unimportant factors. Shade trees, an expanse of green lawn, proximity to a park, cemetery, or high school, frequently sway an opinion toward unwise decisions. Commonly whatever has high visibility misleads an otherwise balanced intelligent individual. Thus a word of caution is in order. The presence of unchurched Protestant people, and that factor alone, constitutes an opportunity for church extension work. Grass, trees, and shrubbery can be added to most sites. Consider carefully therefore the practical implications of each of the six principles and a decision against the background of them all. Beware of superficial and unimportant factors.

1. *A Concentration of People.* The basic ingredient in local church planning is people. No realistic approach to church opportunity can be achieved without objective information about population. Thus to ascertain the number of persons of Protestant background and preference who reside in an area under consideration is fundamental. The significance of new church opportunity is always measured by the number of persons or families out of vital contact with organized religion. Prior to the selection of a site information respecting the number of unchurched Protestants should be in hand. Obviously an effective method for gathering such data is the house-to-house religious census.

The sociological characteristics of the population in the territory under consideration are germane to an intelligent discussion of the problem. Among the more important traits are race, ethnic background, economic status, education, age, and family status of the people. These data are normally available at the public library or at the city-planning commission's office.

In some cases it may be necessary to check the number of permits for new residential construction issued from the office of the city-building inspector. The number of new houses built plus elementary-school enrollment trends by individual schools provide additional valuable insight. Frequently a scrutiny of the master plan of service contemplated for an area by a utilities corporation (gas and/or electricity) is useful here. When required information is not obtainable in the first office visited, the inquirer should try elsewhere. Patience and resourcefulness are indispensable conpanions in gathering sociological materials. The persistent individual can gather necessary facts about Protestant population. The data can and should be found.

2. *Freedom from Barriers.* In determining the location of a new church the denominational executive or pastor should select a site which has a maximum number of persons residing within one-mile radius of the parcel of land. A new church project should be situated at or near the center of a residential area, remote from barriers but not on a side street. Often a neighborhood has vacant land which provides room for additional population growth. If a large park, a cemetery, or a factory is near by, it obviously diminishes the potential number of homes adjacent to the contemplated church site. Such reduction in some communities constitutes the difference between success and failure for the new project. Place the church at the heart of the neighborhood life.

Barriers which bound residential areas and impede the facile movement of population between neighborhoods constitute restrictive influences upon effective church location, especially if they are closer than a mile. Topographical features such as ravines, steep hills, and bodies of water likewise affect adversely the density of population. In church site selection it is imperative to avoid proximity to railroad tracks and yards, to objectionable commercial and recreational establishments, to wide bands of "blighted" housing, and to concentrations of racial and ethnic population groups not normally likely to be served by the contemplated extension project. Boulevards, wide streets, and freeways do not constitute barriers in the sense in which the term is used here.

3. *Freedom from Competition.* Too many Protestant churches in a neighborhood produce debilitating competition. In an examination of the population of a community one should deduct from the gross figures the number of persons who are Roman Catholics, who are Hebrews, who belong to nonassimilable racial groups, who are under ten years of age, and who are already vitally related to neighboring Protestant churches. Then examine the resultant number, for the process will yield a residue of unchurched Protestant people. Thus the extent to which the proposed extension project is needed becomes known.

Crippling competition ensues when the number of churches is too great for the Protestant population potential. Two or three thousand persons in the gross population per church is a safe ratio. The new church may then be expected to grow beyond five hundred members in strength which is commonly regarded as a minimum effective size for urban churches. Mapping the locations of all existing churches will partially reveal the wisdom or folly of entering the proposed territory. If the neighborhood under consideration appears to be adequately churched already, a decision to postpone the launching of another Protestant church would seem advisable.

Freedom from unwholesome or crippling competition is an essential principle to observe in the establishment of new churches. In many cities and towns throughout the United States the ugly results of excessive Protestant competition are clearly evident. Often neighboring churches are permanently destined to smallness and to relative ineffectiveness. Fierce, unchristian rivalry marks the relationship between some congregations. Even where open warfare does not exist, the mere presence of the competing church further divides an already limited opportunity. Under such circumstances the objectives of the Kingdom of God can be but partially realized at best. The denominational administrator should keep in mind that the primary purpose in opening a new church is to reach persons currently out of vital touch with the Protestant faith, and hence it is necessary to establish new units only where neighborhoods are actually underchurched.

4. *A Conspicuous, Accessible Site.* The contemplated new church merits a site where residents of the neighborhood can see it on the way to the store, to school, to work. Whenever a parent goes to buy a loaf of bread or to seek out the elementary school for his children, he should "trip over" the new church. Thus a location is strategic if it is situated on a prominent street or highway, near a shopping center or an elementary school, or at an important intersection. Further, the twin requirements of accessibility from public transportation facilities and centrality of location with respect to residences assist religious leaders in arriving at a wise decision.

In order to serve, a church must be seen. Newcomers quickly discover the new extension project if they pass it in the routine performance of secular errands. This visual reminder of a church in the neighborhood is good publicity and operates in behalf of the institution twenty-four hours a day. A conspicuous site is worth more to the local church than a full-page advertisement in the newspaper every day of the year. Additional attention can be drawn to the institution by means of a bell, a carillon, or a record-playing amplifying system. In short, dignified and continuous publicity begins with the proper site.

To select and to purchase the best possible site is good business. It should be a corner lot of ample size. The trend is toward an acreage site sufficient for future expansion, parking, outdoor recreation, and adequate landscaping. Often an administrator is tempted to accept the gift of an inferior parcel of land and is reluctant to "look a gift horse in the mouth." However, inferior sites have handicapped many churches, and the harvest of frustration and ineffectiveness reaped by congregations so penalized should alone justify reasonable caution in selecting the proper location. Also, when possible, extension needs should be anticipated far enough in advance to permit procurement of land while prices are relatively low.

5. *An Adequate Plant.* There is no way to counteract the depressing effect of an inadequate plant upon the people of the neighborhood. Basement structures and poorly designed temporary buildings come under this category. After the first flush of enthusiasm for the extension project has passed, the ensuing years add more handicaps to the unsatisfactory beginning. Ultimately in many situations disillusionment and discouragement set in and eventually eclipse all expectations for a better plant.

Therefore the denominational executive or pastor should consider carefully the cost of the contemplated project and should enter into the situation with a clearly formulated financial plan. A guiding principle to follow is this: the plant must match or be slightly above the economic level of the homes in the territory. A financial strategy that is adequate should provide for raising sufficient funds to accomplish this reasonable objective. Indebtedness in access of $150 to $200 per family, or three or four times the annual budget for current expense, or one third to one half the value of the church property is to be avoided.

One of the best ways to assure an extension project of success is to launch it with an adequate plant at once. The people can pay for the facilities as they use them. Meanwhile urgent religious needs may be met. However, this solution is not possible in many situations.

Because of this, special planning is required, and consultation with a competent architect from the outset is recommended so that all units fit together into an over-all acceptable edifice. Commonly only part of the facilities can be erected early. Whether the worship facilities or the educational building should be erected first depends upon the circumstances locally. Conditions vary so markedly from city to city that espousal of a single approach is probably ill-advised. In one case the former commends itself; in another the latter.

For example, in a rapidly growing neighborhood or suburb where there are many children it is usually desirable to erect the educational facilities first. The heavy juvenile population places an inescapable responsibility upon the new congregation to serve the rising generation now. Here circumstances underscore the wisdom of constructing a first unit building containing Sunday-school facilities and a commodious room for worship which eventually becomes the fellowship or social hall. Temporarily portable pulpit furniture and other appropriate furnishings can bring a worship atmosphere into this room. Thus through service to children is established the best possible contact with the families who eventually will constitute the membership in a new church. Here is the point at which many new congregations begin: erection of the first unit to provide adequate facilities for an enlarged Sunday school and recreational program.

However, there is another side of the picture. In the very highest type of expensive home additions where there are few children a sanctuary may be called for as the first unit. Further, where the temporary use of a public-school building or some other facility is readily available, it may be wise to erect the worship facilities as a first unit. Clearly it is a matter requiring sound judgment, and therefore a close study of the local situation should guide the Protestant leader respecting this consideration.

6. *An Effective Ministry.* A great deal of enthusiasm may be engendered for a new church. Since the minister must be busy making pastoral calls and cultivating the neighborhood for prospective members, reliance upon laymen becomes a matter of necessity. The extension opportunity calls for an able, aggressive pastor who knows how to put laymen to work.

In a new church everything must be started at once. There is no time for delay, for procrastination. Thus the organizational work of Christian education, of youth, of women, of men, of finances, and so forth provides a broad opportunity for lay participation and lay leadership. For this reason the pastor must prove himself as a discerning administrator, capable of leading in the recruitment of many workers. While some laymen are currently ready to serve as leaders, others must be trained slowly or "grown." There is too much to be done all at once. Therefore the pastor is compelled, fortunately, to rely upon laymen and consequently launches the new project in the wisest way.

An experienced younger clergyman is ordinarily required to start a new church, although success has accompanied the efforts of pastors of varying ages. A person of boundless energy, patience, and resourcefulness, indeed a paragon of all virtues and abilities, is called for. New congregations should be ready to walk alone within five years.

WHERE NEW CHURCHES MAY BE NEEDED

Although various portions of the urban community may be in need of new Protestant churches, the present discussion directs attention to three: (1) blighted areas which have been redeveloped into fine residential neighborhoods; (2) abandoned and under-churched sections of the community; and (3) the suburbs, which constitute the most promising territory for religious extension.

Redeveloped Urban Areas. In many cities large-scale slum clearance projects have enabled more families to live in the redeveloped area than ever dwelled there before. Both private capital and public funds have gone into the erection of these apartment structures. In large cities such as New York thousands of persons have been thus rehoused. Further, some territory previously in nonresidential use has been recovered for residence purposes. Because of the magnitude of such projects many families are no longer within a mile of a church of their faith. Fundamental community changes have redistributed religious opportunities and consequently have placed thousands of persons out of reach of any church.

Redeveloped areas and public-housing projects of varying types merit examination in order to discover whether religious needs are being met. A door-to-door religious census can provide the data from which denominational responsibility may be discovered and assigned. A recent study of a typical housing project revealed that less than 2 per cent of the residents made an effort to find a neighborhood church of their faith, although most of the families desired contact with a minister and wished to participate in a local church near by. An extension project may be needed in or near recently redeveloped areas. Only a careful investigation of the situation will provide knowledge upon which church extension action can be taken.

A visit to the city engineer's office is often necessary in order to spot the location of redeveloped areas on a map and to discover how many families are currently provided housing facilities in each area. Monthly rental per dwelling unit provides a clue to the economic status of families. Generally a month's rent represents approximately one fourth of the monthly income. However, this ratio may be distorted somewhat under existing housing conditions. Redeveloped urban areas merit examination for possible church extension possibilities.

Abandoned or Underchurched Urban Neighborhoods. In neighborhood areas where church work by the major denominations has been abandoned or reduced beyond the point of necessity, need for a new church may be discovered. For example, territory fringing the central business district may be underchurched. Persons residing in rooming houses and cheap apartments have religious needs. Families living in low rental neighborhoods may cherish the ministries of the Christian church. Unless a religious institution identifies itself with the fortunes of these people by actual geographical location and by ministries fashioned to meet human needs, resources for Christian living may be withheld from an important segment of the population.

In some communities great patches of land lie unused within the municipal boundaries. Usually these territories are located just inside the city limits and were the result of hasty annexations. Since World War II residential building activity has begun in these sections. Real-estate brokers and contractors have erected block after block of new homes. Similar activity is occurring in many cities where the general population increased significantly during the

210

war years. Such territory, which at one time was adequately served, may now need additional churches.

Thus the redistribution of religious opportunity calls for an inventory of existing locations of Protestant churches to evaluate the current denominational coverage. Low income territory in the urban community is most frequently neglected or abandoned by Protestants, yet this type of area provides a real test of the vitality and relevance of religion to the human situation. It challenges the church to be inflexible with respect to the basic Christian gospel and to be flexible with respect to its patterns of churchmanship. Every urban neighborhood merits adequate facilities for a religious ministry.

The Suburbs. A third portion of the city which may need new church work is at the periphery. Urban communities tend to grow somewhat like a tree—on the perimeter. The urban fringe has proved to be a most important territory in terms of church extension possibilities. Hence a careful study of the suburbs is required in the development of a complete denominational coverage of the city. Protestants live in all parts of the urban environment.

Older portions of the city undoubtedly have many established churches. It is in the developing urban fringe that a churching lag occurs. Organized religion frequently falls behind its opportunity. Public schools are started when they are needed. New business enterprises are promptly launched to service the population. Often the church is the last project to be started in the suburbs. This lag brings regrets to representatives of organized religion, for it results in missed opportunities.

Therefore investigate the perimeter of the city. Explore every important highway leading out of the community. No avenue, boulevard, or street extension should be overlooked. Although a committee may have looked over the territory recently, examine it again. In an eastern city I discovered that 350 homes had been erected on the urban fringe during the time which elapsed between two visits to the community which were made four months apart. The urban fringe requires frequent investigation.

Secure a street map of the city and record the new residential developments which are occurring in the suburbs. Where a housing development of some size appears, locate it. Draw in newly opened streets. Drive around each block, counting the number of families

211

or housing units. Write the number in the appropriate place on the map.

When this enumeration process has been completed, record also the location of the shopping district, the public schools, and the Protestant churches. Indicate new homes under construction. Determine the location of elevated ground; of topographical, industrial, and other significant barriers; and of the approximate market value of the homes. These materials should underlie judgment in appraising church extension opportunities in the suburbs.

Homes of varying types are built in the urban fringe. There are the highly restricted areas where homes costing twenty, thirty, or fifty thousand dollars only can be erected. Lots are large, homes exceptionally attractive and beautifully landscaped, and population thinly distributed. Many of these residents are members of downtown and prestige churches. Therefore unless a new church is established while the territory is developing, it will be difficult to reach the people with a neighborhood ministry. The religious plant must be on a level at least equal to the economic value of the homes in the area, for the church edifice must be an asset to the community.

Most cities feature a suburban area of middle-class homes. Building lots are medium in size, and the residences represent a corresponding income level. Many young families from the white-collar occupations establish homes in this portion of the urban fringe. Usually Protestant in religious background or preference, these residents are easily accessible for new church work and can support a religious project after it is started. The work of the Sunday school is prominent in such areas. Many persons are potential religious leaders and workers.

The urban fringe also is likely to have an area of very modest homes, including structures ranging from the basement and shack types up to tiny but well-built two- to four-room homes. Lots are small. Many of the residents have fled city slums and substandard urban apartments. Children are numerous. Many adults are likely to have lost vital contact with organized religion. Therefore exceptional pastoral skill and patience may be required to win the people to the church. Church work is difficult, judged from the viewpoint of conventional standards, but it can be done. The opening of a new church here involves outside financial assistance. While persons of low-income status can support only a project of modest proportions, the full ministries of religion should still be made available, however it is accomplished. The unchurch-mindedness of persons in this part of the urban fringe should not cut them off from the resources of religion. Besides there is an important ministry to children which can be emphasized.

The urban fringe is the first and most important portion of the city to investigate in the search of a site for a new church. After a developing residential territory has been located, house-to-house religious census can assist in determining the extent of the Protestant opportunity. No new church should be located or started without objective information respecting the number of unchurched Protestant families or individuals resident in the area under consideration. In as much as there is no dependable rule-of-thumb method for locating new churches, reliance upon a thorough perusal of basic and relevant facts in the situation should be stressed.

Where the population of the area under consideration is found to be largely Protestant, the religious opportunity is propitious. Where the Protestants are to a significant extent made up of persons out of reach or out of touch with a neighborhood church, the success of a new church project is further assured. Too many churches of a similar type in an area fractionalize or divide the Protestant opportunity to a point of weakness. Protestantism in many cities has been greatly handicapped by the ineffective size of its churches. Extension work may mean both increasing the size of existing congregations and the establishment of new ones. In the former case, it may mean revitalizing and rebuilding a former rural church now surrounded by new homes. In the latter case a new congregation starts from scratch.

SELECTION OF A NEW CHURCH SITE

At least six factors are involved in the choice of a church site. Decisions should be made upon the broadest possible basis, and therefore Protestant leaders are urged to investigate the extension opportunity thoroughly. Consideration of the following suggestions may be regarded as essential preparation prior to a decision.

Location of New Population Development. Emergent concentrations of population occur on the edge of the urban community. This is the most prevalent type of extension opportunity. New homes are found along prominent streets, avenues, and boulevards which lead out of the city into the countryside. At first development is limited to a few scattered houses strung along the highway. Subsequently the territory fills in with many residences. Areas of relatively high ground and attractive surroundings are likely to build up first. The eventual appearance of short dead-end streets, running out at right angles with the highway, indicates an early transition stage from a "shoestring" development into a neighborhood. A study of the accompanying Figure No. 21 may illuminate this phenomenon for the reader. Should no primary barriers exist within the area, the subdivision is likely to build up on both sides of the highway with most homes situated adjacent to the shopping district. Suburban families favor reasonable proximity to a grocery store and a school. Thus the identification and location of new population developments is an important preliminary step in the discovery of a church site. A new church should be situated within a concentration of people.

People and Walking Distance. Extensive studies of parish dispersion maps indicate that a majority of the members live within one-mile radius or walking distance of the plant in the neighborhood type of church. All new churches should be launched with this consideration in mind. An extension site should be selected at a point within the territory which focuses the greatest number of residents within one-mile radius. Usually this point is at or near the shopping center or beside the elementary school.

Findings from a religious census of the territory should provide the basis for a judgment to locate a new church. Quite obviously a sufficient number of unchurched people should live in the particular neighborhood to guarantee success to the new project. Translated into numerical terms, this means that the church must have the reasonable hope of reaching eventually a membership strength of from five hundred to one thousand persons. To be assured of success the new project must have a significant rootage in the neighborhood with many prospective members near by. This is one of the most important of all factors involved in effective religious work. In launching a new church it is desirable to start the project with not less than a hundred interested families.

When transportation experts point out that people generally will

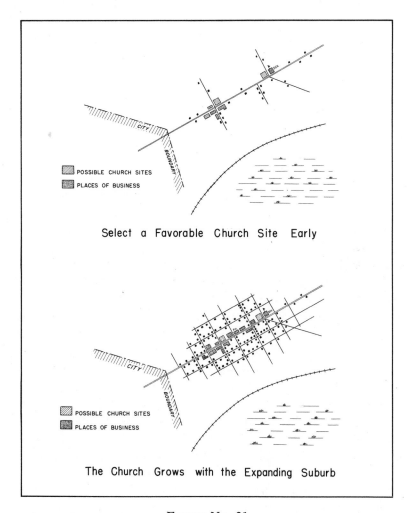

Select a Favorable Church Site Early

The Church Grows with the Expanding Suburb

FIGURE No. 21

SELECTION OF A CHURCH SITE IN A GROWING SUBURB

not walk more than one-fourth mile to board mass transportation facilities, and when public education authorities indicate that urban elementary schools are located universally with one-half mile walking distance in mind, then religious planners should give proper consideration to the factor of service distance. The new congregation should be started among the unchurched Protestant persons who reside

215

within a mile radius of the proposed new church site. Therefore the extension project location should be strategic and central. To expect children and adults to travel a greater distance for attendance and participation in the local church is to be unrealistic. A recent study reveals that people will go farther to buy groceries, to attend the theater, to a place of employment, to visit friends, than to attend the local church. This finding emphasizes the importance of considering extension projects in terms of a church of the neighborhood type.

Promise of the Territory. How many additional persons will take up residence eventually in the territory under consideration? Is there a sufficient number to provide a reasonably good future for the local church now contemplated? How many building lots remain unused although they are generally desirable for residential construction? Have tracts of vacant land been subdivided? Is this portion of the urban community building up quickly or slowly? Has residential building activity been arrested in the recent past? Is the territory a potential slum? How does the territory compare economically with other portions of the community?

Answers to these and related questions should be sought as a guide in determining the promise of the territory. When a new church project is launched, it is assumed that the territory will need religious services and ministries for several decades. The extent of the public-school facilities, the size of the commercial area, the economic level of the housing, the presence of primary barriers which delimit the size of the neighborhood, the number of unused building lots, and population trends provide clues to future prospects of the territory. These materials should be carefully evaluated and interpreted in relation to the selection of a church site.

Existing Protestant Churches. The presence of existing Protestant churches in the area under consideration needs to be noted. Record the location of each church on a map. Where cities have interdenominational comity agreements for the allocation of new church territory, the contemplated project should be cleared through the proper committee and an assignment procured. Where little or no comity understanding exists, care should be taken to project existing pieces of Protestant work from needless competition. Co-operation is desirable and should characterize new church establishment procedure. Pioneering may be necessary among the denominations in order to bring into existence comity agreements by which protection is secured not only for one's own contemplated project but also for those of the weaker denominations.

A properly conducted religious census can reveal whether the Protestant opportunity is already divided beyond the point of safety by existing churches. If a territory shows reasonable promise of growth, then a new project may be launched despite the presence of other Protestant churches. However, every reasonable precaution should be taken to avoid undermining the religious work of another denomination. When an urban church remains under five hundred persons in member strength, it is unlikely to register a significant religious impact upon the community. Therefore the contemplated new project should be assured of growth beyond the margin of bare existence. Overchurching issues in a war of attrition among the churches. Apparently competition bears more acceptable fruit in the secular world than in the spiritual.

Strategic Site Location. The preceding paragraphs have indicated the importance of four relevant considerations in the selection of a new church site. A study of hundreds of urban church parishes reveals that the ideal site is geographically at or near the center of the neighborhood the local church seeks to serve. Therefore avoid physical proximity to industrial, topographical, and kindred primary barriers. Seek a site at least one mile distant from them.

A strategic church site requires a location in or near a commercial area, on a prominent street or highway, and accessible to public transportation facilities. Proximity to an elementary school or to a commercial area is desirable provided that an adequate corner lot and off-the-street parking facilities are secured. A church that is strategically located may be found and reached easily and promptly. A church that is set upon a corner cannot be hid.

An Adequate Parcel of Land. A lot large enough to permit building expansion is desirable. Some urban communities now require off-the-street parking facilities (a minimum of thirty-four square feet of parking space per sitting in the sanctuary) to reduce traffic hazards in the neighborhood. If the alert minister or denominational administrator has gathered the data already suggested, he can now determine what size parcel of land will be adequate for present and foreseeable future needs of the congregation. However, attention should be drawn to possible future expenses for paving, curbs, gutters, and sidewalks.

The absolute fee simple title with no reservations or restrictions is generally recommended by the national headquarters of the denominations. A letter written to the proper office will bring detailed information to the reader. The purchase price of the land parcel under consideration must be viewed from the vantage point of long-term strategy rather than merely in terms of present cost. A church at the proper location may easily justify original high land costs. A poorly located site will exact a crippling penalty throughout the life of the institution. Make certain prior to purchase that the site is zoned for a church building, or where necessary petition to remove restrictions.

PROVISION FOR MINISTRIES

Finally let us highlight several important considerations. Among experienced leaders attention focuses upon the selection of a minister, the procurement of a first building unit, and long-range planning. Wisdom here pays large dividends.

An Experienced Minister. The launching of a new church is not a task for the novice. An experienced, energetic pastor should be selected. He will need immediately to call from door to door, organize the various departments of the church life, launch a financial program, conduct worship services, and challenge laymen with a vision of what is to come. It is too costly for the fledgling to learn to run a church while seeking to establish one. Therefore it is imperative that the minister be carefully chosen and sympathetically supervised during the beginning years of the extension project. A church can fail or succeed during the first few months of existence. Victory depends upon the proper pastoral leader.

An important aspect of the problem concerns itself with housing facilities for the minister. To a new congregation this means the early expenditure of funds for the purchase or the rental of a manse or parsonage. Experienced administrators recognize it as part of the cost of launching the new church and urge that the prompt procurement of a home will add considerably to the well-being of both congregation and pastor. Commonly during the initial period when public facilities are lacking, the home becomes a temporary center of activities and the dynamic nerve center of the new congregation. Thus a well-chosen minister adequately housed in pleasant surroundings opens the way for a successful extension project.

The Initial Church Building. A competent architect should prepare an over-all plan for the entire church plant, which in turn can be divided into units to be erected one at a time as funds are raised. A section of the master plan can be built, paid for, and then another should be undertaken. This step-by-step approach raises the problem of whether to erect the worship facilities or the religious education unit first. The problem arises only when the total church plant cannot be erected at once. As indicated earlier in the chapter, one should study the local situation carefully prior to making a decision to build the initial unit. Circumstances may warrant either an educational building or a sanctuary.

An inferior or inadequate plant proves a handicap to urban church work. Never therefore penalize the extension project with a basement structure, but rather invest such hard-gotten funds in a building above ground. Only as a last resort should temporary or makeshift buildings be erected. Consider the grand purpose of the venture.

In short the initial structure should be churchlike in appearance even though it is modest in size and appointment. When the congregation has grown and its building requirements can be more accurately ascertained, attention should be given to a permanent sanctuary. At that time the all-purpose edifice erected earlier to meet an urgent need can be converted to a social hall or religious education building. However, for the present one should stress realism in procuring facilities.

Long-Range Planning. When a new church is established in a particular neighborhood, people expect it to minister to needs currently unmet. In order to fulfil this expectation definite plans for the future should be formulated. Specific objectives in terms of membership increase, religious education enrollment advance, functioning of organizations, ministry to individuals, plant expansion and construction, and so forth should be set and a time schedule established. The newly organized congregation must continue to think in terms of its complete religious role in the community. Plans for five, ten, and twenty years ahead should be thought through by the committee. The local church may thus be enabled to move into its future with growing effectiveness and strength. An extension project is a noble undertaking. Many reach the status of an independent, self-supporting organization within five years after inception. Such is a worthy goal of every new congregation.

DECALOGUE FOR ESTABLISHING NEW CHURCHES

1. Investigate the urban fringe for possible new church projects.
2. Investigate abandoned and underchurched urban neighborhoods for extension possibilities.
3. Investigate redeveloped urban areas and large-scale housing projects of varying types for conditions which warrant a new church.
4. Use a house-to-house religious census to discover the nature and extent of the Protestant opportunity.
5. Do not enter the territory unless there is a sufficient number of Protestant persons out of touch or out of reach of a local church to promise eventually a congregation of at least five hundred members.
6. Secure a prominent corner parcel of land with an absolute fee simple title for the new church site.
7. Do not locate a new church on a side street or near primary barriers— that is, railroad yards, cemetery, park, industrial plant, golf course.
8. Do not locate a new church nearer than one and three-fourths miles to another plant of the same denomination.
9. Secure a territory allocation through the local council of churches and avoid needless competition with other denominations.
10. Build an attractive structure above ground for either educational or worship purposes as circumstances warrant, if the entire plant cannot be constructed immediately.

CHAPTER VIII

Protestant Strategy and Denominational Teamwork

URBAN Protestantism is confronted by an urgent need to devise effective denominational teamwork patterns and a forward-looking interdenominational strategy. Discussion of this complicated problem was purposely postponed to the closing chapter of the book in order to build up a pragmatic orientation to city church problems against which a significant exploration might be wisely pursued. Thus essential materials presented in the foregoing pages may have stimulated in turn a serious consideration of the principal difficulties and possibilities inherent in downtown church work, in a religious ministry to apartment residents, and in local church work to neighborhoods and to the suburbs. The unfinished task remaining consists in the development of an over-all pattern of Protestant work related to the total urban community.

DEMAND FOR CITY-WIDE CHURCH PLANNING

Scientific planning is no longer novel in the fields of education, business, and government. Public-school administrators commonly take annual censuses to discover the number of preschool children residing in various parts of the urban community. Such information is used in making wise decisions. When a need for additional teachers and physical space becomes objectively apparent, plans are drafted to procure the necessary personnel and facilities. In short, research and planning characterize the best in the educational field today.

Likewise in the commercial world scientific studies underlie many important decisions. The proper geographical location of manufacturing establishments, restaurants, branch banks, gas stations, neighborhood businesses, and kindred enterprises is determined commonly by a thorough investigation of the prospects for success at various site locations. Adequate consideration is given to the type and size of the establishment also. It is the purpose of the site engineers to explore the situation objectively, gathering all relevant facts. If other commercial enterprises have failed in a particular neighborhood, the causes of failure are scrupulously ferreted out and evaluated before a new business is launched. When it comes to a matter of dollars and cents, sentiment as a guiding principle is infrequently tolerated. In the grim sphere of profit and loss decisions to establish a business are formulated after weighing carefully the discernible prospects for material success. Obviously where money is involved, foolish risks are shunned.

Consider the field of municipal government where research projects of manifold types are constantly being carried on. Scientific investigation of living conditions, population trends, land-use patterns, traffic flow, residential building activity, and kindred phenomena underlies proposals for change in the city. Wise expansion of public-serving facilities, annexation of land, and urban improvements derive from such factual studies. Indeed public agencies have discovered a great new ally in municipal planning. Not only has this scientific approach become an accepted pattern today in cities, but the idea has been adopted by many urban counties also. Joint regulations pointing in the direction of orderly development coordinated between city and county planning agencies are gaining in acceptance. This is the mark of forward-looking municipal and county government. Good cities are planned cities.

In view of these remarkable developments one wonders why scientific planning has come so tardily to organized religion. Surely no necessary hiatus exists between pragmatic wisdom and piety. An approach which brings so much benefit in other spheres of urban life merits wider study and eventual appropriation by religious leaders. Already the prolonged use of haphazard methods of Protestant church work in the city has proved as costly and fruitless to religion as to business. No Protestant leader wants to make a poor decision when he can make a wise one.

Today religious planning is an urgent consideration. Because scientific surveys reveal that critical churching problems exist in nearly every American city, Protestantism must confront this disturbing reality and develop an effective strategy of work. Changes brought about by the recent urban revolution in America aggravate the local community and place churches under fresh jeopardy. Recent national mergers of major and minor denominations have introduced shocking competition into heretofore relatively placid situations. Even the ascension of sect groups into denominational status, as revealed by a broadening emphasis upon an educated clergy and upon the use of nontabernacle edifices, has complicated further the work of urban Protestantism. Also, carried over from the past are manifold unsolved churching problems. It is this very accumulation of difficulties which underscores the present urgency for scientific religious planning. Evidently mere passage of time avails little in problem solving. Meanwhile funds and leadership are consumed in a prodigal fashion. With so many communities reporting distress and continued churching difficulty Protestantism can no longer postpone an orderly geographical arrangement of its religious institutions and a scientific attack upon its problems. For a better tomorrow the faith must formulate plans today.

CITY CHURCHES IN TROUBLE

The need for urban Protestant planning is better understood if attention can be drawn to several critical churching problems. Surely the experienced leader is familiar with conditions which commonly harass congregations and disturb administrators. Within recognizable categories let us consider five of these problems which are amenable to survey processes and over-all planning.

Churches in Financial Distress. Certain urban churches appear incapable of financing their own way. This is evident where the local congregation repeatedly fails to meet the budgetary requirements of the ministry called for by the neighborhood. In such cases what is an enlightened policy of mission support? Under what circumstances does subsidy result in pauperization? Is there an acceptable procedure for handling churches which across many years have received aid but have been handicapped by a part-time or inadequate ministry (students, retired ministers, and lay preachers)? Should institutional religious work to needy neighborhoods be financed and carried on within denominations or under interdenominational auspices? How does subsidized work fit into an over-all strategy for Protestantism in the city?

Frequently financial distress is a symptom of a fundamental church-ing difficulty, for example, poor location, needless competition, chang-ing neighborhood, and general planlessness within Protestantism. These conditions invariably produce small churches which in turn encounter distressing financial limitations. Thus the first step toward solution consists in a discovery of primary causes of financial trouble. Since most city church difficulties are interrelated, wise leaders look for the taproot. An approach through scientific survey and planning can aid in the separation of symptoms from basic causes.

Churches in Poor Locations. To the experienced churchman a poor location means serious trouble sooner or later for the congregation. Who has not noted the churches which are within a few blocks from success, and yet Dame Fortune disdains to smile upon them? When the buildings are hidden from view, one soon discovers the pragmatic significance of the maxim: in city church work out of sight means out of mind. Among the congregations so handicapped may be found these typical situations: locations on a side street, in the mid-dle of a city block, at the end of a dead-end street, pocketed off in an obscure corner of the neighborhood, caught in a sparsely settled area where residential development has been arrested, or jammed against a primary barrier (factories, railroad tracks, lake shore, river bank, large cemetery or park, and so on). If newcomers and strangers have difficulty in finding the church or in reaching it by means of public transportation facilities, one should study the situation to dis-cover whether the church has a strategic location. Some survey specialists regard poor location as the most common cause of urban church difficulty. It is the taproot of many distressing problems.

Churches in Competition. When city churches within the same denomination are situated too close to one another, or there is a dearth of Protestant constituents in a territory occupied by several congregations, a condition of competition ensues. This is conspicu-ously evident in neighborhoods severely circumscribed by primary barriers. Small neighborhoods produce small churches. An experi-enced pastor knows that only so many actual and potential members are resident. Sister churches placed in close proximity invariably divide the Protestant opportunity, thereby fractionalizing it to the point of debilitating competition. Thus a hectic scramble for new-comers becomes the pattern for a normal parish ministry. As a result some congregations fall by the wayside or shrivel to ineffective size. In such an atmosphere teamwork appears as a theoretical consideration and ecumenicity remains largely a vocal effort. The plight of the individual congregation is so desperate that mere survival appears a worthy goal. Who has not witnessed such chaos in city church work?

Further, the needless multiplication of Protestant churches downtown, in neighborhoods, and in the suburbs discloses a ruthless type of interdenominational competition which produces distress and demoralizes religious work. Competition surely makes an anomalous contribution to the common good. The temptation to exaggerate the benefits of Protestant rivalry is greatest when one approaches the problem from a parochial and short-range viewpoint. Often the evil effects of competition remain obscured during the growth of a community. But alas, churches struggling in static or declining neighborhoods derive scant consolation from this source. Obviously, without planning, Protestantism in the city becomes a series of emulous contests between congregations with the outcome, no matter who wins, a Pyrrhic victory.

Churches in Transitional Situations. Nearly every city has churches which are in transitional situations. Population changes frequently alter otherwise promising Protestant territory. Where large or continuing in-migration of people of contrasting ethnic background, racial stock, or economic status occurs, the ratio among faiths is disturbed, becomes unbalanced, and inevitably imposes hardship upon congregations. Under changed conditions efforts at program adjustment on the part of individual churches may take on herculean proportions. Certainly no experienced leader thinks it is easy to change over from a bilingual ministry to one featuring English solely; to go from one ethnic specialty to another; to shift from religious work among Caucasians to a ministry for Negroes, Puerto Ricans, Mexicans, or Orientals; to make the hazardous transition from a conventional church to an institutional program. So desperate may conditions be in some cases that adjustment may actually mean discontinuance or merger with another church or even relocation to a new territory. Yet whatever form the metamorphosis takes, the congregation enters a difficult period of transition. Urban change means fundamental religious adjustment.

But this problem has an additional aspect. When the city bursts its boundaries, it engulfs the adjacent countryside. As a result suburban churches which may have started out as open country or village institutions become menaced by "culture clash." Such internal conflict is endemic to the suburb. Aggressive urban newcomers begin competition for religious leadership positions against older residents who perhaps are prone to favor a leisurely church pace into whatever modest or mighty future lies ahead. Not so among the vigorous newcomers. As in the business world so in the religious field they are go-getters. New construction or major improvements of existing church facilities are urged by them, and espousal of progressive patterns of churchmanship are enthusiastically advocated. The disturbing impact of these new ideas ruffles the rural complacency, provoking a conflict between the groups commonly described as "culture clash." To all appearances progress and change have been thrust upon unwilling old-time members, galvanizing them into unhoped-for action. Though the ultimate outcome may prove highly worth while and generally acceptable to all persons concerned, the process of achieving this goal is often scarcely a road of roses. Evidently churches in transition are exposed to shock, turmoil, and reintegration. Vision, tact, and patience are relevant virtues under the circumstances. Among the congregations facing this difficulty are recent mergers, recent relocations, altered opportunities, and suburban churches. Here again scientific survey and planning can prove a boon by interpreting the adjustment process and by lifting up long-range objectives.

Number of Churches—Too Many or Too Few. What administrator has not wrestled with the problem of how many Protestant churches are needed in a city? Patently some communities have too many congregations, others have too few. That the difficulty has been greatly complicated by the wide circulation of spurious principles is apparent to leaders who consider the problem with adequate reference to trends and to basic neighborhood structure. Recent sociological studies disclose that population growth and decline are differential across the city, and hence Protestant leaders are impelled to develop a more discriminating approach than was held previously. Some parts of the urban community grow rapidly while others remain static or even register population loss. Thus multiplicity or dearth of churches invariably applies to specific neighborhoods of the urban community. Likewise the question of number of congregations is related to local standards of overchurching and underchurching and to principles of comity adopted by the denominational leaders involved. An enlightened approach is needed in many American cities.

Hence answers need to be found for a number of important questions. What objective criteria reveal that a neighborhood is overchurched and vice versa? What considerations enter the decision to shift any congregation out of a competitive situation? Where should a new church be located? How near may it be placed to existing Protestant churches? In what ways may churching problems find solution through scientific survey and planning? Before this chapter is closed, at least a partial answer may be found to these basic questions.

The present account of five common difficulties opens the topic for more detailed exploration by the reader. Action deriving from ignorance of the facts and the processes involved generally produces a postponement rather than a solution of churching problems. Surely this is not the objective desired by harassed city church administrators. In contrast scientific procedure frequently eliminates several problems through one wise decision, yielding long-range benefits as a bonus. Individual congregations prosper when critical problems are solved in a broad objective frame of reference. Fewer churches require mission subsidy, and denominational teamwork moves toward actualization. Clearly a scientific approach can guide urban Protestantism into the future with co-ordinated strength, confidence, and a new sense of reality. Planning is indispensable to religious progress.

CHURCHING PROBLEMS AND COMMUNITY KNOWLEDGE

The Protestant church functions in an environment which can be objectively known and measured. People and things make up this milieu. Set down among the homes of its constituents, the church has a location as definite as that of the near-by elementary school. This close identification of church with environment calls attention to the importance of a working knowledge of the community. To be effective Protestantism must know its setting.

Physical Structure of the City. Acquaintanceship with the structure of the city is a fundamental type of information which Protestant leaders should possess. Specifically it consists in the composite body of knowledge abstracted from an adequate study of primary barriers, topographical features, zoning regulations, actual land use, plus the position and extent of residential neighborhoods. Eventual discovery of pockets of residential territory derives from such a survey. Actually the physical structure of a community is God-given (that is, lakes, rivers, elevated ground, cliffs, irregular terrain, and so on), being modified somewhat by man-made barriers (for example, railroad tracks, sidings, industrial installations, large parks and cemeteries, and so on). A thorough study of both factors prepares one for understanding the city. The urgent need for sound Protestant strategy makes a knowledge of neighborhood structure essential.

Communities above 5,000 inhabitants are generally multineighborhood in structure. For instance, the recent analysis of a city of 70,000 residents disclosed 7 basic neighborhoods in addition to the downtown area. Further, a community of 180,000 boasts 10 such territories, while a city of 1,000,000 persons may have 18 or more. Fortunately the boundaries of each residential territory can be delineated from data already available in the local community. This fact should be of considerable interest to religious leaders since knowledge of physical structure underlies proper church placement and long-range Protestant strategy. Many church problems cannot be solved without such information.

Population Changes. Whatever happens to persons is of interest to Protestant planning since the basic ingredient of urban church work is people. Population trend information for a city, neighborhood, or suburb by ten-year periods may be found in the reference room of the public library. Trends covering the past twenty to fifty years are usually studied. An estimate of the current population can be furnished by the city engineer's office or the chamber of commerce. However, at best these are general figures. Church leaders need to examine the trends within racial and ethnic groups also. In larger cities the data are usually available by wards or by census tracts. Resource persons to contact include the librarian, the city engineer, and a professor of sociology in the near-by college.

Further, sociologists call attention to the fact that racial and ethnic groups occupy definite areas of settlement.[1] It is essential therefore to prepare a map showing the location (by street boundaries) and extent of each concentration of homogeneous population. Because the fortunes of some congregations are adversely affected by proximity to nonassimilable groups, Protestant planners need to reckon with the situation. Not only do population growth and decline have an effect upon congregations, but also the changing composition which results in displacement of one racial group or one faith group by another leaves its telltale impression. Most churching mistakes could have been avoided if leaders had kept themselves informed respecting population changes. The people of the urban community are the people of the church. Usually the neighborhood determines the type of ministry required.

The Domicile Factor. Income determines largely in what part of the urban community an inhabitant will live. Though the city man may be dissatisfied with present housing facilities, he knows that he must earn more money in order to live in a better home. This economic factor should not be lost sight of in an intelligent discussion of urban housing. It is basic to local church finances.

Further, the conditions under which people live may reveal the type of religious ministry required. Do housing facilities encourage people to move frequently or to stay put? A discovery of whether the urban population lives in apartment structures, public-housing projects, single-family homes, multifamily buildings, or substandard dwelling units is essential in formulating basic Protestant strategy. Types of housing are localized to various portions of the community, and this fact both complicates the task of the local church and opens the possibility for an amazing range of ministry. Close observation should be given to multiple-housing areas and to suburbs. A survey can reveal to what extent the trend toward use of apartments is increasing. The erection of many new homes on the periphery of the city furnishes a clue respecting extension work and also the wise relocation of competing churches. Information procured from the public library, the city engineer, the building inspector, the local housing authority, and other sources can prove

[1] Consult the latest housing supplement, U. S. Census, for your city. It is entitled *Block Statistics.*

useful in drafting a city-wide Protestant strategy and in dealing with local churches in trouble. A study of the domicile factor can add definiteness to the ministry of religion in the city.

Supplementary Information. Certain additional data can provide enrichment of insight. In the discussion of some churching problems it is essential to discover the number of births to residents of the particular city or neighborhood. Information available from the health department can be procured for each year covering a fifteen- or twenty-year span. Differentiation between Caucasian and nonwhite persons is usually available also. Further, public-school enrollment trends should be gathered by individual school and by race, showing separate breakdowns for elementary and secondary pupils. These data may be procured for each year over a trend period of fifteen or twenty years. Still further, special studies of deteriorated areas, of juvenile delinquency, and so on should be sought out and scrutinized. In short, local Protestant leaders must leave no stone unturned in the search for relevant facts and useful insights.

These four basic types of data plus a thorough knowledge of Protestant work constitute the minimum range of information essential to undergird an adequate church strategy in the city. Since these facts may prove useful to all denominations, they should be placed in a common repository—the offices of the local council or federation of churches. Clearly a local church does not function in a sociological vacuum. Rather its environment can be described in objective terms, and at any time religious leaders can achieve a working knowledge of the milieu. General competence in this field will assist greatly in the solution of churching problems.

Finally Protestantism must learn to work the community the way the city grows. Protestant strategy should commence at the heart of the city and extend outward. Start with a downtown church. This anchor unit should be situated within the geographical boundaries of the downtown territory. Next additional churches within the denomination should be dispersed to residential neighborhoods throughout the city and thence into the suburbs. Where a communion extends itself in a pattern congruent with city growth, churching problems are kept to a minimum. Contrariwise where

Protestantism ignores or works against the direction in which the city develops, serious trouble is soon encountered. The laws of city development cannot be flaunted even by a church without penalty.

Federations and councils of churches may render significant practical service by helping denominations learn and relearn this fundamental lesson. In portions of the city where population displacement occurs and neighborhoods change over from Protestant to Jewish or Roman Catholic, some Protestant churches may be forced to withdraw from the territory and to seek relocation sites in the suburbs. However, withdrawal should never take place without conclusive objective information procured by means of religious census. The suburban fringe requires constant vigilance and occasional launching of new congregations in order to keep pace with the growth of the city. Selection of church sites should be made against a knowledge of the pattern of community growth. This strategy will reduce the number of churching mistakes.

STRATEGY OF CHURCH PLACEMENT

Against the aforementioned background of essential community information let us now evaluate the geographical dispersion of urban Protestant churches. These buildings or plants function primarily as rallying centers for the congregation. They become the focus of parish life and of religious activities, thus calling attention to the importance of proper location in basic strategy. Because Protestantism in the city often remains unco-ordinated with urban neighborhood structure, a chaotic pattern seems to characterize dispersion. This is evident wherever churches apparently are located without due regard to barriers and to concentrations of population. Strange as it may appear, some pastors and administrators find no cause for alarm in the situation, having already accepted the topsy-like arrangement as inevitable. Such an attitude is fraught with considerable peril and eventually must give way to a rational viewpoint which arises from an objective analysis of the situation.

Despite the helter-skelter scattering of Protestant churches to various parts of the urban environment, a remnant of the current pattern can probably be retained. Obviously not all churches are misplaced; neither do all maintain a ministry under conditions of competition, financial distress, or other kinds of imminent jeopardy. Indeed congregations well placed and well spaced furnish a nucleus around which the beginnings of a sound strategy can be established. Thus preparation for a well-conceived church placement strategy may involve thinking about one's own community as the ensuing presentation unfolds and endeavoring to apply the practical generalizations to one's local situation. Experience discloses that at least four fundamental considerations deserve the attention of alert Protestant leaders—that is, the position, spacing, clustering, and ratio of churches in the urban environment.

1. *Position of Churches.* Each city church occupies a definite parcel of ground. By its very location this site determines largely the extent and type of ministry possible under the circumstances. To overlook this insight is to miss completely the point of the present discussion. A downtown location indicates a community-wide ministry, whereas a neighborhood site points to an indigenous religious program with a limited geographical outreach. Location in a tiny or sparsely built-up neighborhood or changing territory means a precarious existence mitigated only in part by mission subsidy, yet inevitably a ministry under the shadow of continuous financial hazard. Furthermore the erection of a building at any particular site means that the facilities are intended to serve a generation of residents. This is a reasonable expectation. If, however, the location proves a poor one, the congregation will be severely penalized throughout the years. Because so much is at stake, the position (geographical location) of churches should always be determined with great care.

Thus the relative significance of each site in terms of effective church work should be assayed by means of an investigation of the number of persons who reside within the service radius (one mile). People are the ultimate test of a proper church location. Hence the question: where is to be found a substantial concentration of unchurched Protestants? A corollary query naturally follows: is the church site at the best location to serve these persons? If not difficulty will be encountered in catching the residents' attention and in holding their interest. That indicates why the more people who reside within the service radius of the church, the better prospects for success the institution has. This consideration is still the most important factor in city church planning.

Further, a site should be examined for its proximity to primary barriers. It has been discovered that churches situated too close (nearer than one mile) to large parks, bodies of water, irregular terrain, factories, railroad yards, and so forth sacrifice part of a normal parish opportunity.[2] Obviously barriers prevent city land from being used for homes and also block access to adjacent neighborhoods. An inevitable result is fewer people from which to build a congregation. Few urban churches can withstand such losses. Rarely do misplaced churches compensate for the sacrifice by attracting a larger number of persons from beyond the service radius in other directions. On the contrary extensive field research reveals that when any territory within a normal service radius is given up, it is irrevocably lost. To put the matter plainly, if an inordinate amount of territory within one-mile service radius is, and may be expected to remain, in nonresidential use, one may properly question the strategic value of the particular site. Both old congregations and new extension projects come under this principle. Constituents cannot be drawn from territory where no one lives. Somehow this valuable insight eludes the serious attention of Protestant leaders when church locations are being selected.

An additional consideration calls attention to the predicament of Caucasian churches stranded against the invading edge of crowded Negro neighborhoods and of the Negro churches adjacent to stable Caucasian territories. The principle may apply to other racial groups also. Areas of prominent change scramble church fortunes and place church futures under jeopardy. Large-scale changes of population, especially to persons of another faith or race, accentuate distress and may hasten the death of a congregation. It is readily seen that whatever happens within the one-mile service radius of a local church impairs or improves the lot of the congregation. This basic insight underlies the drafting of a sound strategy of church placement in the city.

A misplaced church wastes money and leadership. Such prodi-

[2] Consult pp. 163-66 for a detailed discussion of this problem.

gality is unwarranted today and can be avoided by intelligent action. Therefore when the position of a city church is under consideration, scientific investigation should be made of (a) its proximity to primary barriers, (b) the potential of Protestant population in the neighborhood, and (c) the amount of land not in residential use within a one-mile service range of the site. Without a factual report covering these three basic factors, local leaders should abstain from investing funds for renovation, remodeling, or new work. Protestants should investigate thoroughly the relative merits of each location before any construction is undertaken. Here is the fundamental question: is the church where it ought to be? A well-chosen site becomes a tremendous religious asset.

2. *Spacing of Churches.* This term refers to linear distance between churches of the same denomination. The principle does not apply interdenominationally. Congregations within a city and metropolitan area need to be spaced to avoid competition. Wide experience plus extensive scientific investigation reveal that not less than double the service radius of a neighborhood church or approximately one and three-fourths miles should be normative. In cases where Protestant opportunity is severely circumscribed (for example, communities in which Mormons, Roman Catholics, and Jews predominate numerically) the minimum spacing should be two miles. This generalization applies also to residential developments where population is thin because homes are erected on large acreage-type plots. So fundamental to urban church effectiveness is this principle of spacing that denominational leaders are wisely advised to insist upon its universal application. The facts warrant this contention.

There appear to be at least two reasons for emphasizing adequate spacing. First, competition within a denomination is thereby prevented or else reduced to a level of insignificance. If the churches are not spread out spatially, they will interfere with each other's ministry. Thus in a city-wide application of the principle each resident finds himself within the service radius of but one church of his communion. Should the individual desire to attend some other church of the denomination, he must go out of his neighborhood. Such travel would be farther than is normal for the rank and file of urban residents. This is a distance penalty which must be paid by persons who do not patronize the neighborhood church within whose service radius they currently reside. Clearly no two churches of the same communion should be so placed as to cause overlapping of each other's service radius. Each congregation should have a neighborhood of its own in which to serve. A duplication of ministry is both wasteful and unwarranted.

Second, proper spacing permits flexibility in denominational strategy. Where a church is surrounded by a large number of Protestants, it can grow rapidly and soon count its membership in thousands. On the other hand the local church set down in a more restricted neighborhood may achieve its maximum growth when its membership aggregates a few hundred constituents. In the first instance the congregation is in a strong position to withstand any significant reduction of opportunity which the passing years may bring. In spite of neighborhood changes, possibly necessitating membership and budget reductions, the stronger church can still continue its ministry on an effective level. Its fortunes rise and fall with the fluctuating neighborhood conditions. The resultant reduced staff and more modest program furnish a denominational flexibility so sorely needed in the city. However, neighborhood changes cannot be contained where churches are too close to one another. This is the tragedy of intradenominational competition.

Where there are too many churches of the same communion, some congregations have to move, or merge, or go out of existence. This eventuality is not relished by anyone. For the loss of capital funds involved in closing or relocating churches, as staggering as it proves to be, is small compared to the loss of morale and spiritual *esprit de corps* entailed. Tiny and/or competitive city churches find it difficult to survive neighborhood changes. They have so few reserves to draw upon. Indeed, having lived for so long on the edge of urban ineffectiveness and financial insolvency, they find that any notable reduction of religious opportunity seriously jeopardizes their very existence. Smallness itself is one of the fruits of misplacement or intradenominational competition. Thus the proper or adequate spacing of churches makes possible a flexibility of denominational work which is a fundamental urban requirement. Sound Protestant strategy starts with sound denominational strategy.

3. *Clustering of Churches.* In earlier paragraphs attention was

drawn to the wisdom of drafting church strategy according to the basic structure of the city and congruous with the way a community grows. An adequate knowledge of these dual factors becomes our starting point. Simply stated, this is how a desirable Protestant pattern works. The denomination establishes or retains a church in the downtown area. Further, additional congregations are established or retained in each of the principal neighborhoods throughout the city and adjacent suburbs. The achievement of this geographical pattern represents a sound principle of urban church planning. It is one which covers the entire community, leaving no territory without a ministry.

Obviously when various denominations utilize the strategy outlined above, several Protestant churches are likely to be found both in the downtown territory and in each of the neighborhoods. This multiple church phenomenon is common to religious work in the city. Described as clustering, it is inevitable but does not necessarily result in debilitating competition. Clustering arises from the paucity of proper church locations. Strategic church sites are found within a relatively circumscribed area both downtown and elsewhere. Ideal downtown locations are found in proximity to the "green," to the post office or other prominent public buildings, one of which is often the focus of public transportation facilities. Further, experience discloses that a neighborhood church is advantageously placed when situated adjacent to an elementary school or in or at a shopping center. Obviously the number of corner lots of the proper size and ideal location available in each neighborhood is definitely limited, and for that reason Protestant churches commonly appear in clusters. Each congregation wisely seeks the best possible site. In so doing edifices become focused into a relatively small area in neighborhoods across the city (Figure No. 22). So typical of urban religious work is this propensity that the church not found in the cluster is likely to function under needless handicap.

However, only churches of diverse denominations should be encouraged to cluster. Within a denomination congregations are competitive when found close together. Clustering is a principle kept for interdenominational use only. Here is surely a point at which the local council or federation of churches can serve as an educational agency, encouraging the development of a sound pattern

236

of Protestant work throughout the entire urban community. Obviously the council cannot prevent mistakes, but it can furnish technical advice which may perceptibly reduce the number of serious churching blunders. There is abundant evidence showing

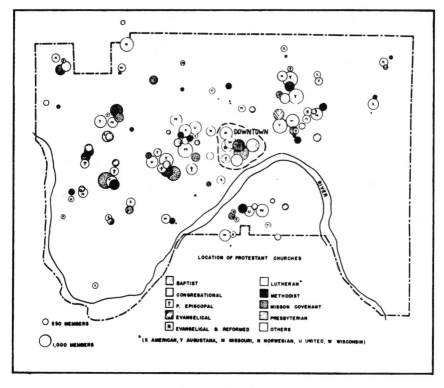

LOCATION OF PROTESTANT CHURCHES

☐ BAPTIST	☐ LUTHERAN*
☐ CONGREGATIONAL	■ METHODIST
⊞ P. EPISCOPAL	▨ MISSON COVENANT
▨ EVANGELICAL	▨ PRESBYTERIAN
⊠ EVANGELICAL & REFORMED	☐ OTHERS

○ 250 MEMBERS

◯ 1,000 MEMBERS

*(X AMERICAN, Y AUGUSTANA, M MISSOURI, N NORWEGIAN, U UNITED, W WISCONSIN)

FIGURE No. 22

PROTESTANT CHURCH CLUSTERING IN A LARGER CITY

that religious leaders will not make a foolish decision when available information points to an intelligent one.

4. *Ratio of Churches.* The proper ratio of churches for an urban community is ultimately derived from a study of the gross number of churched and unchurched residents. The former is discovered by an inspection of membership rolls, but the latter requires a special project. A house-to-house religious census is widely used to discover unchurched persons and where they reside. Suggestions for the organization and administration of such a project are given

elsewhere (Chapter III) in this book. Yet it is important to emphasize here that factual information procured by means of a religious census must underlie a scientific approach to the ratio of churches. With such data in hand Protestant leaders can analyze the materials and determine upon an appropriate course of action. Generally speaking, unchurched persons reside in all parts of the city. This surprising fact raises several problems.

What should be done about unchurched individuals who reside within the one-mile service radius of a small Protestant church? Prompt cultivation of the opportunity is demanded. An obvious answer is to encourage the congregation to strive toward effective size (five hundred active members or more). However, whether the church is large or small, it has a responsibility to absorb as many unchurched persons as possible. Certainly before additional churches are established in a territory, small congregations should get a chance to expand their constituencies. This logical precaution needs to receive more serious consideration in American cities. Who has not noted that approximately one half of the Protestant churches in many communities are too small to conduct an effective urban ministry?

Further, the ratio problem is related to the current dispersion of Protestant congregations. This disturbing consideration impels local religious leaders to re-examine the geographical position of all existing churches. To what extent are the religious units co-ordinated with urban neighborhood structure, that is, spaced or clustered according to the principles described above? A local survey may reveal that the proper ratio of churches for the reader's city has already been reached, and what may be required now is merely a thoroughgoing evangelistic program on the part of each congregation. By such a project all persons out of touch with organized religion can ultimately be drawn into religious fellowship. This primary consideration should be explored fully before a new church is contemplated.

If both a church survey and a religious census reveal the necessity of establishing one or more new churches, it remains to be pointed out that the principles of position, spacing, and clustering should be regarded in the selection of sites. Further, practical suggestions for new church work are described fully in Chapter VII. In every case the presence of a substantial concentration of unchurched Protestant people, and that factor alone, constitutes an opportunity for church extension work. Whether these persons are Caucasian, Negro, Oriental, or Spanish-speaking Americans, the problem of launching a new congregation is essentially the same. Each new congregation should have the prospect of reaching effective size (five hundred active members or more) within a reasonable time limit. This basic principle determines objectively the proper ratio of churches in the city and suburbs. Urban churching blunders usually stem from inadequate information and sheer ignorance of sound guiding principles. Forward-looking administrators, however, are discovering the inherent values of a scientific approach. Today's Protestant leaders do not desire to repeat the mistakes of their forebears.

Here then are four important considerations useful to Protestant leaders in establishing a sound interdenominational strategy in the urban environment. It is church planning based upon sociological facts, administrative experience, and an over-all view. Out of this discussion may arise the desire to survey one's own community. If so, the reader can readily prepare a map showing exact church locations. A special symbol or color assigned to each communion will reveal denominational patterns and spacing. Clusters of churches will undoubtedly appear in the downtown area and in various neighborhoods. As noted above, clustering is endemic to urban Protestantism because downtown churches tend to "skim" the entire city, whereas neighborhood units feature an indigenous ministry restricted to a one-mile service radius. Congregations of the latter type, if located in close proximity to primary barriers, are deprived of a full religious opportunity. Further, the correct ratio of churches with respect to the population of a city depends upon the Protestant potential of the community. Since considerations of this sort may be explored and studied factually, analysis of one's own community can prove a rewarding investigation. Discovery of local conditions may open the way for constructive change and may challenge Protestant leaders to provide a more effective ministry in the city. Adequate preparation for the future starts with wise planning.

A PATTERN OF DENOMINATIONAL TEAMWORK

When cities grow beyond approximately five thousand inhabitants, urban structure becomes complex, and a notable result is multiple neighborhoods. A corresponding intricacy within denominational work should be expected and actually does take place. More people mean more churches. Whereas formerly a single church was adequate to the needs of the population in the village or town, the present enlarged community may necessitate the establishment of an additional church or two. Multiplication of urban neighborhoods catches the attention of Protestant leaders and indicates that the city is growing beyond the reach of the ministry of existing churches. An extension project may need to be placed in each emerging neighborhood.

When a communion's work in the city reaches the proportions of two or more churches, teamwork appears as an inescapable consideration. Both major and minor denominations have developed concern recently over internal co-operation. Somehow the need for joint planning and a city-wide strategy is becoming apparent, and the concern goes deeper than a selfish desire to set merely one's own house in order. Organized Christianity aspires for effectiveness through co-ordinated effort. This is a worthy ambition.

Individual congregations often set forth unmodestly to do all the religious work of the city. Primary ignorance of the basic structure of the community combined with a misapprehension respecting the types of urban ministry required frequently leads churches to embark upon a solo role. No genuine harm is intended, the intention is merely to avoid intrachurch entanglements and ecclesiastical red tape, and perhaps to demonstrate the efficacy of one's own program. Some ministers sincerely regard denominational and Protestant-wide co-operation as fruitless unless it returns tangible benefits to their own congregations. Co-ordinated endeavor is favored only up to the point where it enhances the reputation of the host church or furnishes prospective persons for membership. Although this viewpoint is understandable, it is scarcely laudable. Few pastors are ready to say that a single congregation, however strong, can minister to an entire city. •

Mistakes in judgment and interpretation arise when preoccupation with parochial matters becomes a ruling concern. A healthy interest in the welfare of all the churches of one's denomination in a city must underlie a sound pattern of denominational teamwork. This interest should be implemented by willing and adequate participation in the varying fortunes of the denomination as she undertakes her task in the total metropolitan environment.

Perhaps the urban predicament can be illustrated by a simple parable. The story is told of a fowler who found it easy to capture game. Each time the net was cast, his effort resulted in amazing success. Yet the huntsman was of but ordinary gifts. The explanation is simple: as the net settled down over them, the birds became panic-stricken and struggled chaotically and individually to escape. It was every bird for himself, with teamwork but the remotest objective of terror-filled hearts. Thus the hunter pursued his facile occupation, capturing thousands of relatively helpless game.

Eventually in birdland a state of crisis was reached, and the matter of survival became a haunting concern. Since the birds habitually gathered in flocks and therefore were quite susceptible to capture, several of the number determined that a desperate attempt be made to alter the current intolerable situation. After long deliberation a plan was formulated by which their very gregarious propensity could be utilized as an instrument of survival. It was agreed that when the fowler cast his net again, all birds would co-ordinate their efforts to escape. Since no individual was sufficiently strong to guarantee victory, it was necessary to pool many modest strengths in the interest of the flock.

Soon the hunter returned to the vicinity and cast his net over the flock. Immediately each bird thrust its head through the nearest mesh and beat its wings furiously. This concerted surprise action lifted the net quickly into the air, out of reach of the fowler, and the birds flew away and deposited it in a near-by treetop from which it was easy to escape. Co-operation accomplished what isolated effort proved incapable of achieving. Further, all the birds escaped harm, and this act of concerted action lowered the hazard of survival for all individuals. When subsequent attempts to capture prey failed, the fowler moved to a fresh hunting ground where the game had not discovered the merits of teamwork.

Evidently this parable contains an important truth applicable

241

to urban Protestantism. A single church of any denomination can scarcely serve the entire city. Many of the units become defeated and fall by the wayside when each congregation works in solitude. Reliance upon a unilateral churchmanship in the modern American city is ludicrous. Research reveals the futility of isolated religious effort. What experienced leader does not know that the urban community is too big, too complex, too anonymous, too institutionalized, too dynamic, and too secularized to respond to so naïve a pattern of religious work? Many Protestant churches are tiny and easily become swallowed up in the city. As a matter of fact there are few urban churches large enough to be effective here. However, when churches are united into a denominational team, an inclusive and effective ministry can be furnished throughout the entire city. Yet each local church should handle its own neighborhood. What can be accomplished by teamwork defies achievement by solitary performance. Co-operation is the recipe of urban church success, and this has proved a hard lesson for Protestantism to learn.

It is natural that some urban churches should have a glamorous and eye-catching ministry while other congregations engage in an unheralded ministry to the economically and socially disenfranchised. Still other churches render religious service to residents of ordinary neighborhoods. Few congregations can successfully feature a conspicuous city-wide ministry characterized by radio broadcasts, community religious and secular meetings, and kindred public relations activity. Not more than one or two churches within a denomination should venture so precarious a ministry.

In spite of the inequities with respect to glory and status among individual churches a comprehensive ministry to the entire city by the denomination should be instituted and maintained. The range of needs is broad enough to require the dedicated labors of both "Mary" and "Martha" churches (see Luke 10:38-42). Differences are not qualitative but essentially sociological and economic. A Christian ministry has religious significance irrespective of the temporal status of the recipients.

Thus an important primary step toward united Protestantism consists in the co-ordination of church work within a denomination. Techniques for working together should be found and utilized. Denominational teamwork is not unlike co-operation on the interdenominational level, for it draws upon a sense of community and upon many congruous activity patterns. The desire to work together is an acquired characteristic and derives from the process of co-operation itself.

For the Protestant leader interested in establishing a sound urban pattern of denominational teamwork there are five basic suggestions which merit consideration. First, examine the spacing between the churches of the denomination. This investigation will be aided by locating congregations on a city map. Churches that are situated closer than one and three-fourths miles to one another (and not separated by primary barriers) are probably competitive. This linear distance should be regarded as normative and strictly adhered to within the denomination. Observance of the spacing principle when relocation sites are sought and when new extension projects are launched is plainly essential. The reader may find Figure No. 23 suggestive at this point. Field research discloses that two thirds of all urban problems which interfere with denominational teamwork derive from improper spacing of churches.

Second, examine each local church for membership size. Small churches should be brought up to the level of urban effectiveness. This level is attained when a congregation reaches or exceeds five hundred active members. Small churches tend to have a fractional ministry and therefore should launch immediately aggressive programs of visitation evangelism from which to procure prospective members to enlarge the congregation. A reasonable time limit of one to several years should be set for continuance at the current ineffective level. Several congregations I know required less than three years from date of organization to reach the level of effectiveness. Early discovery of a weakened condition and the prompt launching of remedial measures are mandatory. To this end each neighborhood church can be held responsible for exhausting the full evangelical opportunity within one mile of the church plant. No person within the service radius should be permitted to remain out of active relation with a church of his preference. It is not possible to exaggerate the importance of this objective to the congregation's welfare.

Third, examine each church for range of ministry. The unit should furnish a complete ministry to all persons who come under its care. Can a family find all its religious needs cared for? Is it a church

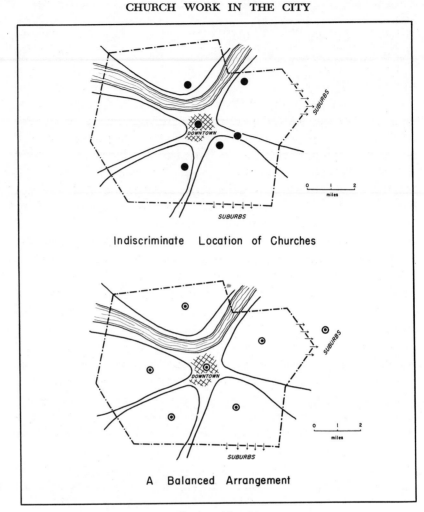

Indiscriminate Location of Churches

A Balanced Arrangement

FIGURE No. 23
CHURCH COMPETITION WITHIN A DENOMINATION
Against the neighborhood structure of a medium-sized city are shown both an
unfavorable and an ideal arrangement of urban churches within
a single denomination

only for older adults? Organizationally the full range of religious experience which is considered normal and significant for children, youth, and adults should be provided. The full set of clubs, societies, and organizations which normally characterize the work of the denomination should provide the framework for the detailed

244

ministry to individuals by the church. Churches organized under an episcopal system should co-ordinate local ministry with the work of the denomination at large.

Fourth, examine the long-range objectives of each church. Espousal of denominational objectives should characterize a teamwork pattern within the communion. Training and experience in this pattern become adequate foundations for co-operation on an interdenominational basis. Ministers and laymen who have failed to learn the co-operative pattern within a communion are equally individualistic and uncharitable in relation to Protestantism. Where administrative pressure must be applied constantly to procure teamwork, the proper co-operative spirit is lacking. Voluntary co-ordinated ministry is the stuff from which interdenominational co-operation ultimately must be made. Progress has been slow in this direction chiefly because close concerted action within the various communions remains to be realized. Many denominational objectives today are of such character as to commend themselves to Protestantism generally. This is increasingly apparent to ecumenically-minded observers.

Fifth, examine the world-wide interests of each church. Ultimately the local congregation must find challenging centers of interest and ministry outside its own neighborhood and enter into the active support of missionaries, mission enterprises, and social service. This is essential to the spiritual welfare of the church. Nearby home-mission projects are in urgent need of financial contributions plus the temporary loan of local church leaders for church extension in the suburbs and for mission-subsidized work among poor or handicapped people. These centers of interest and ministry outside the normal bounds of the parish are instrumental in making denominational teamwork a reality. In some cities downtown and neighborhood churches contribute thousands of dollars annually and provide hundreds of leadership service hours for such purposes. This pattern of sacrifice and resource sharing is a fundamental requirement for united Protestantism.

Enlightened denominational teamwork underlies strong interdenominational cohesion and understanding. Unless local churches achieve willing and effective subordination of personal prominence to the efficiency of the denomination, it is unrealistic to expect high-level co-operation across denominational boundaries. This fundamental lesson has proved to be one of the hardest for urban Protestantism to learn.

PROTESTANT CO-OPERATION IN THE CITY

Complete interdenominational co-operation in urban places apparently cannot be achieved overnight. Yet it must be brought to pass. To accelerate progress at the community level Protestant teamwork should be translated into ecumenical projects, processes, and purposes. Further theorizing now is fruitless. Relationships among churches and leaders should be studied, systematized, and ordered with reference to co-operation. A common foundation for planning within local Protestantism should be found—that is, a common basis which makes possible profound, reputable, and continuous teamwork within the denominations. Let us turn ecumenicity into a "grass roots" movement.

Project Co-operation. An elementary form of Protestant co-operation in the city is revealed through the prevalence of manifold faith-wide undertakings. Appeal for teamwork is made solely upon a temporary basis and according to the intrinsic merits of isolated projects. Many denominations and independent churches otherwise chary of co-operation embark willingly upon a religious census of the city or a simultaneous church financial canvass. Further, a united Protestant approach can often be mustered with respect to attendance at a public hearing on zoning ordinances or crime investigation, observance of Reformation Day, union services for Thanksgiving and other special days, choir festivals, and kindred enterprises.

Thus in the realm of isolated projects is found an elementary form of Protestant co-operation. Participating communions can always supply or withhold support since no continuity of association is involved. This level of course is where many communities have to begin if there is ever to be any kind of Protestant unity at all. The activity lays the groundwork for the eventual achievement of unity. Unfortunately at the completion of each project co-operation has to be resolicited. Absence of continuity proves a serious handicap. The day should come when ecumenical action achieves the dimension of continuity. City life demands it.

Process Co-operation. A second level of Protestant co-operative activity consists of joint participation in certain ecumenical processes. Here denominations and sects unite in manifold teamwork undertakings which involve relatively sustained co-operation within narrow spheres of activity. Co-operating communions agree on principles for locating new suburban churches and seek to arbitrate difficulties in ministering to overchurched territories. In many cities a program of weekday Christian education procures the support of many denominations and independent churches. Thousands of elementary-school children who otherwise undoubtedly would never be adequately exposed to the resources of religion receive Bible instruction regularly. Religious surveys designed to investigate the total Protestant situation are frequently made under the sponsorship of a council or federation of churches. In this connection denominational experts are often loaned to the local community in order to organize and conduct such scientific studies. When findings have been condensed into a published report, copies are circulated among all churches. Radio and television programs are planned and staffed regularly by Protestant leaders of all denominations, thereby rendering an ongoing religious service to the general public with but negligible emphasis upon theological eccentricities and other differences. In some cities an enlightened and co-ordinated plan for mission subsidy to needy churches has been developed by denominational leaders lest needlessly competing projects be maintained by mission funds.

Here then are a few of the ways in which unity on the process level is currently practiced within American Protestantism. Clearly this sustained participation in important activities has ecumenical value. Representing a more evolved pattern of co-operation than is evidenced on the project level, it may encourage leaders to search for additional ways of widening and lengthening the process. Many churchmen find in this activity an important clue to possible future patterns of urban teamwork.

Process co-operation should spread to include the total range of essential Protestant activities. Formerly denominational differences issued in a clash or concord of opinions according to the extent to which amicability characterized relationships. Unfortunately orientation to social facts and objective religious information has been minimized in the past. Today a suspension of judgments and solutions is mandatory until facts essential to a working knowledge of the community can be gathered. The joint discovery of facts and principles which underlie effective urban church work should be undertaken. Discussion of critical problems should be postponed until primary data are assembled and analyzed. It is this process which is vital to denominational relationships.

Following scientific research an achievement of an adequate knowledge of effective urban church patterns emerges. Understanding of the community and of religious work furnishes the leader an appropriate background against which to discuss the problems of the denomination and eventually those of united Protestantism. Rarely do intelligent persons differ respecting major points when all the relevant facts in the situation have been studied. Since problems which confront one denomination frequently harass other communions as well, wiser long-range solutions can be found when several religious bodies unite in an investigation. A common solution is often more permanent and economical. This is the wide-open secret of urban Protestantism. To make common cause is to accomplish mutually beneficial ends.

Purpose Co-operation. Protestant co-operation on the highest level is found in terms of common purpose. Continuing concern and activity at this level hasten the coming of ecumenicity across the street and around the world.

Many denominations are already co-operating in various ways on this level. Sunday-school materials are jointly prepared and published. Books and pamphlets dealing with church architecture, religious education, worship, audio-visual aids, religious census methods, comity principles, and religious radio procedure are issued in growing volume for the use of all bodies. Translations of the Bible and the preparation of religious encyclopedias, commentaries, and dictionaries also need to be mentioned here. In journalism *The Christian Century, Religion in Life, The Ecumenical Review, Church Management, The Christian Herald,* and other trade journals demonstrate that Protestants have found a relative homogeneity of thought and purpose with respect to fundamental tenets of the faith. Good religious journalism wins approbation from discerning church leaders. Materials purporting to call all church members to a day of prayer and to world-wide communion are kindred manifestations. Most denominations have seasons of common emphasis, such as Advent and Lent, and during these periods direct their constituents in the reading of comparable Bible selections and devotion booklets. Common Protestant purpose underlies such co-operation.

It is not surprising that several of the leading theological seminaries are interdenominational in conception of task and that they train clergymen for service in more than thirty-seven denominations. Graduates go forth to serve in all parts of the world. Further, there are state, county, and city councils of churches which co-ordinate the work of the various constituent communions in more than seven hundred American communities. At the present time more than a dozen national commissions and committees are studying ways and means by which additional denomination-wide mergers may be achieved. At the local church level federation and merger across denominational lines are normal procedure as well as withdrawal from overchurched neighborhoods. Denominational leaders consult one another respecting these matters. This emerging new pattern of Protestant co-operative relationship reaches all the way from the local church to the national headquarters, from the parish minister to the top executive. It effects significant change in American Protestantism. It is an ecumenical pattern with a future.

Not only do numerous laymen cross denominational lines with relative ease in cities today, but also clergymen commonly transfer from one communion to another. Emphasis has been shifted from the sectarian differences which divide Christians to commonly held spiritual beliefs which unite religious people into an all-embracing fellowship. Strangely enough differences are more conspicuous today in the administrative structure of denominations than in fundamental tenets of faith. Differentiation is in polity rather than in piety. The vast enlargement of lay activities, in addition to the new prominence accorded such leaders recently, has resulted in drawing church members of various persuasions closer and closer together. Thus relatively homogeneous religious outlook serves as a uniting factor on the level of purpose.

Enlightened Protestant leaders are becoming aware of the need to face the city as an organized team. Remnants of the old-time attitude of unilateral isolationism are vestigial and passing, for surely a tolerant fellowship of Christians is on its way in. Extremely complicated and difficult tasks in the realm of the development of an urban-wide strategy, of long-range planning, and of Protestant unity in the city require nothing less than co-operation on the level of purpose. Heretofore ecumenicity across the street has not been worked out with reference to basic denominational objectives in the urban community. Now denominations should be afforded a chance to tie into the enlightened work of Protestantism. This is an important potential which can become a primary basis for future Protestant fellowship. Many denominations are genuinely interested in the development of an urban-wide strategy and wish to keep pace with community changes and developments. To serve God by reaching effectively the unchurched and by avoiding competition is a laudable objective.

Urban Protestantism needs all the united support it can muster from activity on these levels of project, process, and purpose. Effective teamwork within denominations should be encouraged, since it may become the practical path leading to a high level of interdenominational co-operation. Eventually the religious public will be adequately educated in the ways of co-ordinated activity. It is hoped that many cities will establish demonstration projects showing that new advances toward total co-operation are possible. This is the unfinished task of Protestantism.

Selected Materials for Further Reading

GENERAL

Angell, Robert C. *The Moral Integration of American Cities.* The American Journal of Sociology, Vol. LVII, No. 1, Part II.

Hatt, P. K., and Reiss, A. J. *Reader in Urban Sociology.* Glencoe, Ill.: Free Press, 1951.

Mills, C. Wright. *White Collar.* New York: Oxford University Press, 1951.

Niebuhr, H. Richard. *Social Sources of Denominationalism.* New York: Henry Holt & Co., 1929.

FAITH AND DENOMINATIONAL STUDIES

Abrams, Ray H., ed. *Organized Religion in the United States.* Philadelphia: The Annals of the American Academy of Political and Social Science, 1948. Vol. 256.

Blackwell, Gordon W., et al. *Church and Community in the South.* Richmond: John Knox Press, 1949. (Presbyterian U. S.)

Fichter, Joseph H. *Southern Parish.* Chicago: University of Chicago Press, 1951. Vol. I. (Roman Catholic.)

Gordon, Albert I. *Jews in Transition.* Minneapolis: University of Minnesota Press, 1949. (Jews.)

Mays, B. E., and Nicholson, J. W. *The Negro's Church.* New York: Institute of Social and Religious Research, 1933. (Protestant.)

PROTESTANTISM IN THE AMERICAN CITY

Abell, Aaron I. *Urban Impact on American Protestantism.* Cambridge: Harvard University Press, 1943.

Bower, William C., ed. *The Church at Work in the Modern World.* Chicago: University of Chicago Press, 1935.

Clark, Elmer T. *The Small Sects in America.* Rev. Ed. New York and Nashville: Abingdon-Cokesbury Press, 1949.

Douglass, H. P., and Brunner, E. de S. *The Protestant Church as a Social Institution.* New York: Harper & Brothers., 1935.

Kincheloe, Samuel C. *The American City and Its Church.* New York: Friendship Press, 1938.

Leiffer, Murray H. *City and Church in Transition.* Chicago: Willett, Clark & Co., 1938.

URBAN CHURCH PROBLEMS

Blanton, Wyndham B. *The Making of a Downtown Church.* Richmond, Va.: John Knox Press, 1945.

Douglass, H. Paul. *Protestant Co-operation in American Cities.* New York: Institute of Social and Religious Research, 1930.

————. *The Suburban Trend.* New York: Century & Co., 1925.

Douglass, Truman B. *Mission to America.* New York: Friendship Press, 1951.

Murphy, Bonneau P. *Building and Care of Methodist Church Property.* New York Board of Missions and Church Extension, The Methodist Church, 1951. (Pamphlet.)

SURVEY METHODS FOR THE CITY CHURCH

Douglass, H. Paul. *How to Study the City Church.* New York: Institute of Social and Religious Research, 1928.

Leiffer, Murray H. *The Effective City Church.* New York and Nashville: Abingdon-Cokesbury Press, 1949. Chaps. 14-19.

Perry, Everett L. *Some Suggestions for Church Community Surveys.* New York: Board of National Missions, Presbyterian Church, U.S.A., 1948. (Pamphlet.)

INDEX

253